CHINESE WOMEN
A Thousand Pieces of Gold

CHINESE WOMEN
A Thousand Pieces of Gold

AN ANTHOLOGY SELECTED AND EDITED
BY

Barbara-Sue White

OXFORD
UNIVERSITY PRESS

Oxford University Press is a department of the University of Oxford.
It furthers the University's objective of excellence in research, scholarship,
and education by publishing worldwide in

Oxford New York

Auckland Bangkok Buenos Aires Cape Town Chennai
Dar es Salaam Delhi Hong Kong Istanbul Karachi Kolkata
Kuala Lumpur Madrid Melbourne Mexico City Mumbai Nairobi
São Paulo Shanghai Taipei Tokyo Toronto

Oxford is a registered trade mark of Oxford University Press

Published in the United States
by Oxford University Press Inc., New York

© Oxford University Press 2003

First published 2003
This impression (lowest digit)
1 3 5 7 9 10 8 6 4 2

All rights reserved. No part of this publication may be reproduced,
stored in a retrieval system, or transmitted, in any form or by any means,
without the prior permission in writing of Oxford University Press,
or as expressly permitted by Law, or under terms agreed with the appropriate
reprographics rights organization. Enquiries concerning reproduction
outside the scope of the above should be sent to the Rights Department,
Oxford University Press, at the address below

You must not circulate this book in any other binding or cover
and you must impose the same condition on any acquirer

British Library Cataloguing in Publication Data
available

Library of Congress Cataloging-in-Publication Data
Chinese women: a thousand pieces of gold: an anthology/selected and edited
by Barbara-Sue White.
p. cm.
Includes bibliographical references.
ISBN 0-19-591487-2
1. Women—China—Social conditions.   2. Women—China—History—Sources.
I. White, Barbara-Sue

HQ1767.C4479 2003
305.42'0951—dc22   2003060941

Printed in Hong Kong
Published by Oxford University Press (China) Ltd
18th Floor, Warwick House East, Taikoo Place, 979 King's Road, Quarry Bay
Hong Kong

For my mother, Doris Edith Mount, who raised me with an appreciation of Chinese people and culture, and to my husband, Lynn T. White III, who has shanghaied me for our many years spent in Hong Kong and China.

I would like to thank the following people and institutions:
Cambridge University Library
James Chuck
Jennifer Day
Phyllis M. Deer
Anastasia Edwards
Firestone Library, Princeton University
Gest Library, Princeton University
Martinus Heijdra
Hong Kong University Library
Nancy Pressman Levy
Rebecca Lloyd
Jane Mitchell
Doris E. Mount
Susan Naquin
The late Marguerite Goodner Owen
Roberta and Norman Owen
Priscilla Roberts
Karen Szeto
Kevin M. White
Lynn T. White III
Janice Wickeri
Wu Yanhong

Special thanks to the Centre for Asian Studies University of Hong Kong for my appointment as a Visiting Scholar

A NOTE ON THE ROMANIZATION

This anthology uses romanizations found in the original sources. China's official *pinyin* romanization, which is now most common, may at first seem odd to English readers, because it refers *c*s, *q*s, *x*s, *z*s, and *zh*s to unexpected sounds. The Wade-Giles system, an older alternative that was developed by British diplomats and missionaries, may be distinguished by the apostrophes and hyphens that are absent in *pinyin*. Many 'post office' spellings (Peking, Amoy, Hongkong) follow neither of these systems. Below are the letters that most differ from what English speakers expect. The first five are consonants, always occurring at the beginnings of syllables. After these, four syllable endings are also listed. A speaker who follows this table—and says other *pinyin* letters as in English—will be making a good try at the pronunciation.

Pinyin = SOUND

Five sounds to start syllables:	*c-*	= TS-	(a hard, plosive <u>ts</u>- sound)
	q-	= CH-	(also plosive, as in '<u>chi</u>me')
	x-	= SH-	(a soft 'sh-,' almost an 's')
	z-	= DZ-	(as in 'a<u>dze</u>', but initial)
	zh-	= J-	(a hard sound, as in 'jam')
Four sounds to end syllables:	*-ian*	= -IEN	(have a '<u>yen</u>' for this)
	-ong	= -UNG	('Ach<u>tung</u>!' as in German)
	-ui	= -WAY	(as in 's<u>way</u>')
	-i	= -EE	(but '-R' after retroflexes, or '-UH' after dental sibilants; don't worry about *-i*!)

Two major Chinese dynasty names in *pinyin* (and Wade-Giles) are the *Song* (Sung) and the *Qing* (Ch'ing).

CONTENTS

A Note on the Romanization   vi
Introduction   xvii

PART I: EXCEPTIONAL WOMEN

1. Shen Rong   6
   Ten Years Deducted
2. Anonymous   24
   The Ballad of Mulan
3. Jiang Fang   27
   Prince Huo's Daughter
4. Liu Xiang   37
   The Wife of Ta Tzu
5. Liu Xiang   39
   Jade
6. Liu Xiang   41
   Elder Sister
7. Xiao Yan   43
   Ultimate Causes
8. Howard Levy   44
   The Cowardly Braggart
9. Chinese Profiles   46
   Pretty Third Daughter
10. Ross Terrill   48
    Madame Mao
11. Herbert Giles   50
    A Lady Had a Lover

PART II: CHINESE WOMEN—AS OTHERS SEE THEM

12. Anonymous   53
    Book of Odes

CONTENTS

13.	Julia Corner *The Condition of Ladies*	54
14.	Arthur H. Smith *'Reviling the Street'*	56
15.	George Kates *Shopping*	58
16.	Mencius *The Rules of Behaviour*	59
17.	George Staunton *The Subservience of Women*	60
18.	John Davis *Bound Feet*	61
19.	Edward D. Prime *A Mark of Distinction*	63
20.	Arthur H. Smith *A Useless and Cruel Custom*	65
21.	William Jennings Bryan *Unbound Feet*	66
22.	Eliza Bridgman *A Barbarous Custom*	67
23.	Alicia Little *The Natural Feet Campaign*	68
24.	Isabelle Williamson *Leather Boots*	72
25.	Eliza Bridgman *Beautiful Attire*	74
26.	John Davis *Painted Faces*	75
27.	Julia Corner *Opium Smoking*	77
28.	Dorothea Hosie *Small Six and Her Mother*	79
29.	Marco Polo *Handsome Women*	81

CONTENTS

PART III: CHINESE GIRLS—TINY FEET AND PROPER BEHAVIOUR

30.	Ban Zhao *On the Cultivation of Women*	85
31.	J. Dyer Ball *The Wrong Sex*	87
32.	George Staunton *Childbirth*	89
33.	A. B. Freeman-Mitford *The Little Slave Girl*	90
34.	Arthur H. Smith *The Birth of a Daughter*	92
35.	Zhang Wentao *Advice to Girls*	93
36.	Adele Fielde *Ball Games*	94
37.	Charles Taylor *Hair and Hats*	95
38.	Charles Taylor *Little Annie*	97
39.	George Morrison *Infanticide*	98
40.	Eliza Bridgman *Stories of Little Girls*	100
41.	Arthur Waley *The Place of Girls*	105
42.	Yuan Chen *Miss Oriole*	106

PART IV: BETROTHAL—THE EDGE OF WOMANHOOD

43.	Arthur H. Smith *Is She Betrothed?*	120
44.	Adele Fielde *The Go-Between*	121

CONTENTS

45.	Arthur H. Smith *A Proposal of Marriage*	122
46.	Justus Doolittle *The Fate of Foundling Girls*	125
47.	Richard Wilheim *New Customs*	127
48.	The Facts of Betrothal *Encyclopedia Sinica*	129
49.	Adele Fielde *Marriage Superstitions*	130
50.	Arthur H. Smith *A Lucky Day*	131
51.	Charles Gutzlaff *Marriage Rituals*	133
52.	Tianjin Ribao *Shicong is a Clear-thinking Girl*	137
53.	Herbert Giles *Misunderstandings*	139

PART V: MARRIAGE—THE CURTAINED SEDAN CHAIR

54.	Adele Fielde *The First Days of Marriage*	143
55.	Marguerite Owen *A Chinese Wedding*	148
56.	Huo Da *A Muslim Wedding*	152
57.	George Kates *The Most Hazardous Gamble of All*	162
58.	Encyclopedia Sinica *Posthumous Marriage*	164
59.	Charles Taylor *The Chinese Never Kiss*	165
60.	Susan Townley *Poor Little Chinese Bride*	168

CONTENTS

61.	Lord Macartney *Marriage Laws*	173
62.	Arthur H. Smith *A Bride and Her Mother*	174
63.	J. Dyer Ball *Divorce*	177
64.	Jane Tracy *The French Bride*	178
65.	Arthur H. Smith *The Injured Wife*	179
66.	George Morrison *Attempted Suicide*	181
67.	George Kates *The Useful Concubine*	182
68.	Adele Fielde *The Status of Concubines*	184

PART VI: THE YOUNG BRIDE AND THE MOTHER-IN-LAW

69.	Ban Zhao *On the Reverence Due to Father- and Mother-in-law*	187
70.	Arthur H. Smith *The Cruel Mother-in-Law*	189
71.	Adele Fielde *The Story of a Cruel Daughter-in-Law*	191
72.	Dorothea Hosie *The Manchu Bride*	193
73.	Tie Ning *The Pregnant Woman and the Cow*	196
74.	Charles Taylor *Etiquette*	203
75.	Arthur H. Smith *Mistrust and Suspicion*	204
76.	W. Scarborough *Hawking*	205

CONTENTS

77.	Ban Zhao *On the Instruction of Children*	206
78.	John Thomson *Protecting Women*	207
79.	Hiram Parkes Wilkinson *Motherhood*	208
80.	George Morrison *The Power of Mothers*	209
81.	Arthur H. Smith *Eight Strings of Cash*	210
82.	Adele Fielde *Sundry Superstitions*	212
83.	George Morrison *Multiple Wives*	214

PART VII: WORKING WITH ONE'S HANDS

84.	Charles Taylor *Work in a Western Home*	219
85.	Charles Taylor *Irresistible Babies*	220
86.	Arthur H. Smith *Women's Work*	222
87.	Royal Asiatic Society *Toil*	224
88.	George Staunton *Working on a Boat*	225
89.	Annie Brassey *Life on a Boat*	226
90.	Justus Doolittle *Mediums*	227
91.	J. Dyer Ball *Desperate Measures*	229
92.	Lord Macartney *Idle Men*	230

CONTENTS

93.	Richard Wilheim *Ladies of the Teahouse*	232
94.	Marco Polo *Unlawful Pleasures*	237
95.	Arthur H. Smith *Hard and Tiresome Work*	238
96.	Arthur H. Smith *New Year Fun*	240
97.	Hiram Parkes Wilkinson *Policewomen*	241
98.	Chinese Profiles *The Ticket Seller*	242

PART VIII: WIDOWS AND THE LATER YEARS

99.	Cheng Naishan *Hong Taitai*	247
100.	Li Qingzhao *To the Tune of 'A Lonely Flute on the Phoenix Terrace'*	256
101.	George Morrison *The Greatest Honour*	258
102.	The Lady Pan *The Autumn Fan*	260
103.	Dorothea Hosie *The Manchu Lady*	261
104.	Julia Corner *Adopt an Elderly Princess!*	264
105.	Eliza Bridgman *Mourning Rituals*	266

PART IX: DRAGON LADIES AND COURT LIFE

106.	Shu Qiong *China's Most Famous Courtesan*	269
107.	René Grousset *The Empress Wu*	274

CONTENTS

108. George Staunton *The Palace of Chastity*	279
109. Bland & Backhouse *The Dowager Empress Cixi*	280
110. Daniele Vare *Stories from the Palace*	282
111. Katharine Carl *Painting the Empress*	283
112. Reginald Johnston *The Death of Cixi*	286
113. Susan Townley *Visiting Princesses*	288
114. Katharine Carl *Ladies of the Qing Court*	292
115. Pu Yi *My Mother*	295
116. Pu Yi *My Nurse*	297

PART X: GODDESSES, GHOSTS, AND BELIEFS

117. Jin Shoushen *The Bell Goddess*	303
118. Lord Macartney *Chinese Temples*	307
119. Adele Fielde *Taoist Deities*	308
120. George Morrison *The Terrors of Belief*	310
121. Robert Douglas *The Benevolent Guanyin*	311
122. Howard Levy *A Contest of the Gods*	312
123. Matteo Ripa *The Business of Confession*	314

CONTENTS

124. Marguerite Owen — 316
     Letters from Anhui
125. Astrid Peterson — 320
     Letters from Sichuan
126. Herbert Giles — 326
     A Supernatural Wife

Bibliography — *328*

INTRODUCTION

The mother of the Chinese philosopher Mencius (Mengzi, 370–290 BC) enumerated the 'Three Obediences' that shaped the lives of Chinese women for centuries. As a child, a girl obeyed her father; as a married woman, she was ruled by the wishes of her husband; and in her later years as a widow, she was supposed to heed the advice of her eldest son.

In practice, some girls committed suicide rather than marry their fathers' choice. Wives could be headstrong, and some widows remarried over the objections of their sons. But the ideal persisted: the family was decidedly patriarchal, and centered around ancestor worship and the precepts set down by Confucius and his followers in the second century BC. Women were seen to have complementary 'yin' characteristics to the 'yang' of men. Female qualities were passive, dark, weak, and generally negative.

Having survived infanticide in times of desperation, girls were restricted in childhood, rarely educated, and treated as annoying expenses, really belonging to their future parents-in-law. Some were bought as children by their future in-laws and were treated as servants. Others were bought outright as slaves.

Traditionally, many women were required as servants in the houses of rich merchants, provincial magistrates, and, of course, the imperial household. Some female servants had been purchased as slaves and, if they proved unsatisfactory, could be resold again and again. Kidnappers sometimes drugged and smuggled girls before selling them. Both male and female slaves had government-issued certificates, but those of women were usually not regulated. Women who ran away from their owners could be beaten a legally prescribed eighty strokes.

Female servants sometimes entered homes as *mui tsai* (*meizi*) or 'younger sisters'. These were unwanted girls who had been bought to work in homes, theoretically until marriage, but were at the mercy of their employers. Among the wealthy, concubines were often part of family life, with all complications that such a role might bring. The essential role of a woman was to produce sons to serve her husband's venerable ancestors.

INTRODUCTION

In homes where boys received some education, girls learnt embroidery, sewing, or other domestic skills. The rare girl, allowed to hold a calligraphy brush herself, was usually the daughter of enlightened, educated parents. In a few cases, a girl's tentative brush strokes matured into full literacy and even poetry.

Any girl writing poetry probably had bound feet. Opinions vary on the origins of foot-binding, but some scholars date it back to the Han dynasty between 206 BC and 24 AD. Others suggest that a Tang emperor, Li Yu, ordered his favourite concubine to dance with her bound feet on an image of a lotus flower, creating a sensation that was immediately imitated at the imperial court. Another legend exists that an empress with a deformed foot bound her feet, and again was imitated by court ladies. Foot-binding became widely fashionable during the Song dynasty (960 AD–1279 AD).

Men considered a woman's swaying walk elegant, a sign of gentility, and foot-binding became essential for marrying well. By the end of the Ming dynasty in 1644 AD, even the daughters of some poor families had their feet bound. When the Manchus came to power in the Qing dynasty (1644–1912 AD), their ladies usually retained natural feet, although some Manchu men encouraged binding. By then the 'three-inch lilies' were entrenched among the Chinese.

Girls from mountainous regions needed natural feet, and some groups such as Hakkas ignored foot-binding. A number of writers criticized the process as early as the sixteenth century. Later, in a novel sympathetic to women, *Flowers in the Mirror*, satirist Li Ruzhen (1763–1830 AD) ridiculed the notion that short, fat women could sway with allure on golden lilies.

Western missionaries settled in China after the treaty ports opened in the mid-nineteenth century. By the end of that century, better-educated missionaries, doctors, and scholars arrived, and an anti-foot-binding movement, fostered by foreign women, started to take hold. Even so, I remember seeing an elderly woman with bound feet on the streets of San Francisco in the 1960s, and a few remained in China into the 1990s.

Although the literature of the elite describes women as being extremely secluded and rarely leaving the inner court, a majority of females worked to exhaustion in fields, tended silk worms, spun yarn, or rowed boats. A day spent planting rice was followed by an evening of child-care, food preparation, housework, and sewing.

For some, the pressure was too much, and China continues to have the highest female suicide rate in the world. The threat of suicide was one of a girl's few weapons. The pattern of actual suicides was bimodal over women's lifespans, with the first peak around the time of a forced marriage or a refusal to tolerate an impossible mother-in-law. A second peak occurred after the death of a woman's husband, perhaps because of an inability to adjust to the change in family politics or a socially lauded refusal to live after the death of her husband. Other women were sustained by hope: their sons would grow up to love and care for them and bring honour to their families.

The position of women, as defined by their economic rights as well as legal and social status, continued to be oppressive until the social unrest at the beginning of the twentieth century. The Song dynasty (960–1279 AD) saw widespread implementation of Confucian ideals such as non-remarriage of widows. Conversely, women gained some property rights at that time.

Sometimes, however, the repression of women was encouraged by literature. Liu Xiang (77–6 BC) compiled the *Biographies of Women*, suggesting model but restrictive deportment for women. This was followed by poet and historian Ban Zhao's (*c.* 49–120 AD) *Admonitions for Women,* another conservative collection of advice which became a highly influential work destined to keep women in their assigned places.

Patterns of government also shaped the roles of women. In the China of the pre-Qin period (221–206 BC), dynastic marriages were made between men and women of royal status, to cement or expand relationships between states. This gave women the backing of their politically important relatives. When emperors later ruled a centralized state, imperial wives were selected from the ladies of the realm, and their kin had to content themselves with jockeying for power through the hierarchy of ministers. Even so, the Empress Lu gained power for herself in the Han dynasty after the death of the emperor Liu Bang in 195 BC by ruling during the reign of her son and two succeeding infants as well.

Because ladies of court were confined to the inner parts of the palace, those who wished to pursue power were constrained by their ability to gain access to and manipulate the emperor. As emperors became more exalted and remote court ladies sometimes became go-betweens for the ministers. Since young women in the imperial palace could potentially accrue power and riches for their families, parents dreamt that a daughter might become an imperial consort and the mother of the heir apparent, as her power would increase if he inherited the throne.

In the latter part of the Han dynasty, towards 220 AD, the power of the ministers was largely replaced by the eunuchs within the palace, resulting in future emperors being raised by women of the court while eunuchs became powerful advisors. This pattern continued intermittently until the fall of the Qing dynasty in 1912.

By the second century AD, a writer complained that the imperial harem contained over 5000 ladies, although the number of ranks had been reduced to 'honourable lady', 'beautiful lady', and 'chosen lady.' Girls between the ages of eleven and eighteen were inspected each fall for qualities including virginity, character, and beauty before being ranked.

Women's dependence on men was central to their role in society, and independent women such as unmarried servants or courtesans were excluded from established society, and, like all women, were forbidden to own or inherit land. Women could possess their own jewellery, but this rarely mattered to the servant class. When a woman was released from the responsibilities of marriage, through widowhood or advancing age, a period of creativity or spiritual exploration could ensue. Li Qingzhao (Li Ch'ing-chao, 1083–1149 AD), considered China's greatest female poet, composed most of her poetry after she was widowed at the age of forty-seven.

In more recent centuries, both political and industrial changes affected women. Many of them contributed to family earnings through spinning at home. But as machines were introduced during the Industrial Revolution, some jobs which women had been able to do at home were transferred to factories, sometimes creating child-care, transport, and other problems.

Another radical change occurred with the Taiping Rebellion in the middle of the nineteenth century. Hong Xiuquan (Hung Hsiu-ch'üan), the Taiping founder, imagined himself as Christ's younger brother. He preached in fanatical opposition to slavery, gambling, alcohol, opium, and repression by the ruling Manchus. Hong and his disciples encouraged disaffected peasants to fight imperial troops and to create a new order, which proclaimed equality between men and women. Girls were suddenly

INTRODUCTION

encouraged to attend school, including examinations, while women were allowed to own land and declared legally equal to men. Concubinage, foot-binding, prostitution, and the sale of brides were all made illegal, and the remarriage of widows was condoned. Women could join all-female armies, which might participate in battles but were more apt to work behind the lines.

Although the Taipings were suppressed in 1864, women had become more aware of their legal and social restrictions. Possibilities for women expanded. A year after the Communist Party was established in 1921, its Women's Department was created. The Party inveighed against the oppression under which Confucian precepts had placed women, and many people were willing to work for change. Women continued to be primarily responsible for the family and household tasks, while work for remuneration was secondary.

In China's growing economy, traditional women were often unprepared to compete for better-paying jobs, but a conscious attempt was made to improve the status of women. Poor women still worked hard; Shanghai textile workers put in over twelve hours a day during the 1920s. Meals were eaten standing up, workers had two days off a month, and tuberculosis and other diseases were rampant. Some rural girls were sold to factory owners to work free for a number of years.

Even in Shanghai in recent decades, less than a quarter of the Communist Party members were women. Few women were candidates for advanced university degrees. But changes had occurred. The Chinese Communist Party pressed for the liberation of women, campaigning against wife-beating, foot-binding, and arranged marriages, while trying not to antagonize men in the countryside. Membership in the paid labour force was seen as essential for the liberation of women.

After 1950, women were granted formal equality in the Constitution. They were given the legal right to choose their own husbands and to initiate divorces. Finally, foot-binding began to decrease. During the Cultural Revolution (1966–76), young women, now with natural feet, roamed far from home as Red Guards, challenging authority figures and acting with unprecedented self-assurance.

After the Cultural Revolution, women's employment opportunities increased, but educational opportunities were curtailed by beliefs that boys were simply brighter than girls, and thus more worthy of education. Women could now dress and spend more freely, but those who had postponed marriage past their late twenties found themselves with few offers.

As China welcomed foreigners in large numbers, women's personal lives became subject to comparison and constant discussion in the popular press. Afterwards, with the enforcement of the one-child policy, late-term abortions and female infanticides increased. In rural areas, young women were still subjected to family interference with marriage plans, domineering mothers-in-law, and a continued high level of domestic abuse.

In recent decades, women in the labour force have become commonplace. More women have undertaken advanced studies, entered professions, and followed opportunities abroad. Even so, women hold up perhaps more than half the sky as they juggle families, household duties, and work.

The short fiction by female Chinese authors is reprinted here in translation without abridgement. It often comes from available collections of Chinese stories in English. There are numerous women writing in contemporary China, and the reader will enjoy further reading from books suggested in the bibliography.

Excerpts in this anthology from memoirs by nineteenth and twentieth century visitors to China were taken from the original editions, available in libraries. The pleasure of handling and perusing the actual works, often in leather bindings with a wealth of old illustrations, is something readily available to readers. For example, the 1854 version of Marco Polo used for this collection was printed hundreds of years after the first edition, but it expresses continuous interest in this work in a tangible way. I hope these brief passages will lead readers to the complete works, some penned while writers wiled away months aboard ships and China became a distant memory.

Even though women's lives were more difficult than men's, the following excerpts portray Chinese women as brave, imaginative, ingenious, and diligent. Some women were treacherous and deceptive, while others were benevolent. Together, they represent the women of China.

Barbara-Sue White
Hong Kong 2003

PART I

EXCEPTIONAL WOMEN

'In books there are women who appear as jewels.'

CHINESE WOMEN

Women of extraordinary abilities dot Chinese history in surprising ways. The martial arts skills portrayed by women in films such as *Crouching Tiger, Hidden Dragon* have a long tradition in Chinese fiction. Other heroines are more firmly based in reality.

An early military leader was a woman, Fu Hao, living in the late Shang Dynasty (c.1480–1050 BC). Emperor Wu Ding expanded his empire to include more tribal regions, solidifying his position through marriage to a woman from each tribe. Fu Hao, as one of these wives, took advantage of matriarchal elements still in society to become a military commander. She also presided over court divination ceremonies in which she interpreted divine messages from cracks in heated tortoise shells or bones. When the emperor went to war, she led an army of over 10,000 troops raised from her own and adjacent tribes.

After her triumphs as a warrior, Wu Ding granted her additional personal lands and riches which furthered her economic independence and fortune. However, the succeeding Zhou Dynasty negated the right of women to own personal property, instead establishing a strongly patriarchal clan-centred society.

Another woman, known to us only as Madame Lian, became famous as a strategist in the sixth century AD. As a member of the Li tribe, she married the son of a Han governor and together they arbitrated disputes between the two groups. When the governor of Guangdong Province rebelled, Madame Lian travelled to his palace with conciliatory gifts carried by a thousand porters. Once inside the compound, the porters transformed themselves into soldiers, suppressing the rebellion under Madame Lian's command. She subsequently became leader of the Li tribe, quelling further rebellions, but ended her days as a spiritual leader in a mansion built for her by the grateful emperor.

'Better than a boy' is the translation of Tang Sai'er's name, expressing her parents' joy at her arrival. She came from an impoverished Ming Dynasty family (1368–1644) and her father taught her martial arts. Later she and her husband joined other peasants in attacking government offices to demand grain. After her husband was killed in this unsuccessful assault, Sai'er inspired peasants with some of the tenants of the White Lotus Sect, encouraging equality of men and women and striving to create a better, more balanced society. Many peasants followed Sai'er,

EXCEPTIONAL WOMEN

joining her insurgent army in an uprising against Ming troops. After several battles in which they were outnumbered, her troops were defeated. Her ultimate fate is unknown, but her village was renamed in her honour.

Although the scattered names of female military heroines have trickled down through history, perhaps the most striking incident of armed heroism took place in the middle of the nineteenth century among the tens of thousands of women who joined the Taiping Rebellion against the Qing dynasty (1644–1912). The rebellion, lasting over a decade, began in Guangxi Province in southern China, spread to many parts of the country, with Nanjing the declared capital of the Heavenly Kingdom.

Guangxi was one of the poorest provinces in China, but because of the mountainous terrain, most of the poor women escaped having their feet bound. This meant that they were eager and able to fight for a movement which emphasized the equality of men and women. Women served in separate detachments. Hu Damei, mother of a major leader, led 2,500 troops under her personal command. At one time, a city near Nanjing was guarded exclusively by women. Many women were admired for their ability to fight on horseback, distinctive with their scarlet turbans and straw sandals. Towards the end of the Taiping Rebellion, women carried supplies balanced on bamboo poles into enemy cities as a front for Taiping spying activities.

Hong Xuanjiao, sister of the Heavenly King of the Taiping, commanded an army of tens of thousands of women. After learning equestrian and martial skills as a child, she assumed her husband's leadership following his battlefield death. Hong Xuanjiao is remembered in a popular ballad:

Let's follow Hong Xuanjiao,
Who could fire arms or a sword.
At the battle in the Niupai Mountains,
She beat the Qings and broke their backs.

Also known as a strategist, Hong Xuanjiao raised money for her military actions based on her own intelligence work. After the rebellion was quelled in 1864, she became principal of a Nanjing school for women.

EXCEPTIONAL WOMEN

Poet and rebel Qiu Jin

The People's Republic of China still honours the early twentieth-century agitator and poet Qiu Jin. The daughter of literary parents, she was also thoroughly trained in swordsmanship and equestrian skills. Qiu Jin and other young intellectuals planned an armed uprising against the oppression by the Qing government. She was captured and executed in 1907, thereby assuring her martyrdom. Tales of modern military heroines continue to enliven Chinese history today.

1
TEN YEARS DEDUCTED

Shen Rong
1980

Translated by Gladys Yang

Shen Rong, an exceptional woman herself, writes of the effect of political issues on people's lives. During the ten years of the Cultural Revolution (1966–76) the government designated categories for everyone based on their class backgrounds, education, and jobs. While people with 'bad' labels, such as capitalist, were shamed and often punished, others with 'good' labels, such as worker, were required to denounce members of the first group to prove themselves worthy. Some women, especially young ones, were particularly shrill in these demonstrations.

By the 1980s, when this story is set, men and women were treated as equals by the Communist government. Everyone's age was common knowledge and jobs usually went to the youngest person—even by a margin of a few months.

Word wafted like a spring breeze through the whole office building. 'They say a directive will be coming down, deducting ten years from everybody's age!'

'Wishful thinking,' said a sceptic.

'Believe it or not,' was the indignant retort. 'The Chinese Age Research Association after two years' investigation and three months' discussion has drafted a proposal for the higher-ups. It's going to be ratified and issued any day now.'

The sceptic remained dubious.

'Really? If so, that's the best news I ever heard!'

His informant explained:

TEN YEARS DEDUCTED

'The age researchers agreed that the ten years of the "cultural revolution" wasted ten years of everyone's precious time. This ten years debit should be cancelled out. . . .'

That made sense. The sceptic was convinced.

'Deduct ten years and instead of sixty-one I'll be fifty-one—splendid!'

'And I'll be forty-eight, not fifty-eight—fine!'

'This is wonderful news!'

'Brilliant, great!'

The gentle spring breeze swelled up into a whirlwind engulfing everyone.

'Have you heard? Ten years deducted!'

'Ten years off, no doubt about it.'

'Minus ten years!'

All dashed around to spread the news.

An hour before it was time to leave the whole building was deserted.

Ji Wenyao, now sixty-four, as soon as he got home, yelled towards the kitchen: 'Minghua, come here quick!'

'What's up?' At her husband's call Fang Minghua hurried out holding some spinach she was cleaning.

Ji was standing in the middle of the room, arms akimbo, his face lit up. Hearing his wife come in he turned his head, his eyes flashing, and said incisively:

'This room needs smartening up. Tomorrow go and order a set of Romanian furniture.'

She stepped forward in surprise and asked quietly:

'Are you crazy, Old Ji? We've only those few thousand in the bank. If you squander them. . . .'

'Bah, you don't understand.' Face flushed, neck dilated, he cried, 'Now we must start a new life!'

Their son and daughter as if by tacit consent hurried in from their different rooms not knowing what to make of their father's announcement. Was the old man off his rocker?

'Get out, this is none of your business.' Old Ji shooed away the inquisitive young people.

He then closed the door and, quite out of character, leapt forward to throw his arms round his wife's plump shoulders. This display of affection, the first in dozens of years, alarmed her even more than his order to buy Romanian furniture. She wondered:

What's wrong with him? He's been so down in the dumps about reaching retirement age, he's never demonstrative like this in the daytime, and even in bed he just sighs to himself as if I weren't there beside him. What's got into him today? A man in his sixties carrying on like those romantic characters in TV plays—she blushed for him. But Old Ji didn't notice, his eyes were blazing. Half hugging, half carrying her, he lugged his impassive wife to the wicker chair and sat her down, then whispered jubilantly into her ear:

'I'll tell you some top-secret news. A directive's coming down, we're all to have ten years deducted from our age.'

'Ten—years—deducted?' Minghua let fall the spinach, her big eyes nearly popping out of her head. 'Well I never! Is it true?'

'It's true. The directive will be arriving any minute.'

'Oh my! Well I never!' She sprang to her feet to throw her arms round her husband's scrawny shoulders and peck at his high forehead. Then, shocked by her own behaviour, she felt as if carried back thirty years in time. Old Ji looked blank for a moment then took her hands and the two of them turned three circles in the middle of the room.

'Oh my, I'm dizzy.' Not till Minghua pulled free and patted her stout chest did they stop whirling merrily round.

'Well, dear? Don't you think we ought to buy a set of Romanian furniture?' Ji looked confidently at his rejuvenated wife.

'We ought.' Her big eyes were shining.

'Oughtn't we to make a fresh start?'

'We ought, we ought.' Her voice was unsteady and there were tears in her eyes.

Old Ji plumped down on the armchair and closed his eyes while rosy dreams of the future flooded his mind. Abruptly opening his eyes he said resolutely:

'Of course our private lives are a minor matter, the main thing is we now have ten more years to work. This time I'm determined to make a go of it. Our bureau is so slack I must take a firm grip on things. On the back-up work too; the head of our general office is not a suitable choice at all. The airs our drivers give themselves, they need to be straightened out too. . . .'

He flourished his arms, his slit eyes agleam with excitement.

'The question of the leading group will have to be reconsidered. I was forced to appoint the best of a bad lot. That Zhang Mingming is a bookworm with no experience of leadership. Ten years, give me ten years and I'll get together a good leading group, a young one with really new blood, chosen from today's college students. Graduates of twenty-three or twenty-four, I'll groom them myself for ten years and then. . . .'

Minghua took little interest in the overhauling of the leading group, looking forward to the wonderful life ahead.

'I think I'll get another armchair too.'

'Get a suite instead, more modern.'

'And our bed, we'll get a soft one in its place,' She reddened.

'Quite right. After sleeping hard all our lives we should get a soft bed to move with the times.'

'The money. . . .'

'What does money matter?' Ji Wenyao took a long-term view, filled with pride and enthusiasm. 'The main thing is getting another ten years, ah, that's something no money could buy.'

As they were talking excitedly, hitting it off so well, their daughter opened the door a crack to ask:

'Mum, what shall we have for supper?'

'Oh, cook whatever you want.' Minghua had forgotten completely about the meal.

'No!' Old Ji raised one hand and announced, 'We'll go out and eat roast duck. I'm standing a treat. You and your brother go first to get a table, your mother and I will follow.'

'Oh!' His daughter gaped at seeing her parents in such high spirits. Without asking the reason she went to call her brother.

Brother and sister hurried off to the roast duck restaurant, speculating on the way there. He said perhaps an exception had been made in the old man's case and he was being kept on. She thought that maybe he had been promoted or got a bonus. Of course neither of them could guess that the deduction of ten years was worth infinitely more than any promotion.

At home the old couple were still deep in conversation.

'Minghua, you should smarten yourself up too. Ten years off makes you just Forty-eight.'

'Me? Forty-eight?' she murmured as if dreaming. The vitality of her long-lost youth was animating her plump flabby figure, to her bewilderment.

'Tomorrow buy yourself a cream-coloured coat for spring and autumn.' Old Ji looked critically at her tight grey uniform and said decisively, almost protestingly, 'Why shouldn't we be in fashion? Just wait. After supper I'll buy myself an Italian-style jacket like Zhang Mingming's. He's forty-nine this year; if he can wear one, why shouldn't I?'

'Right!' Minghua smoothed her scruffy, lustreless grey hair. 'I'll dye my hair too and treat myself to a visit to a first-rate beauty-parlour. Ha, the young folk call me a stick-in-the-mud, but put back the clock ten years and I'll show them how to live. . . .'

Old Ji sprang to his feet and chimed in:

'That's it, we must know how to live. We'll travel. Go to Lushan, Huangshan, Jiuzhaigou. Even if we can't swim we'll go to have a look at the ocean. The fifties, that's the prime of life. Really, in the past we had no idea how to live!'

Not pausing to comment Minghua went on thinking aloud:

'If ten years are deducted and I'm just forty-nine, I can work another six years. I must go back and do a good job too.'

'You. . . .' Old Ji sounded dubious.

'Six years, six years, I can work for another six years,' she exulted.

'You'd better not,' Ji said. 'Your health isn't up to it.'

'My health's fine.' In her eagerness to get back to work she really felt quite fit.

'If you take up your old job who'll do all the housework?'

'We'll get a maid.'

'But that lot of women from Anhui are too irresponsible. You can't trust one of them to take over here.'

Minghua began to waver.

'Besides, since you've already retired you don't want to make more trouble for the leadership, right? If all the old retired cadres asked to go back, well, that would mess things up.' Ji shuddered at the thought.

'No, I've still six years in which I can work,' she insisted. 'If you won't take me back in the bureau, I can transfer somewhere else. As Party secretary or deputy secretary in some firm—how about that?'

'Well . . . those firms are a very mixed lot.'

'All the more reason to strengthen their leadership. We old people are the ones to do ideological and political work.'

'All right.'

Ji nodded, pleasing her as much as if the head of the Organization Department had agreed. She chortled:

'That's fine then! Those researchers are really understanding. Ten years off, a fresh start—that's beyond my wildest dreams.'

'Well, I dreamed of it.' Quite carried away Ji cried out vehemently, 'The "cultural revolution" robbed me of ten of my best years. Ten years, think what I could have done in that time. Ten wasted years, leaving me white-haired and decrepit. Who's to make good that loss? Why did I have to take such bitter medicine? Give me back my youth! Give me ten years back! Now this research association is giving me back that decade of my youth. Good for them, this should have been done long ago.'

Not wanting her husband to recall painful memories, Minghua smiled and changed the subject.

'All right, let's go and eat roast duck.'

Zhang Mingming, forty-nine that year, couldn't analyse his reaction. It seemed a mixture of pleasure and distress, of sweetness and bitterness.

Ten years off certainly pleased him. Working on scientific research he knew the value of time. Especially for him, a middle-aged intellectual approaching fifty, the recovery of ten years was a heaven-sent opportunity. Look at researchers overseas. A scientist in his twenties could win an international reputation by presenting a thesis at an international conference, then go on to head his field while in his thirties, his name known throughout the world—there were many such cases. Then look at him: a brilliant, most promising student in college with just as good a grounding as anyone else. But unluckily he had been born at the wrong time, and sent to do physical labour in the countryside. When he got down again to his interrupted studies the technical material was strange to him, his brain didn't function well and his hands trembled. Now with this extra ten years he could make a fresh start. If he went all out and research conditions improved, with less time wasted bickering over trifles, why, he could put twenty years' work into ten years and distinguish himself by scaling the heights of science.

He was pleased, just as pleased as everyone else, if not more so.

But a colleague slapped his back and asked:

'Old Zhang, what are you so bucked about?'

'What do you mean?' Why shouldn't he be bucked?

'Deducting ten years makes Ji Wenyao fifty-four. So he won't retire, you won't take over the bureau.'

Quite true. That being the case Ji won't retire. He doesn't want to. He'll stay on as bureau head. And what about me? Of course I won't be promoted. I'll remain an engineer doing scientific research in the lab and library. . . . Yet two days ago the ministry sent for me to tell me that Old Ji would be retiring and they'd decided to put me in charge. . . . Does that still hold good?

He really didn't want an official post. The highest he had ever held was that of group head, and convening a group meeting was the height of his political experience. He had never expected an official title, least of all the imposing one of bureau head. He had always been a 'bookworm'. In the 'cultural revolution' he had come under fire as 'a reactionary revisionist set on becoming an expert'. Since the overthrow of the 'gang of four' he had spent all his time in his lab, not talking to a soul.

But somehow or other when it came to choosing a third-echelon leading group he had been chosen. In each public opinion poll his name headed the list, just as he had always come top in examinations. When he was summoned to the ministry it sounded as if the whole business had been settled. In that case he couldn't understand where or how he had shown any leading ability, to be favoured by the authorities and trusted by the rank and file. Thinking it over he felt most ashamed. He had never had any administrative ability, let alone any leadership qualities.

His wife Xue Minru, moderately good-looking and intelligent, was an admirable wife and mother. She took a keen interest in her husband's affairs and knew the disputes in his bureau very well. Her comment had been:

'It's because you're not leadership material that you've been chosen for a leading post.'

Zhang Mingming was puzzled by this statement. What does that mean, he wondered. Then he thought: maybe there's some truth in it. Because I've no ability to lead or definite views of my own, and I've not jockeyed for position, no one need worry about me. Perhaps that's why I've been given this opening.

Of course there was also an 'opposition party'. It was said that at one Party meeting in the bureau his problem had been disputed all afternoon. What the dispute was about he wasn't clear. Nor what his problem was either. After that, though, he felt that he had become a 'controversial figure'. And this 'controversy' wouldn't be resolved nor would his 'problem' be cleared up till the day he became bureau head.

Gradually as these public opinion polls and arguments went on, Zhang Mingming became accustomed to his role as someone due to be promoted and a 'controversial figure'. Sometimes he even imagined that he might really make a good bureau head, though he had never held such a position.

'Better take the job,' said Minru. 'It's not as if you'd grabbed at it. When you're bureau chief at least you won't have to squeeze on to the bus to go to work.'

But now he wouldn't get the job. Was he sorry? A little, not altogether. What it boiled down to was: his feelings were mixed.

He went home at a loss.

'Back? Good, the meal's just ready.' Minru went into the kitchen to fetch one meat dish, one vegetable dish and a bowl of egg and pickle soup. The meat dish wasn't greasy and the green vegetables looked very tempting.

His wife was an excellent housekeeper, considerate, clever and deft. During the three hard years when their neighbours contracted hepatitis or dropsy, she kept their family fit by cooking coarse grain so that it tasted good, boiling bones to make soup and using melon rind in place of vegetables. Now farm products were plentiful but fish and meat had risen so much in price that everybody claimed they couldn't afford them. However, Minru knew how to cook tasty inexpensive meals. When Zhang saw the supper she had served he lost no time in washing his hands, sitting down at the table and picking up his chopsticks.

'What succulent celery,' he remarked, 'is it expensive? The papers say celery keeps your blood pressure down.'

Minru simply smiled.

'These pickles are good too, they give the soup a fine flavour.'

Still she just smiled and said nothing.

'Bamboo shoots with pork. . . .' He went on praising this simple meal as if he were a gourmet.

She laughed and cut him short to ask:

'What's got into you today? Has anything happened?'

'No, nothing.' He made a show of surprise. 'I was just admiring your cooking.'

'You never do normally, so why today?' She was still smiling.

Feeling driven into a corner he retorted:

'It's because I don't normally that I'm saying this now.'

'No, you're hiding something from me.' She could see through him.

With a sigh he put down his chopsticks.

'I'm not hiding anything, but I don't know what to make of it myself or how to tell you.'

Minru smiled complacently. Her husband might be an expert researcher, a top man in his own field, but when it came to psychoanalysis he was no match for her.

'Never mind, just tell me.' She sounded like a teacher patiently encouraging a child.

'Today word came that a directive's coming down to deduct ten years from everybody's age.'

'Impossible.'

'It's true.'

'Really?'

'Really and truly.'

She thought this over and looked at him with big limpid eyes, then chuckled.

'So you won't be bureau head.'

'That's right.'

'Does that upset you?'

'No. I can't explain it, but I feel put out.'

He took up his chopsticks again to fiddle with the rice in his bowl as he went on:

'To start with I'm not leadership material and I didn't want this job. But they've made such a mess of things these last few years, it seems I ought to take over. Still, this sudden change makes me feel a bit. . . .' He was at a loss for words.

Minru said incisively:

'If you don't get the job so much the better. You think it's a cushy post?'

Zhang looked up at his wife, surprised by her decisive tone of voice. A few days ago when he'd told her about his impending promotion, she had shown genuine elation. She'd said, 'Look at you—you didn't grab at the job and now these laurels have been put on your head.' Now the laurels were lost she wasn't upset or angry, as if there had never been any talk of promotion.

'As bureau head, head of the bureau, you'd have been expected to solve every problem big or small—could you have stood it?' she asked. 'Allocation of housing, promotions, bonuses, private squabbles, financial affairs, finding jobs or kindergartens for people's children. How could you manage all that?'

True, no one could manage it all.

'Stick to your speciality. An extra ten years will make all the difference to what you can achieve.'

Yes, it would certainly make all the difference.

Zhang fell easier in his mind, with a sense of light-hearted well-being.

He went to bed expecting to sleep soundly. But he woke in the middle of the night with a feeling of faint regret and deprivation.

Thirty-nine-year-old Zheng Zhenhai shot out of the bureau and cycled swiftly home. There he took off his old grey jacket and tossed it on to a chair, conscious of inexhaustible energy. This deduction of ten years seemed to call for prompt action to solve many major problems.

'Hey!'

No one answered his call. His ten-year-old son was fooling about as usual in the alley, and where was his wife who usually responded? Out visiting? Hell! What sort of home was this?

His home-made armchair was so misproportioned that his spine didn't reach the back, while the low arms and high seat made sitting there positively tiring. All because she had to keep up with the neighbours and since they couldn't afford an armchair had insisted on his making a set himself. What a philistine! It was sickening the way every family had armchairs like this, as standard as a cadre's uniform. So philistine!

Whatever had made him choose her? Such a vulgar family with no interests in life except food, clothing, pay and perks. Family education was all-important. She was the spitting image of her mother: the same crude way of talking, and fat as a barrel since the birth of the boy, with no good looks, no figure, no character. Whatever had made him choose someone like her?

Hell! It came of being in too much of a hurry. A bachelor nearing thirty couldn't be choosy. Now with ten years off he was only twenty-nine! He must think over this problem seriously. Yesterday she'd squawked and flounced about because he'd bought a carton of good cigarettes, threatening to divorce him— they couldn't go on like this. Divorce? Go ahead! Twenty-nine was just the right age to find a wife, a slender college graduate of twenty-two or twenty-three with a refined, modern outlook. College students should marry other college students. She was half-baked, just from a technical school. He could kick himself for making such a mistake.

He must re-organize his life, not muddle along like this. Where the hell had she gone?

In fact, after work she'd bolted out of the bureau to head for a shop selling women's clothes.

The thought of ten years off had thrown Yuejuan into raptures and fired her imagination. A woman one year short of forty, she was suddenly restored to a girl of twenty-nine. For her this heaven-sent stroke of luck was a boon not all the money in the world could buy.

Twenty-nine—to be so young was glorious! She glanced down at her faded, drab, unprepossessing uniform with a stab of pained resentment. Hurrying into the shop she pounded up to the section displaying the latest fashions, her eyes scanning the dazzling costumes hanging there till a scarlet dress with a white gauze border struck her. She asked to try it on. The salesgirl looked her up and down, her impassive face cold and stony, her cold look implying contempt.

'Well? Aren't I fit to wear this?' Yuejuan fumed inwardly, as she often had in recent years when shopping for clothes, because whenever something took her fancy Zhenhai always ticked her off:

'That makes you look like mutton dressed like lamb.' What was wrong with that? Did she have to dress like an old woman? Generally she went home in a rage without buying anything, to squabble with him all night. How unlucky she was, landed for life with such a stick-in-the-mud.

Why stop to argue with the salesgirl? I'll pay for what I buy, you hand it over and mind your own bloody business! What did the silly fool know? Had she heard about the directive? This is just the dress for someone of twenty-nine. The Chinese are too conservative. In other countries, the older ladies are the more they prink themselves up. Eighty-year-olds wear green and red. What does it matter to you what I choose to wear? However you glare at me, I'm taking this.

Having paid up, Yuejuan went into the fitting room. In the long mirror the scarlet dress which hugged her plump figure so tightly seemed a rather outsize mass of fiery red, but really hot stuff, really smart. Well, she'd have to start slimming. Ten years could be deducted from her age by a directive from the higher-ups, but to deduct ten pounds from her weight she'd have to sweat blood. She'd long since stopped eating animal fat and ate only the minimum of starchy food, even cutting down on fruit. However was she to slim?

She huffed and puffed her way home, threw open the door and burst in like a ball of fire. Zheng leapt up in horror from his armchair to ask:

'What's come over you?'

'What do you mean?'

'Where on earth did you get that dress?'

'I bought it. So what?' She raised the hem of the dress and circled round like a model with a coquettish smile.

He at once poured cold water on her.

'Don't imagine that gaudy colours are beautiful—it depends on who's wearing them.'

'Why shouldn't I wear them?'

'A dress like that is out of place on you; you're past the age for it. Just think of your age.'

'I have thought; that's why I bought it. Twenty-nine! Just the right age to dress up.'

'Twenty-nine?' Zheng was taken aback.

'That's right, twenty-nine. Minus ten years makes me twenty-nine, less one month. I insist on wearing reds and greens—so there!' She was gesticulating like an affectedly coy pop singer careering about the stage.

Confound the woman, at her age, so broad in the beam, what a sight she was carrying on like this because of ten years off! Zheng shut his eyes, then opened them abruptly to glare at her.

'The higher-ups are issuing this directive so as to give full play to cadres' youthful vitality and speed up modernization, not so that you'll dress up!'

'How does dressing up affect modernization?' She sprang to her feet. 'Does the directive forbid us to dress up? Eh?'

'I mean you can't dress up without taking into account your appearance and figure. . . .'

'What's wrong with my figure?' Touched on a sore spot she struck back. 'I'll tell you a home truth. You think me fat; I think you scrawny, scrawny as a pullet, with deep lines like tramways on your forehead, and you can't walk three steps without wheezing. Bah! I wanted an intellectual for a husband. But with you, what better treatment have we had? You're nothing but an intellectual in name. No decent clothes, no decent place to live in. Well? Now I'm twenty-nine, still young, I can find a pedlar anywhere in the street who's better off than you, whether he sells peanuts or sugar-coated haws.'

'Go ahead then and find one.'

'It's easy. We'll divorce today, and tomorrow I'll register my new marriage.'

'Let's divorce then.'

With that the fat was in the fire. Normally Yuejuan kept talking of 'divorce' while to Zheng the term was taboo. Now that devil was using it too. Of all the gall! This wouldn't do.

It was all the fault of those damn researchers. She butted her husband with her head and raged:

'Deducting ten years has sent you round the bend. Who are *you* to want a divorce? No way!'

'You think by deducting ten years you can have your way in everything—you're crazy!'

'Little Lin, there's a dance tomorrow at the Workers' Cultural Palace. Here's a ticket for you.' Big Sister Li of the trade union beckoned to Lin Sufen.

Ignoring her, Sufen quickened her step and hurried out of the bureau.

Take off ten years and she was only nineteen. No one could call her an old maid any more. The trade union needn't worry about a slip of a girl. She didn't need help from the matchmakers' office either. Didn't need to attend dances organized to bring young people together. All that was done with!

Unmarried at twenty-nine she found it hard to bear the pitying, derisive, vigilant or suspicious glances that everyone cast at her. She was pitied for being single, all alone; scoffed at for missing the bus by being too choosy; guarded against as hyper-sensitive and easily hurt; suspected of being hysterical and warped. One noon when she went to the boiler room to poach herself two eggs in a bowl of instant noodles, she heard someone behind her comment:

'Knows how to cosset herself.'

'Neurotic.'

She swallowed back tears. If a girl of twenty-nine poached herself two eggs instead of having lunch in the canteen, did that make her neurotic? What theory of psychology was that?

Even her best friends kept urging her to find a man to share her life. As if to be single at twenty-nine were a crime, making her a target of public criticism, a natural object of gossip. The endless idle talk had destroyed her peace of mind. Was there nothing more important in the world, no more urgent business than finding yourself a husband? How wretched, hateful, maddening and ridiculous!

Now she had been liberated. I'm a girl of nineteen, so all of you shut up! She looked up at the clear blue sky flecked with small white clouds like handkerchiefs to gag those officious gossips. Wonderful! Throwing out her chest, glancing neither to right nor left, she hurried with a light step to the bicycle shed, found her 'Pigeon' bicycle and flew off like a pigeon herself through the main gate.

It was the rush hour. The crowded streets were lined with state stores, collectively run or private shops. Pop music sounded on all sides. 'I love you. . . .' 'You don't love me. . . .' 'I can't live without you. . . .' 'You've no place in your heart for me. . . .' To hell with that rubbish!

Love was no longer old stock to be sold off fast. At nineteen she had plenty of time, plenty of chances. She must give top priority now to studying and improving herself. Real knowledge and ability could benefit society and create happiness for the people, thereby earning her respect, enriching her life and making it more significant. Then love would naturally seek her out and of course she wouldn't refuse it. But it should be a quiet, deep, half-hidden love.

She must get into college. Nineteen was just the age to go to college. There was no time to be wasted. If she did well in a television college or night school she could get a diploma. Still those weren't regular universities, not up to Beijing or Qinghua. Her life had been ruined by the interruption to her education. Strictly speaking she had reached only primary school standard, because in her fourth year in primary school the 'cultural revolution' had started; but after skipping about in the alley for several years she counted as having finished her primary education. In middle school she felt as dizzy as if in a plane, unable to grasp nine-tenths of what they were taught, yet somehow or other she managed to graduate. Sent down to the country to steel herself by labour, she had forgotten the little she'd learned. When the 'revolution' ended she went back to the city to wait for a job, but none materialized. She contrived to get into the service team under the bureau, though that was a collective, not state-run. Reckoning up like this, it seemed there was only one way for her to spend the rest of her life—find a husband, start a family, wash nappies, buy oil, salt, soya sauce, vinegar and grain, change the gas cylinder and squabble.

Was that all there was to life? It wasn't enough for Sufen. One should achieve something, leave something behind. But with her primary school level, unable to grow rice or to mine coal, she was neither worker nor peasant, an 'intellectual' with no education, a wretched ghost cut off from humankind.

She'd started from ABC. Spent practically all her spare time attending classes, and most of her pay on school fees and textbooks. Chinese, maths, English, drawing—she studied them all. But this method of catching up was too slow, too much of a strain. She wanted a crash course. Her age was against her. If she couldn't get quicker results, even if she ended up fully proficient it would be too late for her to win recognition.

She concentrated on English, hoping to make a breakthrough. Studied different textbooks, radio materials, TV classes and crash courses all at the same time. After a month she discovered that this breach was already besieged by countless others. All elderly bachelors or unmarried girls like her, trying to find a short cut to success. And this wasn't a short cut either. Because even if you gained a good grasp of English what use would it be in China which is still backward as far as culture is concerned? Translate English into Chinese? Chinese into English? There were plenty of good translators among the graduates from foreign languages colleges. Who was going to look for new talents among young people waiting for employment?

She transferred to the 'Correspondence College for Writers'. Why not write stories or poems to disclose all the frustrations, uncertainties and aspirations of our generation? Let the reading public and youth of the twenty-first century know that for one brief phase in China the younger generation was unfairly treated and stupefied by history. Through no fault of their own they had lost all that should have been theirs by right and been burdened with a heavy load they hadn't deserved. They would have to live out their lives weighed down by this crushing burden.

TEN YEARS DEDUCTED

To talk of writing was easy. But how many works written by her age group made any appeal? When you picked up your pen you didn't know where to start. She'd torn off so many sheets from her pad that her family were desperately afraid that she was possessed. Apparently not everyone could be a writer.

Then what about studying accountancy? Accountants were in great demand. . . .

She couldn't make up her mind. She vacillated, frustrated and unsure of herself, not knowing what she wanted or ought to do. Someone advised her, 'Don't be senseless. At your age, just muddle along.' Someone else said, 'Once you're married you'll feel settled.'

But that was the last thing she wanted.

Now this stupendous change: flowers were blooming, birds singing, the world had suddenly become infinitely beautiful. Subtract ten years and I'm just nineteen. To hell with all hesitation, frustration and wretchedness. Life hasn't abandoned me, the world belongs to me again. I must treasure every single moment and waste no time. Must set my life goals, not turn off the right track again. I mean to study, go to college and get myself a real education. This is my first objective.

Yes, starting today, as of now, I'll press towards this goal.

Cycling along and smiling all over her face, she headed for the textbook department of the Xinhua Bookstore.

The next morning the whole bureau seethed with excitement. Upstairs and down, inside and out, all was bustle, talk and laughter. Cardiac cases climbed up to the fifth floor without wheezing, changing colour or heart palpitations, as if nothing were wrong with them. Men of over sixty who normally talked slowly and indistinctly now raised their voices and spoke so incisively that they could be heard from one end of the corridor to the other. The doors of all the offices stood wide open and people wandered about as if at a fair to share their excitement, elation, dreams and illimitable plans.

Suddenly someone suggested:

'Let's parade through the town to celebrate this new liberation!'

At once everyone went into action. Some wrote slogans on banners, some made little green and red flags. The head of the recreation committee fetched out from the storeroom a drum the size of a round table and the red silk used for folk dances. In no time they all assembled in front of the bureau. Written in yellow characters on the red banners was the slogan, 'Celebrate the return of youth'. The small flags voiced their inmost feelings: 'Support the brilliant decision of the Age Research Association', 'Our new youth is devoted to modernization', 'Long live youth!'

The big drum beat a rousing tattoo. Ji Wenyao felt his blood was boiling. Standing at the top of the steps he meant to say a few inspiring words before leading this grand parade, when suddenly he saw dozens of retired cadres rush in. Charging up to him they demanded:

'Why weren't we notified of this deduction of ten years?'

'You . . . you've already retired,' he said.

'No! That won't do!' the old men chorused.

Ji raised both hands and called from the top of the steps:

'Quiet, comrades. Please. . . .'

They paid no attention, the roar of their voices rising to the sky.

'Ten years deducted applies to everyone. It's not fair to leave us out.'

'We must carry out the directive, not just do as we please.' Ji's voice had risen an octave.

'Where's the directive? Why hasn't it been relayed?'

'Show us the directive!'

'Why don't you let us see it?'

Ji turned to the head of the general office.

'Where's the directive?'

The man answered bluntly:

'I don't know.'

They were in this impasse when shouts went up from some newly recruited workers in their late teens:

'Ten years taken off—nothing doing!'

'Have we grown up for eighteen years and landed a job, just to be sent back to primary school—no way!'

The children of the bureau's kindergarten trooped up to Ji too like a flock of ducklings. Clinging to his legs and grabbing his hands they prattled:

'Ten years off, where can we go?'

'Mummy had to be cut open when I was born.'

In desperation Ji called again to the head of the general office:

'The directive—hurry up and fetch the directive.'

Seeing the man at a loss he thundered:

'Go and get it, quick, from the section for confidential documents.'

The man rushed off to hunt through all the directives there, but failed to find it.

Well-meaning suggestions were made:

'Could it have been put in the archives?'

'Could it have been lent out?'

'Dammit! Suppose it's been thrown away!'

In all this confusion Ji kept a cool head. He ordered:

'Everybody's to make a search. Look carefully, all of you, in every corner.'

'Shall we call off the parade?' asked the head of the general office.

'Why should we? First find that directive!'

2
THE BALLAD OF MULAN

Anonymous
Sixth century AD

In the fifth century AD, Mulan disguised herself as a man to take her father's place in battle, maintaining the ruse for a dozen years. These verses, penned a hundred years later in northern China, are one of many tributes to one of the great folk heroines of China. Further tribute was paid in the animated 1998 Disney movie and in the fiction of Maxine Hong Kingston.

Click, click, for ever click, click;
   Mulan sits at the door and weaves.
   Listen, and you will not hear the shuttle's sound,
But only hear a girl's sobs and sighs.
'Oh, tell me, lady, are you thinking of your love,
Oh tell me, lady, are you longing for your dear?'
'Oh no, oh no, I am not thinking of my love,
Oh no, oh no, I am not longing for my dear.
But last night I read the battle-roll;
The Khan has ordered a great levy of men.
The battle-roll was written in twelve books,
And in each book stood my father's name.
My father's sons are not grown men,
And of all my brothers, none is older than me.
Oh, let me to the market to buy saddle and horse,
And ride with the soldiers to take my father's place.'
In the eastern market she's bought a gallant horse,
In the western market she's bought saddle and cloth.
In the southern market she's bought snaffle and reins,
In the northern market she's bought a tall whip.
In the morning she stole from her father's and mother's house;
At night she was camping by the Yellow River's side.

She could not hear her father and mother calling to her by her name,
But only the voice of the Yellow River as its waters swirled through the night.
At dawn they left the River and went on their way;
At dusk they came to the Black Water's side.
She could not hear her father and mother calling to her by her name,
She could only hear the muffled voices of foreign horsemen riding on the hills of Yen.
A thousand leagues she tramped on the errands of war,
Frontiers and hills she crossed like a bird in flight,
Through the northern air echoed the watchman's tap;
The wintry light gleamed on coats of mail.
The captain had fought a hundred fights, and died;
The warriors in ten years had won their rest.
They went home, they saw the Emperor's face;
The deeds of the brave were recorded in twelve books;
In prizes he gave a hundred thousand cash.
Then spoke the Khan and asked her what she would take.
'Oh, Mulan asks not to be made
A Counsellor at the Khan's court;
I only beg for a camel that can march
A thousand leagues a day,
To take me back to my home.'
When her father and mother heard that she had come,
They went out to the wall and led her back to the house.
When her little sister heard that she had come,
She went to the door and rouged her face afresh.
When her little brother heard that his sister had come,
He sharpened his knife and darted like a flash
Towards the pigs and sheep.
She opened the gate that leads to the eastern tower,
She sat on her bed that stood in the western tower.
She caste aside her heavy soldier's cloak,
And wore again her old-time dress.
She stood at the window and bound her cloudy hair;
She went to the mirror and fastened her yellow combs.
She left the house and met her messmates in the road;
Her messmates were startled out of their wits.

CHINESE WOMEN

They had marched with her for twelve years of war
And never known that Mulan was a girl.
For the male hare sits with its legs tucked in,
And the female hare is known for her bleary eye;
But set them both scampering side by side,
And who so wise could tell you 'This is he'?

3
PRINCE HUO'S DAUGHTER

JIANG FANG
EARLY NINTH CENTURY AD

Short stories flourished in China during the Tang Dynasty (618–907 AD) becoming more complex than earlier tales and influencing later writers. Based on a true story, often retold in China, this one is set in Chang'an (now Xian), the capital and cultural centre during the Tang Dynasty. Its heroine, named Ciao, falls in love with Li Yi, a renowned poet, but his parents plan to use his fame to attract a prosperous bride. The story includes many strong and intelligent female characters such as the matchmaker, mother, maid, and with a touch of the supernatural, the loyal heroine.

During the Da Li period (766–779), there was a young man of Longxi whose name was Li Yi. At the age of twenty he passed one of the civil service examinations and the following year the best scholars of his rank were to be chosen for official posts through a further examination at the Ministry of Civil Affairs. In the sixth month he arrived at the capital and took lodgings in the Xinchang quarter. He came from a good family, showed brilliant promise, and was acknowledged by his contemporaries as unsurpassed in literary craftsmanship. Thus even senior scholars looked up to him. Having no mean opinion of his own gifts, he hoped for a beautiful and accomplished wife. But long and vainly did he search among the famous courtesans of the capital.

In Chang'an there was a match-maker named Bao, who was the eleventh child in her family. She had been a maidservant in the prince consort's family, but a dozen years before this had redeemed herself and married. Clever and with a ready tongue, she knew all the great families and was a past master at arranging matches. Li gave her rich gifts and asked her to find him a wife, and she was very well disposed towards him.

One afternoon, some months later, Li was sitting in the south pavilion of his lodgings when he heard insistent knocking and Bao was announced. Gathering up the skirt of his gown, he hurried to meet her. 'What brings you here so unexpectedly, madam?' he asked.

Bao laughed and responded, 'Have you been having sweet dreams? A fairy has come down to earth who cares nothing for wealth but who admires wit and gallantry. She is made for you!'

When Li heard this he leaped for joy and felt as if he were walking on air. Taking Bao's hand he bowed and thanked her, saying: 'I shall be your slave as long as I live!'

Asked where the girl lived and what her name was, Bao replied: 'She is the youngest daughter of Prince Huo. Her name is Jade, and the prince doted on her. Her mother, Qinchi, was his favourite slave. When the prince died, his sons refused to keep the child because her mother was of humble birth, so they gave her a portion and made her leave. She has changed her name to Zheng, and people do not know that the prince was her father. But she is the most beautiful creature you ever saw, with a sensibility and grace beyond compare. She is well versed too in music and the classics. Yesterday she asked me to find a good match for her, and when I mentioned your name she was delighted, for she knows you by reputation. They live in Old Temple Lane in the Shengye quarter, in the house at the entrance to the carriage drive. I have already made an appointment for you. Go tomorrow at noon to the end of the lane, and look for a maid called Guizi. She will show you the house.'

As soon as the match-maker left, Li started to prepare for the great occasion, sending his servant Qiuhong to borrow a black charger with a gilt bit from his cousin Shang who was adjutant general of the capital. That evening he washed his clothes, had a bath, and shaved. He could not sleep all night for joy. At dawn he put on his cap and examined himself in the mirror, fearing all might not go well. Having frittered away the time till noon, he called for the horse and galloped to the Shengye quarter. When he reached the place appointed, he saw a maid standing there waiting for him, who asked, 'Are you Master Li?' He dismounted, told the maid to stable the horse, and went quickly in, bolting the gate behind him.

The match-maker came out from the house, smiling at him from a distance as she cried, 'Who is this gatecrasher?' While they were joking with each other, he found himself led through the inner gate into a courtyard where there were four cherry trees and a parrot cage hanging on the northwest side.

At the sight of Li, the parrot squawked, 'Here's a guest! Lower the curtain!'

Naturally bashful, Li had felt some scruples about going in, and now the parrot startled him and brought him to a standstill until Bao led the girl's mother down the steps to welcome him, and he was asked to go inside and take a seat opposite her. The mother, little more than forty, was a slender, attractive woman with charming manners.

'We have heard of your brilliance as a scholar,' she said to Li, 'and now that I see what a handsome young man you are too, I am sure your fame is well deserved. I have a daughter who, though lacking in education, is not ill-favoured. She should be a suitable match for you. Madame Bao has already proposed this, and today I would like to offer my daughter to you in marriage.'

'I am a clumsy fellow,' he replied, 'and do not deserve such a distinction. If you accept me, I shall count it a great honour as long as I live.'

Then a feast was laid, Jade was called by her mother from the east chamber, and Li bowed to greet her. At her entrance, he felt as if the room had been transformed into a bower of roses, and when their eyes met he was dazzled by her glance. The girl sat down beside her mother, who said to her, 'You like to repeat those lines:

When the wind in the bamboos rustles the curtain,
I fancy my old friend is near.

Here is the author of the poem. You have been reading his works so often—what do you think of him now you see him?'

Jade lowered her head and answered with a smile: 'He doesn't live up to my expectations. Shouldn't a poet be more handsome?'

Then Li got up and made several bows. 'You love talent and I admire beauty,' he said. 'Between us we have both!'

Jade and her mother looked at each other and smiled.

When they had drunk several cups of wine together, Li stood up and asked the girl to sing. At first she declined, but her mother insisted, and in a clear voice she sang an intricate melody. By the time they had drunk their fill it was evening, and the match-maker led the young man to the west wing to rest. The rooms were secluded in a quiet courtyard, and the hangings were magnificent. Bao told the maids Guizi and Wansha to take off Li's boots and belt. Then Jade herself appeared. With sweet archness and charming coyness she put off her clothes. Then they lowered the bed-curtains, lay down on the pillows and enjoyed each other to their hearts' content. The young man felt that he was in bed with a goddess.

During the night, however, the girl suddenly gazed at him through tears and said, 'As a courtesan, I know I am no match for you. You love me now for my looks, but I fear that when I lose them your feelings will change, and then I shall be like a vine with nothing to cling to, or a fan discarded in the autumn. So at the height of my joy I cannot help grieving.'

Li was touched, and putting his arm round her neck said gently, 'Today I have attained the dream of my life. I swear I would sooner die than leave you. Why do you talk like that? Let me have some white silk to pledge you my faith in writing.'

Drying her tears, Jade called her maid Yingtao to raise the curtain and hold the candle, while she gave Li a brush and ink. When not occupied with music, Jade was fond of reading, and her writing-case, brushes and ink all came from the palace. Now she brought out an embroidered case and from it took three feet of white silk lined with black for him to write on. The young man had a gift for contemporary composition, and taking up the brush wrote rapidly. He swore by the mountains and rivers, by the sun and the moon, that he would be true. He wrote passionately and movingly, and when he had finished he gave Jade his pledge to keep in her jewel box.

After that they lived happily for two years like a pair of kingfishers soaring on high, together day and night. But in the spring of the third year, Li came first in his examination and was appointed secretary-general of Zheng County. In the fourth month, before leaving to take up his post and to visit his parents in Luoyang, he gave a farewell party for all his relatives at the capital. It was the season between spring and summer. When the feast was over and the guests had gone, the young man and the girl were filled with grief at their coming separation.

'With your talents and fame,' said Jade, 'you have many admirers who would like to be related to you by marriage. And your old parents at home have no daughter-in-law to look after them. So when you go to take up this post, you are bound to find a good wife. The pledge you made me is not binding. But I have a small request to make, which I hope you will consider. May I tell you what it is?'

Li was startled and protested, 'In what way have I offended you, that you speak like this? Tell me what is on your mind, and I promise to do whatever you ask.'

'I am eighteen,' said the girl, 'and you are only twenty-two. There are still eight years before you reach thirty, the age at which a man should marry. I would like to crowd into these eight years all the love and happiness of my life. After that you can choose some girl of good family for a wife—it will not be too late. Then I shall retire from the world, cutting my hair short and becoming a nun. This is the wish of my life and I ask no more.'

Cut to the heart, Li could not hold back his tears. 'I swear by the bright sun,' he assured the girl, 'as long as I live I shall be true to you. My only fear is that I may fail to please you—how can I think of anything else? I beg you not to doubt me, but rest assured. I shall reach Huazhou in the eighth month and send to fetch you. We shall be together again before very long.' A few days later he said goodbye to her and went east.

Ten days after Li's arrival at his post, he asked leave to go to Luoyang to see his parents. Before he reached home, his mother had arranged a match for him with a cousin in the Lu family—a verbal agreement had already been reached. His mother was so strict that Li, though hesitating, dared not decline; accordingly he went through with the ceremonies and arranged a date for the wedding. Since the girl's family was a powerful one, they demanded over a million cash betrothal money and would call off the marriage if this were not forthcoming. Because Li's family was poor he had to borrow this sum; and he took advantage of his leave to look up distant friends, travelling up and down the Huai and Yangtse River valleys from the autumn till the next summer. Knowing that he had broken his promise to fetch Jade at the appointed time, he sent no message to her, hoping that she would give him up. He also asked his friends not to disclose the truth.

When Li failed to return at the appointed time, Jade tried to find out what had become of him, only to receive contradictory reports.

She also consulted many fortune-tellers and oracles. This went on for more than a year, until at last she fell ill of sorrow; and, lying in her lonely room, went from bad to worse. Though no tidings had come from Li, her love for him did not falter, and she gave presents to friends and acquaintances to persuade them to find news of him. This she did so persistently that soon all her money had gone and she often had to send her maid out secretly to sell dresses and trinkets through an innkeeper in the West Market.

One day Jade sent Wansha to sell an amethyst hair-pin, and on her way to the inn the maid met an old jade-smith who worked in the palace. When he saw what she was carrying, he recognized it. 'This hair-pin is one I made,' he said. 'Many years ago, when Prince Huo's youngest daughter first put up her hair, he ordered me to make this pin and gave me ten thousand cash for the job. I have always remembered it. Who are you? And how did you come by this?'

'My mistress is the prince's daughter,' replied the maid. 'She has come down in the world, and the man she married went to

Luoyang and deserted her. So she fell ill of grief, and has been in a decline for two years. Now she wants me to sell this, so that she can bribe someone to get news of her husband.'

The jade-smith shed tears, exclaiming, 'Can the children of nobles fall on such evil times? My days are nearly spent, but this ill-fated lady's story wrings my heart.'

Then the old man led Wansha to the house of Princess Yanxian, and when the princess heard this story she too heaved sigh after sigh. Finally she gave the maid one hundred and twenty thousand cash for the hair-pin.

Now the girl to whom Li was engaged was in the capital. After raising the sum he needed for his marriage, he returned to his post in Zheng County; but at the end of the year he again asked for leave to go to Chang'an to get married. And he found quiet lodgings, so that his whereabouts would not be known. A young scholar, however, named Cui Yunming, who was Li's cousin and a kind-hearted man, had formerly drunk with Li in Jade's room and laughed and talked with her until they were on the best of terms. Whenever he received news of Li, he would tell Jade truthfully, and she had helped him so often with money and clothing that he felt deeply indebted to her.

When Li came to the capital, Cui told Jade, who sighed and exclaimed indignantly, 'How can he be so faithless?' She begged all her friends to ask Li to come to her; but knowing that he had broken his promise and that the girl was dying, he felt too ashamed to see her. He took to going out early and coming back late in order to avoid callers. Though Jade wept day and night, unable to eat or sleep in her longing to see him, he never came. And indignation and grief made her illness worse. When the story became known in the capital, all the young scholars were moved by the girl's love while all the young gallants resented Li's heartlessness.

It was then spring, the season for pleasure trips, and Li went one day with five or six friends to Chongqing Temple to see the peonies in bloom. Strolling in the west corridor, they composed poems together. A close friend of Li's named Wei Xiaqing, a native of Chang'an, was one of the party. 'Spring is beautiful and flowers are in bloom,' he told Li. 'But your old love nurses her grief in her lonely room. It is really cruel of you to abandon her. A true man would not do this. Think it over again!'

As Wei was sighing and reproaching Li, up came a young gallant wearing a yellow silk shirt and carrying a crossbow.

He was handsome and splendidly dressed, but attended only by a Central Asian boy with cropped hair. Walking behind them, he overheard their conversation; and presently he stepped forward and bowed to Li, saying, 'Is your name not Li? My family comes from the east, and we are related to the royal house. Though I have no literary talent myself, I value it in others. I have long been an admirer of yours and hoped to make your acquaintance, and today I am lucky enough to meet you. My humble house is not far from here, and I have musicians to entertain you. I have eight or nine beautiful girls too, and a dozen good horses, all of them at your disposal. I only hope you will honour me with a visit.'

When Li's friends heard this, they were delighted. They rode along after this young gallant, who swiftly turned corner after corner until they reached the Shengye quarter. Since they were approaching Jade's house, Li was reluctant to go any farther and made some excuse to turn back.

But the stranger said: 'My humble home is only a stone's throw from here. Don't leave us now!' He took hold of Li's bridle and pulled his horse along.

In a moment they had reached the girl's house. Li was dismayed and tried to turn back, but the other quickly ordered attendants to help him dismount and lead him inside. They pushed him through the gate and bolted it, calling out, 'Master Li is here!' Then exclamations of joy and surprise could be heard from the whole house.

The night before, Jade had dreamed that Li was brought to her bedside by a man in a yellow shirt and that she was told to take off her shoes. When she woke up she told her mother this dream, and said, 'Shoes symbolize union. That means that husband and wife will meet again. But to take them off means separation. We shall be united then parted again—for ever. Judging by this dream, I shall see him once more and after that I shall die.'

In the morning she asked her mother to dress her hair for her. Her mother thought she was raving and paid no attention, but when Jade insisted she consented. And no sooner was her hair done than Li arrived.

Jade had been ill so long that she could not even turn in bed without help. But on hearing that her lover had come she got up swiftly, changed her clothes and hurried out like one possessed. Confronting Li in silence, she fixed angry eyes on him. So frail she could hardly stand, she kept averting her face and then, against her will, looking back, till all present were moved to tears.

Soon several dozen dishes of food and wine were brought in. And when the company asked in astonishment where this feast had come from, they found it had been ordered by the young gallant. The table spread, they sat down. Jade, though she had turned away from Li, kept stealing long glances at him; and finally raising her cup of wine, she poured a libation on the ground and said, 'I am the unhappiest of women, and you are the most heartless of men. Dying young of a broken heart, I shall not be able to look after my mother; and I must bid farewell for ever to my silk dresses and music, to suffer torments in hell. This is your doing, sir! Farewell! After death I shall become an avenging spirit and give your wives and concubines no peace.'

Grasping Li's arm with her left hand, she threw her cup to the ground. Then, after crying out several times, she fell dead. Her mother placed her body on Li's knee and told him to call her, but he could not revive her.

Li put on mourning and wept bitterly during the wake. The night before the obsequies she appeared to him within the funeral curtain, as beautiful as in life. She was wearing a pomegranate-red skirt, purple tunic, and red and green cape. Leaning against the curtain and fingering the embroidered tassels, she looked at him and said, 'You must still have some feeling for me, to see me off. That is a comfort to me here among the shades.' With that she vanished. The next day she was buried at Yusuyuan near the capital. After mourning by her grave, Li went back; and a month later he married his cousin. But he was in low spirits after all that had happened.

In the fifth month, Li went with his wife to his post at Zheng County. About ten days after their arrival, he was sleeping with his wife when he heard soft hoots outside the curtain, and looking out he saw a very handsome young man hiding behind the hangings and beckoning repeatedly to his wife. Li leaped up in agitation and went round the curtain several times to look for the intruder, but no one was there. This made him so suspicious that he gave his wife no peace until some friends persuaded him to make it up and he began to feel a little better. About ten days later, however, he came home to find his wife playing her lute on the couch, when an engraved rhinoceros-horn case, little over an inch in diameter and tied with a flimsy silk love-knot, was thrown into the room. This case fell on his wife's lap. When Li opened it, he found two love-peas, one Spanish fly as well as other aphrodisiacs and love-charms. Howling like a wild beast in his anger, he seized the lute and beat his wife with it as he demanded the truth. But she could not clear herself. After that he often beat her savagely and treated her with great cruelty; and finally he denounced her in the court and divorced her.

After Li divorced his wife, he soon became suspicious of the maidservants and women slaves whom he had favoured, and some he even killed in his jealousy. Once he went to Yangzhou and bought a famous courtesan named Ying, who was the eleventh child of her family. She was so charming and beautiful that Li was very fond of her. But when they were together he liked to tell her about another girl he had purchased, and how he had punished her for various faults. He told her such things every day to make her fear him, so that she would not dare to take other lovers. Whenever he went out, he would leave her on the bed covered up with a bath-tub which was sealed all round; and upon his return he would examine the tub carefully before letting her out. He also kept a very sharp dagger and would say to his maids, 'This is Gexi steel. It's good for cutting the throats of unfaithful women!'

Whatever women he had, he would soon grow suspicious of them, and he was a jealous husband to the two other wives he married later.

4
THE WIFE OF TA TZU

Liu Xiang
77–76 BC

The Lie Nü Zhuan *is a compilation of tales of virtuous historical women told by Liu Xiang. It became a standard text, read by literate women and commended to all as a shining example of illustrious womanhood. In this story the wife's cleverness, bravery and independence saves her from her husband's fate.*

She was the wife of Ta Tzu, an official of T'ao. Ta Tzu had spent three years in subjugating T'ao and his reputation was not very glorious but his family fortune had increased three times. Although his wife admonished him frequently, he did not accept her advice. He served in office for five years and a hundred carts followed him when he returned home on leave. His tribesmen slew a cow and congratulated him but his wife remained alone holding her child and weeping silently.

The mother-in-law in anger said, 'Why this unpropitious omen?'

The wife replied, 'My husband's ability is small and his position great; this is called "stirring up trouble". He is without merit and his family is affluent. This is called "piling up misfortune".'

'Formerly in Ch'u, the Chief Minister, Tzu Wen Chih, ruled the country. His family was poor and the country wealthy; the ruler was sedate and the people respectful; and hence there was prosperity and happiness for his posterity. His name was handed down to later generations. Today, my husband's situation is the contrary, for his family is wealthy and his duty is great but he does not regard the later misfortune that will follow.

'I, the wife, learned that the South Mountain had a black leopard. There was fog and rain for seven days and he did not come down the mountain to eat. Why was that? He wished to make his hair glossy and he became spotted. For this reason he hid and avoided misfortune. If the dog and the pig do not choose their food in order to fatten their bodies but sit in one place they must die. At present, my husband is ruling T'ao. His family is wealthy and the kingdom is poor; the ruler is not sedate and the people are not respectful. It is evident proof of the ruin to come. I desire to escape with my little son.'

The mother-in-law was angry and thereafter cast her out. After a period of years, the family of Ta Tzu was really considered a criminal family to be executed. Only the mother was spared because she was old. The wife then returned with her little son and cared for the mother-in-law. In the end she died a natural death.

5
JADE

Liu Xiang
77–76 BC

Again, from the Lie Nü Zhuan, *a wise woman helps her father and saves her inheritance, despite the machinations of her gullible sisters-in-law.*

In a mud hut on one of the highest mountains there lived an old couple and their only son. (Their daughter lived in a nearby village.) They were members of a tribe which traditionally encouraged each man to marry two wives, and their son observed this tradition. He married twice, calling his wives Big Wife and Little Wife, and returned with his brides to the home of his parents.

But that winter an epidemic took the lives of mother and son. The two wives got all the family property and lorded it over their aging father-in-law. They made him look after the oxen in the bitter cold, fed him on a starvation diet, and forced him to drink sour milk and ox blood. The poor old man almost starved to death.

Finally he could stand it no longer, so he wrote the following letter to his daughter:

'Mother and Elder Brother have passed away, and I am living on sour milk—and ox blood. Oh yes, and sometimes my two daughters-in-law give me water to drink. Can you do anything to help me?'

When his daughter got the letter, she enclosed a precious piece of jade in a brick and had it delivered to her father by a trusted servant. And she warned him never to sell it. The old man understood her perfectly, for here's what he did. He broke open the brick in the woods, secured the jade, and returned home. There he showed the jade to Big Daughter-in-law and told her that when he died it would be hers. She was delighted to hear this and she gave him food to eat and fine clothes to wear, thinking that the end was near.

One day when she was out of the house he showed Little Daughter-in-law the jade and made her the same promise, and she too treated him like a king. So his promise of the jade made his final years comfortable and pleasant.

But then one day the old man got deathly sick and he realized that the end was near. He hid the jade on a rafter, right above a huge water jar, and when both daughters-in-law were out he gave his servant the following message for his daughter:

'Tell her to come and see me. But if I die before she arrives, tell her there's something precious on the neck of the dragon. And its shadow falls on the surface of the water.'

Soon after he died, and the daughters-in-law searched everywhere for the jade but without success. They then went back to their native villages and not a day later Only Daughter came by and by following her late father's instructions recovered the jade from its perch on the rafter.

6
ELDER SISTER

Liu Xiang
77–76 AD

In another story from the Lie Nü Zhuan, *an intelligent woman knows more of propriety and the affairs of men than her younger brother, but custom dictates that she must be ruled by him.*

The elder sister of Kung-ch'eng of Lu was also the elder sister of Kung-ch'eng Tzu-p'i of Lu. All the members of their clan died and the elder sister wept over it very sorrowfully but Tzu-p'i stopped her, saying, 'Be quiet now and I shall arrange a marriage for you, Elder Sister.'

The time for marrying passed and Tzu-p'i had not fulfilled his word. The ruler of Lu wished to use Tzu-p'i as minister and Tzu-p'i asked his elder sister, saying, 'The ruler of Lu wishes to use me as minister. Shall I do it?'

The elder sister said 'Do not do it!'

Tzu-p'i asked, 'Why not?'

The elder sister said, 'When we were still in mourning, you spoke of marrying me to someone; and so in the first place you did not practise propriety. Then the time having passed you did not speak of it; and so in the second place you do not understand men's affairs. At home you do not practise propriety, and outside the home, you do not understand men's affairs, then how could you be a minister of State?'

Tzu-p'i said, 'If my Elder Sister desired to get married, why did she not speak of it sooner?'

The Elder Sister said, 'The duty of a woman is to wait until someone starts to sing and then she accompanies him. How could I use the reason of desiring to marry to urge you on? You really are not versed in propriety and you do not understand men's affairs. If such a person were used as minister of State, who has to manage a great number of people, how would he manage them? It would be like covering a man's eyes in order that he distinguish black and white and yet no misfortune would result from it. You, who do not understand men's affairs, would be an official of the State; if you would not receive a Heaven-sent calamity, you certainly would suffer a man-made misfortune. You should not do it!'

At last he succeeded in becoming a minister but he filled the office for no great period of time and in the end he was executed.

7
ULTIMATE CAUSES
Xiao Yan
464–549 AD

In Xiao Yan's poem, we see that occasionally a woman was educated and able to use her literary talents. Here she muses on the cryptic nature of the universe.

Trees grow, not alike,
    by the mound and the moat;
  Birds sing in the forest
    with varying note;
Of the fish in the river
    some dive and some float.
The mountains rise high
    and the waters sink low,
But the why and the wherefore
    we never can know.

8
THE COWARDLY BRAGGART
Howard Levy
1970s

> *In this retelling of an old folktale, an enterprising and energetic woman reforms and mobilizes her husband.*

A foolish man in Mongolia once married a well-to-do woman. But after they wed he wasn't willing to do a single thing in or out of the house, and he just lay in bed all day long. His wife saw how he was depending on her for everything just like a parasite, and she felt very unhappy about this. She decided that she'd have to do something to make a wage earner out of him.

One day she was walking along a border road frequented by merchants when she noticed that someone had left behind valuable hawk feathers. She didn't pick them up, but immediately rushed home and said to her husband, 'Run down to the highway the merchants use and see what they've left behind, won't you?' The husband obediently but lazily strolled over to that road, discovered the hawk feathers, and sold them to a man who made arrows, earning some money through the transaction. He proudly returned home and gave the money to his wife, boasting about his money-earning capacity, and his wife praised him highly.

A few days later she gave her husband a horse, a bow, some arrows and a few provisions, and told him to go back to the border road and there seek his fortune. He rode until he reached a place where merchants usually camped for the night. This area was far from the city, and there were many woods nearby where bandits roamed; so even though merchants slept there, they were very cautious and fearful of everything around them. He tied his horse to a tree and took shelter behind a large rock hidden by tall grass, so that while he could see people along the road, they couldn't see him. Maybe he wasn't so stupid after all! Soon afterwards a group

THE COWARDLY BRAGGART

of merchants came along and set up camp very close to him. They had brought with them many valuables, including a pearl which was used to accompany priests intoning the Buddhist sutras. He'd never seen anything like it, so he crawled quietly over to the trumpet and blew it, making a kind of eerie, musical sound.

The merchants were just then huddled together, wondering what they'd do if they were attacked by bandits, and when they heard that strange noise, they thought surely it was some signal from the bandits. They were terrified and ran away, leaving behind many valuables.

The lazy husband came out of this hiding place when he saw the merchants run away, and picked up much of what they'd left behind. After, packing it on his horse, he rode swiftly home. He told his wife that he'd attacked a group of bandits, routed them and got their booty in the bargain. Now his wife knew he was a coward and she didn't believe a thing he said, so she decided to have a little fun at his expense.

'Go back there again tomorrow,' she told him, 'but beware of that terrible bandit Su-yeh Pa-lu. He's a notorious killer who's afraid of no one, not even the King of Hell!'

'I'm not afraid of anyone either,' the husband replied, 'and if he comes near me I'll kill him for sure!'

The next day the husband got on his horse and returned to the road he'd travelled the day before. Meanwhile his wife disguised herself as a bandit, got on her horse, and rode toward him from the opposite direction. When he saw her coming, the husband thought she was Killer Su-yeh for sure, and he quivered and quaked. He got down from his horse and groveled in the dirt before her, begging for his life. His disguised wife said she'd let him live only if he kissed her feet, and he hastily did this. She then took his horse and bow and arrows away with her. After he'd walked all the way home, the husband confessed to his wife that he'd met the killer, who had humiliated him and taken his belongings.

The woman never told her husband about the joke she'd played on him. And he never made a false boast again.

9
PRETTY THIRD DAUGHTER

Chinese Profiles
1980s

Chinese Profiles *is the title of a book published in the 1980s containing conversations with a variety of Chinese people. Here, a modern girl handles an enviable problem.*

We are friends so you must be sure not to show me up. I've already suffered a lot for being pretty. Of course it's been an advantage sometimes too. All in all, I couldn't really say whether it's been a good thing or not. That's a proper puzzler.
    Why do you want to write about me anyway?
    'How does it feel to be pretty?'
    What do you mean? Am I so different from other people?
    I was born in Beijing in 1955. I already had two elder sisters and after me a brother was born. Then my father decided that was enough. He had a boy to carry on the family line. None of the others was particularly good-looking. I don't know why I turned out like this. I just don't have the ordinary Wu family looks.
    It was in my second year at junior middle school that I realized I was pretty. Of course people had always said I was a pretty little girl, but I thought they were just being nice. Obviously by the time we were at middle school, we weren't completely innocent about sex, but we didn't know all that much either. I was aware that several of the boys fancied me. I couldn't help knowing. They were always trying to please me and showing off....
    You think I was lucky? Only thirteen and boys were falling in love with me. Of course they were only interested in me for my looks. I wasn't very good at getting on with people....
    Once I was back in the city, I was sent to work in a factory canteen. I couldn't stay in that job. I had to ask for a transfer. The reason was that everyday the queue in front of me was always the

longest, and they were all men waiting for me to serve them. Some of them were so shameless they wrote me little notes on their food tickets. I took no notice at all but afterwards the person who checked the food tickets would say, 'Oh, here's a letter for you, Little Wu.' She was teasing of course. I was transferred on to driving a crane which was very easy. As usual, everyone looked after me. Once the crane cable snapped and a big shaft fell down just missing one of the workers. If it had hit him it would certainly have killed him. He was only a young fellow but he was the only one who dared scold me. You're right. There wasn't anything frightening about me. It's just that the others were so much in awe of my looks. I admired him for having more to him. I didn't want to drive the crane any more after that, so I applied for another transfer and was sent to work on a grinder. That was very light work too, because it was electronically controlled.

Too many men were just knocked backwards by my looks. And women? With women it was the opposite. I felt that all the women hated me. They regarded me as a potential thief because they were afraid I would steal their men. Even the ones who hadn't got boyfriends somehow felt the same.

I got married to a technician when I was 27. It was all based on fantasy. I had wanted to marry someone who knew how to struggle. It was too romantic. I don't want to talk about my husband. I think we've both got an idea of what may happen, even though I'm about to become a mother. Even if we wanted to make it last, it wouldn't work. It can't go on. Don't push me. Don't ask about it.

Yes. Prettiness—this is my advantage, my 'capital'. But I always seem to like the people who don't take any notice of it. The pity is I don't have anything else to give. No, nothing.

10
MADAME MAO

Ross Terrill

1999

Jiang Qing, 1914–91, gained power as the wife of Mao Zedong during the Cultural Revolution. After his death in 1976, she was denounced as one of the counter-revolutionary Gang of Four. They were accused of attempting to usurp power and assassinate Huo Guofeng, the new party chairman. Born into an impoverished Shandong family, Jiang Qing became a film actress in the 1930s before her marriage. The cultural life of China was her particular interest, and some of the control she exercised is described below.

Jiang oversaw the production of *The Red Detachment of Women*, a feminist military saga set in tropical Hainan Island, and *White-Haired Girl*, a harrowing tale about an evil landlord and a persecuted maiden. These dance-dramas were an amalgam of Chinese ritual and Western romanticism. Jiang hated existing ballets, such as *Swan Lake*, full of birds and beasts; ballets should be full of human will, she said. She made her dancers live with army units so they would better portray war and struggle in their movements and facial expressions. After removing scenes of childbirth and sex from the original version of *Red Detachment*, Jiang added a nearly religious finale, glorifying Mao, on the theme of resurrection.

One day in the winter of 1965 Jiang dropped in on the Central Philharmonic Society. 'The capitalist symphony is dead,' she announced. The musicians politely objected that she knew little about music; she retorted that she was bringing them the higher grace of revolutionary fervor. 'You're attacking me with a hammer,' the conductor of the orchestra complained. But nothing pleased Jiang more than to be thought of as a fearsome attacker. She later took up the conductor's remark as a boast, 'With hammer in hand, I set out to attack all the old conventions.' She pounced on 'unhealthy passages' in the existing repertoire. She sent a pianist south to retrace the route of one of Mao's military campaigns so that he could more movingly play the fierce Yellow River Concerto. By sheer force of will, unencumbered by detailed knowledge of the subject, she threw together a model symphony adapted from the opera *Shajiabang*. One shocked violinist could not help murmuring, 'I honestly can't regard *Shajiabang* as a symphony.' Zhou Yang objected on behalf of the orchestra 'We already have a very tight schedule without adding this thing.'

Jiang swept all objections aside. What counted was that *Shajiabang* was hers, her child just as Li Na was her child, and when she adorned it with a flourish here and an accent there, it was just as if she were dressing little Li Na in a fresh outfit, hoping to color the girl in her own image. Eventually she surfaced with two musical models, *Yellow River Concerto* and *Shajiabang Symphony*. Music was to serve the 'revolution'; music was to serve the career of Jiang Qing.

11
A LADY HAD A LOVER

Herbert Giles
1925

Clever quips abound in Chinese literature and have sometimes been collected by Westerners. The following comes from a collection by the prolific sinologue, Herbert Giles.

A lady had a lover who lived next door. Hearing her husband come home, the lover jumped out of the window; and when the husband got in, the first thing he saw was a man's shoe. Cursing his wife roundly, he put the shoe under his pillow and went to sleep, saying, 'Wait till tomorrow, when I will find out whose shoe this is, and settle accounts with you.'

The wife kept awake until he was sound asleep, and then gently drew out the shoe and placed one of her husband's own shoes in its place. In the early morning, the husband got up and began again to curse his wife; but he soon discovered that the shoe was his own.

Repenting of his behaviour, he said to his wife, 'I was wrong in my suspicions of you. I must have been the man who jumped out of the window.'

PART II

CHINESE WOMEN— AS OTHERS SEE THEM

'There is no such poison in the green snake's mouth or the hornet's sting, as in a woman's heart.'

Having glimpsed women with extraordinary qualities, we now see how the position, appearance, and character of Chinese women were viewed by others. Nineteenth-century foreigners were mesmerized by the appearance of Chinese women, with their lavish robes and bound feet. They also witnessed displays of sharp temper and shrill tongues. Some women were morally lax while others were so proper that they rarely ventured outside their home compounds. And, while women could be powerful within the home, men ruled the world outside. Westerners not only observed Chinese women but often objected strenuously to the way they were treated. One, George Morrison, wrote in 1895 that although 'the lot of the average Chinese woman is certainly not one that a Western woman need envy . . . she is happy in her own way nevertheless. Happiness does not always consist in absolute enjoyment—but in the idea which we have formed of it.'

12
BOOK OF ODES
Anonymous

The Book of Odes is a much-quoted classic written in the Zhou dynasty (c. 1122–221 BC) when women were often considered to be bearers of discord. This excerpt was translated in 1923 by Herbert Giles.

A clever man builds a city,
    A clever woman pulls it down.
    Though woman's wit is sometimes heard,
    She's really an ill-omened bird.
Her long tongue's like a flight of stairs
    Which leads to miserable cares.
Disorder does not come from heaven,
    But is brought about by women.
Of all we cannot be trained or taught
    Women and eunuchs are our bane.

13
THE CONDITION OF LADIES
Julia Corner
1853

Even though Julia Corner (1798–1875) published a romantic novel, she was best known for her history books about Europe, India, and China. In this excerpt she implies that Chinese women seem to be something of a mystery to the British.

The real condition of ladies in China, and the position they hold in society, is certainly not yet very accurately known. They are seldom seen in the streets, it is true; but that is sufficiently accounted for by their inability to walk with ease; and as they do sometimes appear abroad, and are often observed at the windows without making any attempt to conceal their faces from the gaze of strangers, it is evident they enjoy far more liberty than the Turkish ladies, although it is not the custom for the sexes to mix together in general society. When a mandarin gives a grand entertainment, his wife frequently invites her friends to witness the theatrical performances, and various amusing exhibitions that are going forward during the dinner. These they can see, without being seen, from a latticed gallery provided for that purpose; and thus they are not entirely debarred from the enjoyment of the festivities, although they do not mingle with the guests.

But we must consider the sex degraded wherever the system of polygamy prevails, and wherever (as in China and all these eastern countries) men stock their harems according to their wealth and rank. Another source of degradation should seem to be the universal practice of buying and selling women. All classes of Chinese purchase their wives from the parents or legal guardians of the young women. A family of handsome daughters, particularly if well trained in ceremonials and Chinese accomplishments, are often a source of great profit to their parents. Some of the mandarins appear to be incapable of understanding that women are not sold in England. Since our war with them, the second mandarin of an imperial war-junk visited one of our ships at Hong-Kong, and was there mightily smitten by one of our fair countrywomen, a young married lady. He immediately offered to purchase her. But though so much smitten, the second mandarin had a frugal mind, and the national turn for bargaining. He began by offering a low price, telling the English gentleman that he did not think that, in the present state of the market, he would get more for her. Finding this proposition rejected, he bade for her at a gradually increasing rate, until he offered what he considered the highest price that ought ever to be given for a wife; namely, 6000 taels, or about 600*l.* English, informing the gentleman, at the same time, that he should require neither her wardrobe nor her jewels. Upon learning that it was not the custom of Englishmen to traffic in ladies, he apologised, and then begged to be allowed to buy her a gold watch and chain.

The condition of the poor women in China is apparent to all visitors, and deplorable enough. They seem to be condemned to an extraordinary share of the hardest labour. They work in the fields, harrowing, hoeing, and even ploughing; they work in the shops of carpenters and blacksmiths; they carry burthens through the streets and along the high roads; they work like the men on board the river junks; and they scull or paddle half of the sampans, or wherries, which ply on the river at Canton. An Irish sailor was heard to declare, that in China nearly all the boats were *manned* with women.

14
'REVILING THE STREET'
Arthur H. Smith
1894

A missionary in China for twenty-two years, Arthur Smith wrote vivid descriptions of Chinese customs. Here he observes that when a woman in China is upset, everyone knows it.

It is a common complaint that women use even viler language than men, and that they continue it longer, justifying the aphorism that what Chinese women have lost in the compression of their feet seems to have been made up in the volubility of their tongues.

The practice of 'reviling the street' is often indulged in by women, who mount the flat roof of the house and shriek away for hours at a time, or until their voices fail. A respectable family would not allow such a performance if they could prevent it, but in China, as elsewhere, an enraged woman is a being difficult to restrain.

When any Chinese is once seized of the idea that he has been deeply wronged, there is no power on earth which can prevent the sudden and often utterly ungovernable development of a certain amount of *ch'i* [energy], or rather of a very uncertain amount of it.

An old woman who will not take 'no' for an answer asks for financial assistance, and throws herself on the ground in front of your carter's mules. If she is run over so much the better for her, for she is thus reasonably sure of support for an indefinite period. An old vixen living in the same village as the writer was constantly threatening to commit suicide, but though all her neighbours were willing to lend their aid, she never seemed to accomplish her purpose. At last she threw herself into one of the village mudholes with intent to drown, but found to her disgust that the water was only up to her neck. She lacked that versatility of invention which would have enabled her to put her head under water and hold it there, but contented herself with reviling the whole village at the

'REVILING THE STREET'

top of her voice for her *contretemps*. The next time she was more successful.

If a wrong has been committed for which there is no legal redress, such as abuse of a married daughter beyond the point which custom warrants, a party of the injured friends will visit the house of the mother-in-law, and if they are resisted, will engage in a pitched battle. If they are not resisted, and the offending persons have fled, the assailants will proceed to smash all the crockery in the house, the mirrors, the water-jars, and whatever else is frangible, and having thus allowed their *ch'i* to escape, they depart.

15
SHOPPING
George Kates
1930s

In his book, The Years That Were Fat, *George Kates, a gentleman scholar, draws one of the most colourful pictures of Beijing in the 1930s. His interest in domestic crafts led him to write a book about Chinese household furniture.*

Only when I had lived in Peking for some time did I realize how my servants divided shopping in general. The most superior manner of purchase, the most intelligent as well as most face-conferring, was the private display of articles not shown in a shop at all. They were brought to the house on appointment by a merchant who usually came with an assistant, his wares wrapped in the large blue cloth bundles, or *pao-fu,* that one so often saw in the streets. In the old days, when women did not leave their houses to make purchases, this was the manner in which silks and satins were submitted to the lady of a household. Even in my time, antiques, pictures—mounted as scrolls—and other precious articles were generally sold in this way.

16
THE RULES OF BEHAVIOUR
Mencius
c. 370–290 BC

Mencius (Mengzi), one of China's great Confucian philosophers, believed that human nature was basically good, but that rules were required to cultivate proper moral behaviour. Propriety, he taught, must be adjusted to the situation.

K'wan said, 'Is it the rule that males and females shall not allow their hands to touch in giving or receiving anything?'

Mencius replied, 'It is the rule.'

K'wan asked, 'If a man's sister-in-law be drowning, shall he rescue her with his hand?'

Mencius said, 'He who would not so rescue the drowning woman is a wolf. For males and females not to allow their hands to touch in giving and receiving is the general rule; when a sister-in-law is drowning, to rescue her with the hand is a peculiar exigency.'

K'wan said, 'The whole kingdom is drowning. How strange it is that you will not rescue it!'

Mencius answered, 'A drowning kingdom must be rescued with right principles, as a drowning sister-in-law has to be rescued with the hand. Do you wish me to rescue the kingdom with my hand?'

17
THE SUBSERVIENCE OF WOMEN
GEORGE STAUNTON
1799

In 1793 George Staunton visited Beijing as secretary to Lord Macartney's expedition from the British government to the court of Emperor Qian Long and offered the instant, expert opinion–of an outsider.

Women, especially in the lower walks of life, are bred with little other principle than that of implicit obedience to their fathers or their husbands. To them they are taught to refer the good or bad qualities of their actions, without any idea of virtue in the abstract. Nor do the men seem to value chastity, except what may tend to their own personal gratification. The case is probably somewhat otherwise in the upper classes of life in China. There is, in fact, a greater difference often between different ranks, in the same country, than between the same ranks in different countries. The Chinese women, of whatever condition in life, are, for the most part, deprived of the benefit of reading, or acquiring knowledge by observation. Their ignorance, their inexperience, their retirement, their awe also of those whom they consider as their superiors, disqualify them, in great measure, from becoming the friends or habitual companions of the leisure of their husbands. Even a relish for their personal charms is subject gradually to diminish; and less horror is felt against unnatural practices, which, however they are, as well as all perverse and impure desires, justly reprobated by the Chinese moralists, are seldom, if ever, punished by the law, at least when committed by the mandarins. Where the ladies never form a part of society with men, mutual improvement, or delicacy of taste and sentiment, the softness of address, the graces of elegant converse, the refinement and play of passions, cannot take place; and unguarded manners in the men are liable to degenerate into coarse pleasantry or broad allusions.

18
BOUND FEET
John Davis
1857

Sir John Davis, a British plenipotentiary and Hong Kong governor, translated Chinese novels and plays and wrote essays and a novel of his own, as well as a memoir of his journey to the interior of China. Here he offers some perceptive comparisons with foreign customs—in particular the dress of Victorian ladies.

But the most unaccountable species of taste is that mutilation of the women's feet for which the Chinese are so remarkable. Of the origin of this custom there is no very distinct account, except that it took place about the close of the Tang dynasty, or the end of the ninth century of our era. The Tartars have had the good sense not to adopt this artificial deformity, and their ladies wear a shoe like that of the men, except that it has a white sole of still greater thickness. As it would seem next to impossible to refer to any notions of physical beauty, however arbitrary, such shocking mutilation as that produced by the cramping of the foot in early childhood, it may partly be ascribed to the principle which dictates the fashion of long nails.

The idea conveyed by these is *exemption from labour*, and, as the small feet make cripples of the women, it is fair to conclude that the idea of gentility which they convey arises from a similar association. That appearance of helplessness which is induced by the mutilation, they admire extremely, notwithstanding its very usual concomitant of sickliness; and the tottering gait of the poor women, as they hobble along upon the heel of the foot, they compare to the waving of a willow agitated by the breeze. We may add that this odious custom extends lower down in the scale of society than might have been expected from its disabling effect upon those who have to labour for their subsistence. If the custom was first imposed by the tyranny of the men, the women are fully revenged in the diminution of their charms and domestic usefulness.

In no instances have the folly and childishness of a large portion of mankind been more strikingly displayed than in those various, and occasionally very opposite, modes in which they have departed from the standard of nature, and sought distinction even in deformity. Thus, while one race of people crushes the feet of its children, another flattens their heads between two boards; and, while we in Europe admire the natural whiteness of the teeth, the Malays file off the enamel, and dye them black, for the all-sufficient reason that dogs' teeth are white! A New Zealand chief has his distinctive coat of arms emblazoned on the skin of his face, as well as on his limbs; and an Esquimaux is nothing if he have not bits of stone stuffed through a hole in each cheek. Quite as absurd, and still more mischievous, is the infatuation which, among some Europeans, attaches beauty to that modification of the human figure which resembles the wasp, and compresses the waist until the very ribs have been distorted, and the functions of the vital organs irreparably disordered.

19
A MARK OF DISTINCTION
Edward D. Prime
1872

Edward Prime, a doctor of divinity from the United States, commented on Chinese women in his book, Around the World: Sketches of Travel. *His estimate that a quarter of the female population had bound feet suggests the practice was far from universal.*

The cultivation of small feet is not altogether peculiar to the higher classes, nor to those who are exempt from labor. It is regarded as a mark of distinction, but only as conformity to fashion distinguishes its votaries. In every city great numbers of

A servant manages daily marketing on her 'golden lilies'

women, perhaps a quarter or more of the female population, may be seen toddling about the streets on their pegs, looking very much as if their feet had been cut off and they were walking on the stumps. It is difficult to balance themselves in walking, and they frequently resort to a third peg in the shape of a cane to keep themselves straight. The custom of closely bandaging the feet from infancy is not so injurious as might be supposed, but it greatly interferes with locomotion.

20
A USELESS AND CRUEL CUSTOM
Arthur H. Smith
1899

The missionary Arthur Smith reflects on the continued popularity of foot-binding at the end of the nineteenth century.

The practice of binding the feet of Chinese girls is familiar to all who have the smallest knowledge of China, and requires but the barest mention. It is almost universal throughout China, yet with some conspicuous exceptions, as among the Hakkas of the south, an exception for which it is not easy to account. The custom forcibly illustrates some of the innate traits of Chinese character, especially the readiness to endure great and prolonged suffering in attaining to a standard, merely for the sake of appearances. There is no other non-religious custom peculiar to the Chinese which is so utterly opposed to the natural instincts of mankind, and yet which is at the same time so dear to the Chinese, and which would be given up with more reluctance.

It is well known that the greatest emperor who ever sat upon the throne of China dared not risk his authority in an attempt to put down this custom, although his father had successfully imposed upon the Chinese race the wearing of the queue as a badge of subjection. A quarter of a millennium of Tartar rule seems to have done absolutely nothing toward modifying the practice of foot-binding in favour of the more rational one of the governing race, except to a limited extent in the capital itself. But a few *li* (miles) away from Peking, the old habits hold their iron sway. The only impulse toward reform of this useless and cruel custom originated with foreigners in China, and was long in making itself felt, which it is now, especially in the central part of the empire, beginning to be.

21

UNBOUND FEET

William Jennings Bryan

1907

William Jennings Bryan served as American Secretary of State and ran three times for president on the Democratic ticket. He espoused liberal causes, including increased freedom for Chinese women, whom he observed on an extensive trip to the country. Here he notes that, although many Chinese men found bound feet enticing, others abhorred the practice.

A prominent Chinaman told me that being opposed to foot-binding, he had, when a young man, tried to find a wife with natural feet but was not able to do so. He has in recent years persuaded his wife to unbind her feet and has kept his daughters from undergoing the ordeal.

The process, as described by a physician and as shown in a photograph and model which I secured, is as follows: At the age of five or six the little girl's feet are tightly bandaged; the second, third, fourth and fifth toes being gradually brought back under the sole of the foot; the heel is then drawn forward under the instep and the natural growth of the foot entirely arrested. The medical missionaries report instances in which the foot has rotted away because of lack of circulation. On one of the boats we met an intelligent Chinese merchant who, after condemning the practice of foot-binding and telling us that, in opposition to his wife's wishes and in opposition to the girl herself, he had saved one daughter from foot-binding, compared this custom to that of lacing, affirming that the latter was much more injurious. He also ventured to suggest that Chinese women do not expose their health and their shoulders in decolleté gowns, but perceiving that he had discovered a weak spot in our own social armor, I hurriedly changed the subject.

22
A BARBAROUS PRACTICE
Eliza Bridgman
1853

In 1830 Eliza Bridgman and her husband, Elijah, became the first non-denominational missionaries sent to China from the United States. She was also one of the first Westerners interested in the education of Chinese girls, and wrote about her attempts to improve their situation in her book, Daughters of China.

Most of the pupils who entered our family as boarders, had their feet already compressed. To this prevalent custom there were some exceptions; at least their feet had not been long bound, and there were five or six whose parents were persuaded to let them remain without being bandaged.

This is a most barbarous practice, but it has such a strong hold upon the people that it will be a long time before it will be relinquished.

Our ears are often assailed by the cries of children who are suffering from compression. In the higher classes this process commences very early, at four or five years of age. The elder women are called upon to do it. The four toes on each foot are bent completely under, and then a long fold of bandage is put on, which is tightened every three or four days. The pain is very severe.

This fashion is the mark of a lady, and considered indispensable to a suitable betrothal, which also takes place early. A girl whose feet are permitted to grow to the usual size, would not be selected *as the wife*. She may be bought for a sum of money if she have a pretty face, for the second, third, or fourth wife, but the large feet affect her rank seriously in domestic life, and hence the prevalence of the custom in the middling and lower classes.

23
THE NATURAL FEET CAMPAIGN
ALICIA LITTLE
1908

In the later nineteenth century, Alicia Little, a long-time resident of China, set off on an anti-footbinding campaign to Chinese cities. She finally arrived in Hong Kong, where the governor's wife, Lady Blake, welcomed Chinese women to Government House.

They explained that the two were sisters, and the second his wife, both daughters of the grey-bearded old gentleman, who was the largest owner of Chinese house property in Hong-Kong, where the two girls had been born and bred, yet as the servants said, without even having once seen a foreign lady. This gave me some idea of the seclusion in which Chinese girls are kept in Hong-Kong, and how little therefore European residents there were likely to know of their condition, unless they had taken some pains to ascertain facts. The steamer captain had told me how those who had travelled with him were 'carried on board pick-a-back by their men servants, just as sacks might be carried, so that I could not believe it when I was told there were no bound feet in Hong-Kong, and now, on being confronted with two rooms full of wealthy Chinese there, I was told at once to bear in mind that nearly all their womenkind were crippled.

'We must have them to a meeting,' said Lady Blake, and at once came to the rescue. She sent out invitations broadcast to Government House, inside which no Chinese women had ever yet set foot, and, to render it easier for them to come, invited Chinese gentlemen to be entertained in one room whilst the ladies should hear addresses in another.

An hour beforehand there sat the English admiral's wife patting a neatly-shod foot on the fender as she said, 'It really won't matter much if none do come,' whilst the Governor's wife said with

THE NATURAL FEET CAMPAIGN

authority, 'Oh, some are sure to come, and we'll have them into the drawing-room and shut up the ballroom, if they're very few.' Meanwhile Miss Blake, who had consented to be Honorary Secretary for Hong-Kong, had just returned with me from seeing the palms and shrubs the gardeners had been all the morning carrying to line the approaches to the ballroom, and we pronounced that it looked *very big*. Half-an-hour beforehand we all felt sure no Chinese ladies would dare to come, and that if they even did start they would never venture past the sentries.

But then we looked out and saw they were beginning to arrive. By some mistake they all left their sedans at the outside gate, and great was the hobbling, whilst the ballroom filled and filled, till no more seats could be found *anywhere*. Then two or three of the Chinese ladies conferred together, and one of them gave out that servants ought not to sit in the presence of their mistresses, and all amahs were requested to stand. This at once cleared out seventy or eighty not-bound-foot women, who thereafter stood down the sides of the ballroom, whilst a large school of little girls were requested to take up their places on the floor, rather to the horror of the children, who regarded sitting on the floor as far odder than English children would. But there was no other place for them.

And though some were urgent to send these little girls away as too young, I was delighted they had stayed, when at the end of the meeting these children counted out their money contributions and actually wrote down their own names as members of our society. Four or five amongst them were already bound, so that there could be no-doubt but that they all understood what they were protesting against. Two ladies with small bound feet took up a prominent position at the end of a front row, and after a Chinese lady from Australia had interpreted Lady Blake's words of welcome and the opening of my address, she could no longer stand the sight of these feet, stuck out straight in front of their owners for comparative ease and thus obtruded between her and the audience, so apostrophised the ladies in the racy colloquial of the south.

Two English ladies, who had thus unexpectedly had the attention of a large audience called to them, would probably have looked very indignant, or if not indignant showed signs of confusion. But, although I think they certainly did blush, these two Chinese ladies showed no indignation and wonderful self-possession, as the elder answered that she was too old to unbind. What reason was given for the younger not doing so I did not understand. It was pitiful afterwards to see the rows of amahs in the hall waiting to support their tottering mistresses to their sedans. But forty-seven ladies joined the Natural Feet Society there and then, and one showed how she had already begun to loosen her feet. At one of the leading Chinese newspaper offices a young man had said to me with a bow, 'My wife and all my sisters have unbound their feet.' A Chinese doctor had contended that Hong-Kong bound feet could not be unbound, but facts prove that he is mistaken, although it seems that feet are bound exceptionally tight there. According to a Chinese writer: 'The child is made to lie in bed during the first year, and only lifted out when it is absolutely necessary.'

According to a gathering of Chinese ladies in Shanghai a woman with a very strong hand is required to bind the feet the first time, and she does it so tightly that the bandage cannot be removed without dipping foot and bandage together into warm water. Unless this precaution were taken all the skin would come off with the bandage and probably great lumps of flesh also. Several of them said they had seen this occur. At a meeting at Foochow

[Fuzhou], lady after lady said she had seen a girl, both of whose feet had dropped off through binding, and one, a Chinese admiral's wife, said, 'Not one or two, but several have I seen among my own acquaintances.' Before mortification sets in and goes so far as to cause the whole foot to fall off it is painful to think what sufferings must have been undergone.

'Were they not exquisitely dressed and do you not think that a room full of Chinese ladies looks much better as far as toilette goes than a room full of English ladies?' Such was one of the remarks after the meeting. But the English admiral's wife, to whom we all deferred on matters of dress, answered with decision, 'That is not at all fair. We were in morning dress. Wait till we come down in our ball-gowns and diamonds. They all were in full dress.' Then she too went into an ecstasy over the embroideries and the blending of tints. All the same the Hong-Kong dresses were simply barbarous to what I afterwards saw at Hangchow and Soochow [Hangzhou and Suzhou].

24
LEATHER BOOTS
Isabelle Williamson
c. 1875

Isabelle Williamson listed her residence as Chefoo, China where she served as a missionary. Now known as Yantai in Shangdong province, it was then not a place where Westerners were a familiar sight.

There are no objects of interest greater than China's daughters. Beautiful they are with a certain beauty of their own. On them, alas! centuries of non-culture have pressed heavily; but now, Undine-like, each Chinese maid and matron seems rising and asking for a soul.

On the journey my interest was chiefly in the women, and I looked at all through a woman's eyes.

As we got near to the house, just on the edge of the hamlet, we found nearly all the villagers assembled. The greetings were

numerous and cordial. Women came round and were introduced as the mothers of sons named to us. Indeed, a woman's title in China is usually the name of her eldest son; and what title is sweeter to a mother's ear?

The family of our host consisted of his wife, a son, and a daughter, the brightest little Chinese maiden I have ever seen. She was greatly interested in my buttoned boots. The particular fault of this little Chinese maid was a tendency to be untidy in her gaiters and shoes. So she at once informed her mother that she would not need to be scolded for her besetting sin if her shoes and gaiters were all in one piece, as mine were, and if they were made of leather. Altogether she took my heart—a cheery, sunny little lassie.

25
BEAUTIFUL ATTIRE

ELIZA BRIDGMAN
1853

This missionary ran a school for Chinese girls and was often critical of native customs. But, as this excerpt from her book Daughters of China *shows, she did admire some aspects of Chinese taste.*

The Chinese lady, in the better classes, is not without attractions; she is generally bland and courteous in her manners; her toilet is often arranged with taste and beauty; though her decorations are usually profuse and gaudy. Her dress is well adapted to the season. In the heat of summer, her attire is simply grass-cloth; as the weather becomes cool, this is exchanged for silk and other richly embroidered materials.

26
PAINTED FACES

JOHN DAVIS
1857

British plenipotentiary and Hong Kong governor, Sir John Davis, had much to say in praise of the appearance of Chinese women.

The women would frequently be very pretty, were it not for the shocking custom of daubing their faces with white and red paint, to which may be added the deformity of cramped feet. In point of health, however, this is in a great degree made up by the total absence of tight lacing, and of all ligatures and confinements whatever about the vital parts. The consequence is that their children are born very straight-limbed, and births are scarcely ever attended with disaster. Their dress is extremely modest and becoming, and, in the higher classes, as splendid as the most exquisite silks and embroidery can make it; for the Chinese certainly reserve the best of their silk manufactures for themselves. What we often choose to call *dress* they would regard as absolute nudity, and all close fitting to the shape as only displaying what it affects to conceal.

Unmarried women wear their hair hanging down in long tresses, and the putting up of the hair is one of the ceremonies preparatory to marriage. It is twisted up towards the back of the head, ornamented with flowers or jewels, and fastened with two bodkins stuck in crosswise. They sometimes wear an ornament representing the foonghoâng, or Chinese phœnix, composed of gold and jewels, the wings hovering, and the beak of the bird hanging over the forehead, on an elastic spring. After a certain time of life the women wear a silk wrapper round the head in lieu of any other dress. The eyebrows of the young women are fashioned until they represent a fine curved line, which is compared to the new moon when only a day or two old, or to the young leaflet of the willow.

Pink and green, two colours often worn by women, are confined exclusively to them, and never seen on men. The ordinary dress is a large-sleeved robe of silk, or of cotton among the poorer sort, over, a longer garment, sometimes of a pink colour; under which are loose trousers, which are fastened round the ankle, just above the small foot and tight shoe. A proverbial expression among the Chinese for the concealment of defects is—'long robes to hide large feet.' Notwithstanding this, the Tartar women, or their lords, have had the good sense to preserve the ladies' feet of the natural size. In other respects, however, they dress nearly as the Chinese, and paint their faces white and red in the same style.

27
OPIUM SMOKING
Julia Corner
1853

In the nineteenth century, opium smoking increased forty-fold. Although expensive, it offered relief from the pressures of increased population, a lower standard of living, and the general demoralization resulting from colonization. It spread throughout society and was not limited to men.

Smoking is not confined to the male sex, nor to the lower class of females; but every Chinese lady has her richly ornamented pipe, which would really be an elegant appendage if it did not involve so unfeminine an indulgence. It is also related that not a few of the ladies intoxicate themselves by smoking opium. The usual employments among the Chinese ladies are, working embroidery, playing on different musical instruments, and painting on silk and rice-paper. It is not supposed that they possess generally any accomplishments more intellectual than these; yet as some ladies are known to write to their husbands when absent, it is clear that there are individual cases where the art of writing has been acquired, and, of course, that of reading; which might lead us to conjecture that, in some of the numerous families where private tutors are now employed, the girls may be allowed to participate, to a certain extent, in the studies of their brothers: but this is a mere supposition, for which there is no authority.

The costume of the Chinese being regulated by law, is not subject to the caprice of fashion or individual taste, except in such trifling particulars as produce no alteration in the general style. The dress of a Chinese lady is not different from that worn in ancient times: it consists of a short loose robe, confined round the throat with a narrow collar. The robe is worn over a long full skirt, and both are frequently made of richly-embroidered silks. The sleeves are wide, and sufficiently long to fall over the hands, and

CHINESE WOMEN

the hair is gathered up in a knot at the top of the head, and is fastened with golden bodkins, and adorned with flowers. They all wear trousers, like the Turkish women; and their tiny shoes are of satin, silk, or velvet, beautifully worked with gold, silver, and coloured silks, the soles being of rice-paper, from one to two inches in thickness, and covered outside with white leather, made from pigs' skin. The little girls are very becomingly attired in short dresses, reaching to the throat, and worn over the full trousers.

28
SMALL SIX AND HER MOTHER
Dorothea Hosie
c. 1912

Lady Hosie, the daughter of a British China scholar, was raised in China at the turn of the twentieth century. Fluent in Mandarin and comfortable with the culture, she wrote several books relating her observations.

In a provincial centre, the officials and their wives are cut off from their relatives and their friends. Custom allows them to visit the families of other officials or go shopping, but the shops are naturally inferior to those of the big centres. And one may imagine, when comparing Kung Tai Tai (the author's friend) with the lady of the soiled brocade sofa, that the womenkind of other yamens do not always prove congenial companions. Above all, while they are in the street, the ladies must either be carried in sedan-chairs or be driven in the uncomfortable closed springless cart on its great iron-studded yellow wheels. They must never walk; they must invariably keep their eyes down, nor must they look about, or the tongues of the populace would wag, and the shameless conduct of the Governor's or the Judge's wife become the subject of popular talk.

'How can he expect to rule us when he cannot exact correct behaviour from his own "Within-Ones"? Letting them gallivant about the streets and stare men boldly in the face like mannerless foreign women!' they would jeer.

In spite of the simplicity of their garments, Chinese ladies take an inordinate length of time dressing, owing to their exacting ideals of hairdressing. I have watched an amah—a serving-woman—after her mistress had finished her toilet, take an hour and a quarter over her own hair. The Kung girls had to do each other's hair, as well as their mother's, for the amahs were not considered clean enough to help. It was odd to find that even Small

Six, aged twelve, was helping to do her mother's hair, and not, as in England, her mother doing Small Six's. In the same way, Small Six helped to wash and dress her mother. This is probably why young Chinese girls, with the trimmest of mothers, often have a tide-mark round their own necks. It is considered their duty to look after their mother, not she after them. There is much to be said for that view.

Tiffin, or *déjeuner*, was at twelve; so that, by the time the ladies had finished their toilets, there was not much time left for study.

Chinese women do not walk in a row or company across the pavement. Preference is given to single file, and remarks from the leader are repeated by the middle person to reach the one in the rear. Sometimes, however, they hold hands, partly in affection and partly for mutual support as they sway. It is undoubtedly a pretty fashion in a Chinese city, but is apt to draw attention in a foreign settlement, when one of the parties is a foreigner.

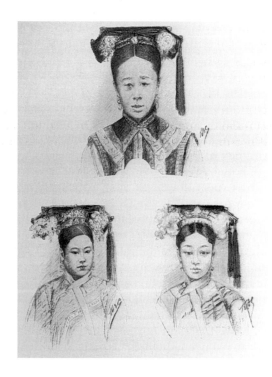

29
HANDSOME WOMEN
Marco Polo
c. 1300

Marco Polo and his uncles left for China in about 1271, finally spending twenty-four years on their voyages. Upon his return to Venice, Marco Polo was captured in battle and incarcerated in Genoa for four years where he wrote his memoirs.

The women of the place are very handsome and live in a state of luxurious ease. . . . wives equally abstain from work. They have much beauty, as had been remarked, and are brought up with delicate and languid habits. The costliness of their dresses in silks and jewellery, can scarcely be imagined. . . . They are friendly towards each other, and persons who inhabit the same street, both men and women, from the mere circumstance of neighbourhood, appear like one family. In their domestic manners they are free from jealousy or suspicion of their wives, to whom great respect is shown, and any man would be accounted infamous who should presume to use indecent expressions to a married woman.

PART III

CHINESE GIRLS—TINY FEET AND PROPER BEHAVIOUR

'A runaway son is still precious; a runaway daughter loses her value.'

CHINESE WOMEN

That the birth of a girl was no cause for great rejoicing in China is patently clear in the following excerpts. An expense to be born until she could be disposed of as a bride or even a slave, a girl's greatest disadvantage was that, as a female, she was expected to venerate the ancestors of her future husband rather than those of her birth parents.

In cases of poverty or a superfluity of females, infanticide was sometimes practised. Girls also died from differential care in which their cries for food or other needs were heeded less than their brothers'. But many girls survived, often with bound feet, and some even prospered.

At fourteen, a girl pinned up her hair to signify readiness for marriage, which usually followed in two or three years. Girls with bound feet embroidered their own tiny shoes, and this, too, was a sign of eligibility for marriage.

Many girls entered other homes as servants or as slaves. Slavery was prohibited by the Qing dynasty in 1910, but the law wasn't seriously implemented until further laws in 1928. The Qing government also instituted homes for runaway slaves, as did various missions, but sometimes the education they received simply meant higher prices for the girls on the slave market.

Children of both sexes toiled with their parents in the fields. When education was a possibility, it went to the boys and rarely to their sisters, although there were some notable exceptions. The few girls who were taught to read concentrated on five classic books for females which emphasized their duties and subservience.

Missionaries established schools for girls: the first, opened in Ningpo in 1844 was run by an English woman, Mary Ann Aldersley, who financed the effort herself. By the 1870s over 2,000 girls were studying in about 120 mission schools. That number doubled in the next quarter century. The first girls' school organized by the Chinese opened in 1898 in Shanghai due to the sponsorship of a male reformer. By 1909, there were over a hundred government-sponsored girls' schools.

In twentieth-century China, during the Cultural Revolution, boys and girls were found studying together in middle schools. Subjects included chemistry, English, the thoughts of Chairman Mao, and a month of supervised labour each year on a commune or in a factory. Time was also spent on song and dance productions on ideological themes with titles such as *To Our Friends Around the World*.

30
ON THE CULTIVATION OF VIRTUE
Ban Zhao
c. 100 AD

Ban Zhao is best remembered as a poet and China's first female historian who completed a dynastic history begun by her father and brother. The emperor appointed her tutor to the empress and the ladies of the court, and Ban Zhao later advised the empress when she became regent to the succeeding child emperor. For her daughter, Ban Zhao wrote Admonitions for Women, long the authoritative guide for the proper deportment of females.

CHINESE WOMEN

All girls, everywhere,
First should learn to cultivate virtue.
Of cultivating virtue's methods,
The most important is
To be pure and upright in morals;
If pure, you are clean inside and outside;
Chastity is your body's glory;
Having it, all your acts shine.
When walking, look straight, turn not your head;
Talking, restrain your voice within your teeth;
Sitting, don't shake your knees—a common fault with men;
Standing, keep quiet your skirts;
When pleased, laugh not aloud;
If angry, still make no noise;
Inner and outer rooms (women's and men's) duties
Fully understand.
Boys and girls must not together be.
With outside business you have no concern;
Therefore, go not beyond the court.
If necessary outside to go,
Exhibit not your form,
But screen your face with fan or veil.
To men who are not with you related you may not speak.
  With women and girls of not careful conduct you may not associate.
  Following virtue, decorum, and uprightness, you so accomplish the end of your being.

31
THE WRONG SEX
J. Dyer Ball
1912

A British civil servant posted to Hong Kong at the end of the nineteenth century, James Dyer Ball published his observations of the Chinese in three books, Things Chinese, The Celestial and His Religion, *and* The Chinese at Home.

China is the land of children. No Malthusian law deters the multiplication of the human race there. All boys are heartily welcomed on their arrival into this world, and none are at once assisted out of it again, unless there be some congenital defect which makes their presence undesirable. With girls it is a different matter; they are unacceptable, and not to be mentioned in the enumeration of one's children, though the poetical name of 'a thousand pieces of gold' is given to them. However, a metaphorical shower of gold of this nature is not desired. If means are ample, they are endured, though not wanted. The ravages of famine, the devastations of floods, straitened circumstances, the local customs, are all factors in the determination whether the child, if of the wrong sex, shall stay in this world or only be here a few minutes or hours or days.

32
CHILDBIRTH
George Staunton
1799

The extent of infanticide depended on the severity of a famine and the area of China. Girls born in the Year of the Horse were sometimes apt to be sacrificed because they were reputed to be headstrong and therefore to make the worst wives. Babies were often born with a minimum of assistance.

No male physician is allowed to attend a pregnant woman, and still less to practise midwifery; in the indelicacy of which, both sexes seem to agree in China. There are books written on that art for the use of female practitioners, with drawings of the state and position of the infant at different periods of gestation; together with a variety of directions and prescriptions for every supposed case that may take place: the whole mixed with a number of superstitious observances.

33
THE LITTLE SLAVE GIRL
A. B. Freeman-Mitford
1860s

A. B. Freeman-Mitford, the future Lord Redesdale, was an ancestor of the literary Mitford sisters and served as the British attaché to Beijing in the 1860s, writing prolifically about his Asian experiences. Here he witnesses the sale of a daughter.

A Cantonese named Ma, whom I know and who has come up to Peking on business, was anxious to buy a little Pekingese slave-girl, and I was present at the negotiations. The child, a bright little creature eight years of age, was brought by her parents to Ma's lodging, and as she gave satisfaction, the question resolved itself into one of price, and here the fun began, for the little thing was so keen to go that she eagerly took part with the purchaser in beating down the vendors; and, finally, a bargain was struck at 28 dollars. At that price she was handed over to her new owner, together with a bill of sale, of which here is a translation:—

'This is a deed of sale. Wan Cheng, of the village of Wan Ping, has a child the offspring of his body, being his second daughter and his seventh child, aged eight years. Because his house is poor, cold, and hungry, relying on what has passed between a third person and his wife, he has determined to sell his daughter to one named Ma. He sells her for twenty-eight dollars, every dollar to be worth seven tiaos and a half. The money has been paid over in full under the pen' (*i.e.* at this time of writing). 'The girl is to obey her master and to depend upon him for her maintenance. In the event of any difficulties or doubts arising on the part of the girl's family, the seller alone is responsible, it does not regard the buyer. It is to be apprehended that calamities may occur to the child, but that is according as Heaven shall decree; her master is not responsible.

THE LITTLE SLAVE GIRL

None henceforward may cross the door to meddle in her affairs. This agreement has been made openly face to face. In case of any inquiries being made this document is to serve as proof.' (Here follow the signatures or rather marks of the vendor, the middleman, and a third person as witness, and the date.) 'The child's birthday is the 11th day of the 6th month, she was born between the seventh and eighth hours.'

Ma declares that as soon as the girl is grown up he shall let her marry. He says, 'My no wanchee do that black heart pidgin.' I believe he will keep his word—it is a matter of business, and in business the southern Chinese trader is scrupulously honest.

As for the child, she was simply in a fever of delight at leaving her parents. I dare say her poor little life had been none too rosy; for what says the proverb? 'Better one son, though deformed, than eighteen daughters as wise as the apostles of Buddha.'

I wonder whether any European ever witnessed such a transaction before.

34

THE BIRTH OF A DAUGHTER

Arthur H. Smith
1899

Missionary Arthur Smith's long experience in China led him to compare life there to life in the West. Here he contrasts the reactions to the birth of a daughter.

The arrival of a first baby is, in the life of a Chinese wife, a very different event from the like occurrence in the life of a wife in Occidental lands. If the child is a boy, the joy of the whole household is of course great, but if on the contrary it is a girl, the depression of the spirits of the entire establishment is equally marked. In such a case, the young wife is often treated with coldness, and not infrequently with harshness, even if, as sometimes happens, she is not actually beaten for her lack of discretion in not producing a son. If she has had several daughters in succession, especially if she has borne no son or none which has lived, her life cannot be a pleasant one.

There is a story of a certain noble English lord, who had more daughters than any other member of the aristocracy. When on the Continent travelling, he walked out one day with six of his daughters. Someone who saw him, remarked to a companion, 'Poor man.' The noble lord overheard the observation, and turning to the person who made it, replied, 'Not so "poor" as you think; I have six more at home!' It is questionable whether any Chinese could be found who would not sympathize with the comment of the bystander, or who would agree with the reply of the father. Indeed, we have serious doubts whether, among all the innumerable myriads of this race, there ever lived a Chinese who had twelve daughters living at once.

35
ADVICE TO GIRLS
Zhang Wentao
18th century

A female poet cautions brides.

Trust not spring clouds, trust not to flowers:
    The butterfly is caught;
    Oh snatch no passing joy in hours
       Of pleasure wrongly sought!

A mien severe and eyes that freeze
    Become the future bride;
No whispering underneath the trees
    E'er yet the knot be tied.

'Tis heaven on earth when woman wed
    Leans on her husband's arm;
Beauty, like flowers, is quickly shed:
    Oh envy not its charm!

36
BALL GAMES
Adele Fielde
1894

Adele Fielde lived in Guangdong Province for fifteen years before returning to New York to write her memoirs of the country.

Little Chinese girls seldom amuse themselves with dolls, but they frequently acquire skill in playing with a single ball, hitting it with foot, forehead, or hand, as it bounds from roof, wall, and floor. The player often whirls quickly around while the ball is in the air, and meeting it upon its rebound, sends it up again. Some girls are expert in tossing marbles, keeping as many as five in air at one time. Both boys and girls play with tops and shuttlecocks, but boys alone fly kites.

37
HAIR AND HATS

CHARLES TAYLOR
1860

Charles Taylor studied ancient languages, then medicine in preparation for missionary work in China. Due to his wife's failing health, he returned to the United States where he wrote his memoirs, Five Years in China.

The heads of Chinese children, girls as well as boys, are shaven *all* over several times before they are a year old. Then, in a year or two more, two small round patches of hair are suffered to grow just above the ears, near the top of the head. When the hair from these becomes long enough, it is braided into two little tufts that project like horns on a cow.

On the heads of girls, the hair is still shaven around the edges, till they become twelve or fourteen years old, and during this time they wear a black silk fringe around the head, hanging over the forehead and temples, and down the back of the neck. The remainder of the hair they put up in a graceful knot a little to one side of the head, and frequently wear flowers in it, giving them a very pretty appearance. When they become young women, the silken fringe is laid aside, the whole of the hair is permitted to grow, is combed back from the face, and put up on the back of the head, being kept in place by several long, ornamental pins of brass, silver, or gold, according to the ability of the wearer. They also wear a thick band around the head, about two inches wide, pointed in the middle upon the forehead, and gradually becoming narrower, till it ends in two strings at the back, where it is tied under the hair. This band is often very beautifully wrought with silk and gilt lace; and generally has a round ornament, somewhat resembling a breast-pin, and sometimes very costly, fastened in the middle at the widest point. The women never wear any other covering on the head, except those who work in the fields during hot weather. These frequently have a kind of straw hat, not unlike a large tin pan turned bottom side upward, with a round hole in the middle, for the braid of hair to project through. This also serves to keep the hat on the head.

The nails are worn long, especially those of the little fingers, and are often seen as long as the fingers themselves. Ladies sometimes wear a golden sheath over the nail to prevent it from being broken.

38
LITTLE ANNIE
CHARLES TAYLOR
1860

Sometimes girls received a very special education from Western missionary families— always combined with an introduction to Christianity.

We have in our family, a little Chinese girl, ten years of age, who has been for a year and a half in the family of another missionary, but as their situation rendered it impracticable for them to keep her any longer, we have taken her at their request, rather than allow her to go back to heathenism, after having been instructed in many truths of the Christian religion. She can read quite well in the Bible, has committed to memory several hymns, the ten commandments, the Apostles' creed, and repeats the Lord's Prayer every morning with us at family worship—all in the English language. She prepares a spelling lesson, one also in reading, writes a composition, and commits to memory a verse of Scripture every day. All these exercises are performed under the superintendence of Mrs. Taylor, who is also teaching her to sew and knit. She then, in turn, is imparting instruction to the nurse of our little boy, who is quite a sensible Chinese woman, and already manifests a strong desire to be taught the '*Yah-soo taw le*'—the 'doctrines of Jesus.' She now sits near me, eagerly studying the ten commandments in Chinese, as they have been read and explained to her by Annie—for this is the name of the little girl.

39
INFANTICIDE
GEORGE MORRISON
1895

Dr George Morrison was an Australian who ended up spending seventeen years in China because he missed a boat to Japan. Despite his inauspicious beginning, he became the respected China correspondent for The Times *of London, and then the Political Advisor to the Government of China after the fall of the Manchu Empire. In the 1990s Cambridge University Press published two volumes of his letters. In this excerpt he notes that if girls from impoverished families survived infanticide, slavery was still a possible fate.*

The selling of its female children into slavery is the chief sorrow of this famine-stricken district. During last year it is estimated, or rather, it is stated by the Chinese, that no less than three thousand children from this neighbourhood, chiefly female children and a few boys, were sold to dealers and carried like poultry in baskets to the capital. At ordinary times the price for girls is one tael (three shillings) for every year of their age, thus a girl of five costs fifteen shillings, of ten, thirty shillings, but in time of famine children, to speak brutally, become a drug in the market. Female children were now offering at from three shillings and fourpence to six shillings each. You could buy as many as you cared to, you might even obtain them for nothing if you would enter into an agreement with the father, which he had no means of enforcing, to take care of his child, and clothe and feed her, and rear her kindly. Starving mothers would come to the mission beseeching the foreign teachers to take their babies and save them from the fate that was otherwise inevitable.

Girls are bought in Chaotong [Sichuan Province] up to the age of twenty, and there is always a ready market for those above the

INFANTICIDE

age of puberty; prices then vary according to the measure of the girl's beauty, an important feature being the smallness of her feet. They are sold in the capital for wives and *yatows* [slave girls]; they are rarely sold into prostitution. Two important factors in the demand for them are the large preponderance in the number of males at the capital, and the prevalence there of goitre or thick neck, a deformity which is absent from the district of Chaotong. Infanticide in a starving city like this is dreadfully common. 'For the parents, seeing their children must be doomed to poverty, think it better at once to let the soul escape in search of a more happy asylum than to linger in one condemned to want and wretchedness.' The infanticide is, however, exclusively confined to the destruction of female children, the sons being permitted to live in order to continue the ancestral sacrifices.

One mother I met, who was employed by the mission, told the missionary in ordinary conversation that she had suffocated in turn three of her female children within a few days of birth; and, when a fourth was born, so enraged was her husband to discover that it was also a girl that he seized it by the legs and struck it against the wall and killed it.

40
STORIES OF LITTLE GIRLS
ELIZA BRIDGMAN
1853

Missionary Eliza Bridgman invited several young Chinese girls to join her intensely Christian household. They also became members of her English classes in which they studied with boys.

Dec. 9th, 1846.—To-day the fortune-teller again made his appearance; and, true to his word, brought his little girl with him. She was a child of fine countenance, poorly clad, filthy as a vagrant, though her father made a respectable appearance. He was unwilling to bind himself to any term of years; said she was betrothed; but, being straitened in his circumstances, he was glad to get her provided for.

It was only in consideration of her brother Twei-lum being with us, that she was willing to remain. With us it was an experiment.

I well remember how her appearance affected me. Her skin covered with dirt, her shoes slip-shod, her clothes, what few she had, I suspect had never been washed; she seemed like one uncared for, and I pitied her, and was glad to welcome her to our habitation.

For a fortnight she was so perfectly ungovernable, I fluctuated between hope and discouragement; the principle of obedience was entirely new and strange to her. I never witnessed in a child so young such bursts of passion as she exhibited. She would throw herself upon the floor, kick and scream in such a way as to draw the attention of Chinese neighbors; her will had never been subdued, and mild measures had no effect.

Her brother would often pacify her by the promise of some toy, or something to gratify her appetite, but such a course, to be continued, I knew would never answer; and I said to my husband, if she did not do better, I must send her home. He begged me to persevere and try a little longer.

STORIES OF LITTLE GIRLS

The progress made by the Fortune-teller's little daughter shows that the mind of woman in China is susceptible to high cultivation. Ah-yee having joined my class of lads in learning English, acquired the sound and meaning of words very rapidly, and in a year was enabled to speak and read English with the fluency of her native dialect. I took great pleasure in the unfolding of her mind, and was not long in discovering what chord vibrated most tenderly. She expressed a strong attachment to her mother and a little brother, the companion of her plays. Her father she avoided, whenever he called, and he seldom took any notice of her. Ah-yee came to us December 9th, 1846. At the same time Liang Ateh, son of Liang Afah, who had been a favorite pupil of my husband, was in the habit of visiting us, and bringing his relatives to see his 'Tuteress,' as he respectfully called me. His relatives—his mother, his grand-mother, his aunts, &c. would come, but his wife never came; he said he would like to have me go and see her, but added that his friends were afraid; they were in humble life, lived in the country, and 'it would make so much talk, and draw so many people around the house to have a foreign lady come there; therefore they preferred I would not come.' However, all were not so particular.

Liang is the family name, Ateh the given name, comes last; by this latter name, Ateh, we always called him.

He had a very pretty little daughter, whom I wished to educate but Ateh thought her too young, and said she would not be separated from her Mother and Aunt.

My little pupil, Ah-yee, had been with us six months, when some Chinese visitors came one day, bringing with them a child very poorly clad. She was more cleanly in appearance than Ah-yee was on her introduction, and she was accompanied by her grandmother, mother, and another relative.

The mother said, 'I heard you wanted a little girl, and I have brought you one; I give her to you, and I hope that you will do well by her and get a husband for her.'

She was not betrothed, and I promised to do by her as if she were my own. She was a homely child, and had lived out of doors so much that her black hair was scorched to a reddish brown by the heat of a tropical sun; but such as she was, I was glad to receive her.

The agreement, though verbal, being perfectly understood between us, when the child's relatives left us she appeared willing to stay. She was the daughter of Liang Ateh's wife's sister; her name was A-lan.

It was now Ah-yee's business to make her little companion happy and comfortable; and pleasing it was to observe her efforts to do so. If I came near A-lan, even to give her food, she would run from me, apparently in terror; so I kept away for a time, and let Ah-yee act the 'go-between.'

A-lan has since told me the cause of her fear. I wore at that time, thin white morning-dresses, the climate being very warm at Canton. White, in China, is the color for mourning. It was I believe, the association in her mind with death and funeral solemnities, that made her new friend, the foreign lady, to whom she supposed her parents had sold her, the cause of so much disquietude.

The closing month of this year brought with it a new and unexpected trial. Very suddenly one bright morning the fortune-teller from Canton presented himself.

The object of his errand, like an electric shock flashed upon my mind, our dear Ah-yee must return to her heathen home. She had been with us four years; was so grown and altered her father scarcely knew her, but seemed much pleased at her improvement. There was no alternative, and we must submit.

The parents of the lad to whom she was betrothed insisted upon her return, that her feet might be compressed, and she made ready for marriage, which will probably take place when she arrives at the age of sixteen.

Their passage was secured, and the child was prepared with an aching heart, for a speedy departure. She begged me not to weep when we parted; said she would come back to school if she could.

Some articles were put in her trunk for her mother, and a few things also for A-lan's relatives. For a long time it had been promised that when she returned home she should have a silver dollar to give to her mother. The money was ready, but she was reminded of her father's avaricious disposition, and it was proposed that a dress should be purchased with it, in order that her mother, very much, might receive the benefit, but the sparkling silver had attractions for her eye, and she wished the pleasure of putting the dollar into her Mother's hand, so she placed it in a little bag, quite in the bottom of her trunk, which was not to be opened till she reached Canton.

STORIES OF LITTLE GIRLS

The dear child left us. We had good report of her behavior on board the vessel, the young, lone, Chinese girl, cheering herself by singing the hymns she had been taught in the school.

On arriving at the house of Mr. Williams at Canton, she was left in a room with her father, and was heard to cry bitterly. The servant reported that the trunk was opened and the child deprived of her dollar, the father having taken it for his own purposes.

We have since received no intelligence from Ah-yee, but we have great hope that the seed sown in her young and tender mind for four years, will yet spring up and bear fruit unto Eternal life.

The little Canton girl, A-lan, who was taught to read and write English, has been introduced to our readers. We will now let her tell a story for herself. It is part of a letter which she wrote to a dear friend in New York, who was much interested in the school at Wongka Moda. The following is an extract in her own childlike style of narration.

'*Nov. 10th.* Mrs. Bridgman says she thinks you always like to hear about the Chinese; and I am going to tell you something about one of our scholars.

'There is a little girl who was brought here by her adopted mother, a woman who had lost all her own children. The child's own mother sold her to her adopted mother for two dollars. Last Saturday evening when we went to our supper, Neepaw was missing; we looked about the house but we could not find her. Mrs. Bridgman was not at home; we were afraid that Neepaw had fallen into the well, and one of the girls looked into the well, and took a stick and moved it about there, but she was not to be found. One of the girls then said she saw her go out of the front door, when the Chinese woman was busy up stairs.

'Two or three persons were sent out to look for her, she had been seen passing along the street with her own mother.

'After searching a long time and asking a great many people, her adopted mother found her hid away in a neighbor's house. The people in the house were not willing to let Neepaw go, but her adopted mother took her away and brought her back to Mrs. Bridgman.

'Her own mother made a great cry in the street, and a great noise, she said 'the foreigners had got her child and were going to take her away to their own country.' A great many people came around to see what was the matter. Dr. Bridgman went down from his study, and told the woman to come into the school-room, and wait until Mrs. Bridgman came back.

'Neepaw was nicely clothed and well-looking. She had rice to eat and her mother had given her money to make her go away, and was going to sell her again. The next morning she was to go into the country. When Neepaw cried and told her mother she wanted to come home, her mother said, 'To-morrow morning go,' but she did not mean to let her go.

'We were all glad to see Neepaw back, and Mrs. Bridgman told her mother she must not take the child away, for she had sold her once, and her adopted mother had signed a written agreement that she should stay in the school three years; so the woman went away, and I hope we shall have no more trouble. I have no more room to write and must close. A-lan.'

The above is a fair specimen of the little dependence that can be placed upon the word or integrity of the Chinese.

41
THE PLACE OF GIRLS
Arthur Waley
1911

This poem was translated by Arthur Waley, author of almost eighty books. He specialized in translations from both Chinese and Japanese.

Then a boy is born,
    Put to lie on a bed,
    Robed in a gown
With jade tablets to finger.
And lusty he wails.
But one day in red knee-caps shall he walk,
Lord or prince, sprung from this house!
Then a girl shall be born,
Put to lie on the floor,
Robed in rags,
With a roof-tile to finger.
No bad thing shall she do,
Nor good thing either.
Enough if she can carry
Wine and plates of food
And give no trouble,
To her father and mother.'

42
MISS ORIOLE
Yuan Chen
Tang Dynasty

The Dream of the Red Chamber *is one of China's most beloved stories. Told in many forms including opera, theatre and song, it has been translated into several English versions. 'Miss Oriole', by Yuan Chen, is the story on which it is based. As an illustrious poet and storyteller of the Tang dynasty (618–907), he wrote this autobiographical story of a Chinese courtship. Later in the Song dynasty, Chen Delin set it as a song cycle, and in the Yuan dynasty, an outstanding playwright transformed it into a play.*

It happened during the Cheng Yuan time of the Tang dynasty. At twenty-three, young Chang still had never had an experience with women. He was a brilliant scholar, handsome and gentle, but at the same time rather sensitive and conceited. When in the company of others who were feasting and flirting, he only smiled and remained untouched. Therefore, he always maintained his serenity and made his friends think that he had no interest in the fair sex.

'Of course, I do,' he would protest. 'Teng-tu Tzu [a fictional character] did not know what a true beauty was, but merely put a beautiful image on his plain-looking wife. When I see an extremely beautiful creature, I never can drive her image out of my mind, so I know that I have more than a passing interest in women. The trouble is that I have not met the girl worthy of my attention.' Thus it was apparent that he was the kind of person who, if he ever fell in love, would fall head over heels.

Then one day Chang took a tour to Pucheng and stayed at a monastery called Puchiu, about ten *li* east of the city. A certain widow, Madam Tsui, who was taking her late husband's coffin back home, happened to stop at the same monastery. They met and, upon introducing themselves, found that Madam Tsui and

MISS ORIOLE

Chang's mother had the same family name, Cheng. Chang therefore addressed her as his distant aunt.

In that same year, General Hun Chien died in Pucheng. Ting Wen-yah, the *chung-jen* [emperor's eunuch] was not able to maintain the morale of the army; consequently, the soldiers broke out in a sudden revolt, plundering and raping. Madam Tsui was in great terror, for she had a beautiful young daughter, rich property, and a large entourage of servants and maids.

She sought help from Chang, for he knew someone in the army. Chang sent an urgent request to his friend, who was on good terms with the commander. The commander sent over half a dozen guards and a formal proclamation warning the troops to keep away from Madam Tsui's house. Some ten days later, the emperor sent Tu Chueh, the circuit commissioner, to succeed the late general, and thus put down the revolt.

The grateful Madam Tsui invited Chang to come to her place for dinner. Before they started the meal, she said to him: 'It is very sad that my husband should die and leave me a widow with two small children. We were in great danger the other day when the rioters came to attack our home. But for your kindness and help, my young daughter and my little son would have lost their lives. Your benevolence to us is great. To show you my gratitude, I will tell my children to address you as Elder Brother.'

So saying, she bade her ten-year-old boy, Huan Lang, to bow to him. Then she turned towards the inner room and called to her daughter: 'Oriole, Elder Brother saved your life the other day. You must come out to pay him your respects.'

But Oriole did not appear. She sent word to her mother that she did not feel well. Madam Tsui was displeased. 'Elder Brother has saved your life,' she exclaimed. 'How can you be so discourteous as not to come and thank him?'

It was still some time before Oriole made her appearance. When she came, she wore an ordinary dress and had no make-up on her face; yet she was strikingly beautiful with her black hair trimmed above her eyebrows and a natural pink glow on her cheeks. The room brightened the moment she entered it. The astonished Chang rose from his seat and bowed to her.

She curtsied in return, but because she had been compelled by her mother to meet a stranger, she looked so gloomy and unhappy that it appeared that she could not support her delicate body. She sat by her mother's side without a flicker of her eyelids. When Chang asked her age, Madam Tsui said, 'She was born at the end of the seventh month of the year of Chia Tzu. This is the year of Keng Chen in the Cheng Yuan era, so she is seventeen.'

Chang tried to start a conversation, but Oriole did not answer. Moreover, she remained silent throughout the dinner. Her aloofness and modest manners enchanted Chang all the more. He fell desperately in love with her.

Finding no opportunity to see Oriole again, Chang tried to bribe her maid, Hung Niang, to convey his love to her mistress. As he had feared, Hung Niang, frightened at his request, ran away from him in great embarrassment. Chang regretted what he had done. The next time he saw Hung Niang, he apologized for his impertinence and mentioned the subject no more. However, she had a suggestion for him.

'Just as I dare not convey your thoughts to my mistress, neither dare I speak of them to others. You are related to Madam Tsui and know her family well. Why not send a matchmaker to ask for Oriole's hand?'

'Of course, that is the proper thing to do. But you see, I have never fallen in love before. Ever since childhood, I have not been able to mix with people easily. Nor did I take a fancy to any of the girls, even those from high society. It was simply a prejudice because I am so unsociable. Yet I did not realize it until the day I met your mistress. All my former prejudices left me. I could hardly control myself during the dinner. The beauty of your mistress has made me so absent-minded that I have completely lost my taste for food, and I cannot sleep. I know that I am going to die from lovesickness if I have to suggest matrimony through a matchmaker, then wait for the decision of a fortuneteller, and send betrothal gifts, and go through all the formalities, which usually take two or three months. By that time, I shall be as dead as a fish in the market. What can I do?'

'My mistress is so virtuous and strict that even her elders cannot say anything improper to her, let alone a maid! But she likes literature and is well-acquainted with poetry. Often she ponders over exquisite lines. Why not send her a poem to open her heart? This seems the only way.'

Chang was delighted. He promptly wrote two poems and gave them to Hung Niang to take to her mistress. That evening, the maid came to him again with Oriole's answer written on a coloured sheet of paper. The title of Oriole's verse was 'The Night of the Full Moon.'

Waiting for moonlight in the western chamber,
Gentle winds blow the doors half open.
The shadow of flowers dances on the wall,
As though the handsome one were coming,

Chang thought it was a message of invitation, for that day was the fourteenth of the second month, and the next evening would be the full moon.

Inside the east wall of Madam Tsui's courtyard stood an apricot tree. The next evening Chang climbed the wall at this place and made his way to the western chamber. The doors were half ajar. Hung Niang was sleeping in the outer room. Chang awoke her, and her eyes opened wide in surprise. 'Why have you come?' she exclaimed. 'How did you manage to get in?'

'Your mistress sent for me,' lied Chang. 'Please tell her that I have come.' Hung Niang rose from her bed and went into the inner room. She came out, shortly, announcing, 'She is here! She is here!'

Chang was excited, thinking that his desire was about to be fulfilled. But when Oriole appeared, she was fully dressed, with a solemn expression on her face. She began to reproach Chang.

'You have indeed saved our family, and we all owe you a great deal. That is why my mother entrusts her children to you for protection. My brother and I are glad to respect you as our elder brother. How can you conceive such an unclean thought as to ask Hung Niang to bring me those poems? You showed us your kindness by protecting us from being humiliated by bandits, but now you want to humiliate us yourself. What is the difference between your motives and those of the rioters?

'If I kept what you wrote me a secret,' she continued, 'it would be silent acceptance. But if I told my mother about it, I would be showing you an ingratitude. I could have asked Hung Niang to tell you how I feel, but then I thought that she might not be able to make it clear, so I sent for you. Suspecting that you might decline to come, I intentionally wrote those romantic lines to attract you. Now, don't you feel ashamed of yourself for having such vile thoughts? I hope from now on you will be better able to control yourself.'

Having finished, Oriole turned her back on the young man and withdrew to her room. Chang was aghast. He stood rooted to the spot for a while, then climbed back over the wall and returned to his room, embarrassed and disappointed.

Some nights later, as he was sleeping alone, someone woke him up. It was Hung Niang, who brought him an embroidered quilt and a pair of pillows. 'She is coming, she is coming,' she declared. 'Why sleep alone?' With a smile, she laid the quilt and the pillows on Chang's bed and left. Chang rubbed his eyes unbelievingly and, drawing on his robe, sat on the bed and waited in suspense. Perhaps he was only dreaming.

Presently Oriole appeared, leaning upon the arm of Hung Niang. She was so overcome with bashfulness and passion that she could hardly hold her head up. All her former dignity and haughtiness had left her and, her hair loose and her eyes gleaming, she had become a perfectly amorous creature. The slanting moon shone brightly on the bed and made Oriole look even more exquisite and enchanting. Chang held her close and believed that he was in paradise. Never had he felt such ecstasy in his life.

Dawn approached, and they could hear the morning bell of the monastery. Hung Niang hurried in to take her mistress back. Sobbing passionately, Oriole left on the maid's arm. She had not uttered a single word throughout the entire night.

Chang, half awake in the early light, exclaimed, 'Am I dreaming?' But when he perceived the mark of Oriole's rouge on his arm, the stain of her tears on the pillows, and the odour of perfume on the quilt, he realized that he had indeed had an intoxicating night.

No word came from Oriole for more than ten days. In remembrance of the romantic union, Chang composed a thirty-line poem entitled 'A Rendezvous with a Fairy.' Just as he finished it, Hung Niang came to see him, and he asked her to take it to her mistress. Impressed by his tender love, Oriole favoured him with repeated trysts. From then on, every night Chang came to Oriole by climbing the wall beside the apricot tree, and every morning he left the same way. They enjoyed their nights together in the western chamber for about a month.

When Chang asked Oriole what made her love him so suddenly and so ardently, she only answered 'I could not control myself.' Though enchanted and enamored, Chang debated inwardly whether he should propose formal marriage to a girl who behaved so capriciously, first being so virtuous and dignified, and then suddenly letting her passions hold sway.

The happy days did not last long. Chang had to go to Changan, the capital, for his literary examination. He broke the news to Oriole, waiting for her reaction. Oriole said nothing to stop him, but her face was so extremely sad that it was pitiful to see. Chang did not get to see her the night before he left.

Chang returned from the west after a few months and stayed in the same monastery in Pucheng. While he was there, he resumed his nightly meetings with Oriole.

Oriole was well versed in literature and could write excellent letters, but she did not want to show off her talent, even at Chang's request. Sometimes Chang composed a verse just to inspire her, but she still did not seem to develop enough interest to reciprocate. She was reserved and kept much to herself. When she learned a skill, even though she mastered it perfectly, she acted as if she knew nothing about it. She could speak brilliantly and wisely, yet she seldom talked. Though she loved Chang with her heart and soul, she did not permit her affection to show. It was difficult to judge from her expression whether she was happy or sad.

One evening Chang heard her playing the lyre alone and was deeply moved by the haunting melody. He asked her to repeat the song for him, but she refused. He was all the more bewildered by her icy character.

Again it came time for Chang to go west for a higher examination. The night before parting, he tried not to mention the unpleasant subject, but only wore a sad face and sighed frequently. Knowing well what he meant, Oriole began to talk to him with a respectful expression on her face and in a calm, cheerful tone.

'I know that you are going to leave me tomorrow. It would not be surprising if you, who initiated our illicit affair, should despise and forsake me. What protest have I except to die with eternal regret? But if you, the gentleman who loved me first, will love me to the end, I shall be grateful to you all my life. So long as we remain faithful to our love, why should we grieve over this parting? Since you feel gloomy tonight and I can do nothing to soothe you, I shall play a song on the lyre for you. You have asked me to do it several times, but I was always afraid that I might not play it well. Now I shall play it for you.'

She then ordered the lyre to be brought in and played on it the famous 'Song of Rainbow Skirt and Feather Garment.' The melody revealed her sorrow to such a degree that after a few chords, she could hardly control the tune. The maids who attended her on both sides were moved to tears. Stopping short, Oriole laid down the lyre and went to her mother's room weeping. She did not reappear that evening.

Next morning Chang left. Failing the examination, he stayed on in the capital, only writing Oriole a love letter. Oriole wrote him a reply.

'I was both happy and sad to read your letter bearing your tender thoughts for me. It was kind of you to send me a box of hair ornaments and the five inches of rouge, which I should be proud to use if you were here. Since you are away, for whom should I decorate myself? When I look at your presents, my longing for you grows.

MISS ORIOLE

'It is good to know that you are well in the capital and are able to pursue your studies. What worries me is that, since I am an old sweetheart far away from you, you probably will forget me as time passes by. If that day ever comes, I will have to content myself with my fate and say nothing.

'Since you left me last autumn, I have been feeling lost all the time. Though I force myself to smile and join in the conversation when I am among company, my tears stream down at night when I am alone. Often I cry in my sleep when I dream that you have come back to me and that we have rejoiced together, as in the old times. But before we have finished enjoying our rendezvous, I suddenly awake and, finding only half of the quilt warm, mourn over the thought that you are no longer here beside me.

'The old year has gone. Changan is a gay city full of excitement and temptation. How fortunate I am that you have not forgotten your humble girl! To express my gratitude, I want to tell you again that I shall remain faithful to our love till the end of my life. It was through my mother that we became cousins. And later on you asked Hung Niang to bring me the poems which led me to lose my self-control and surrender myself to your desire.

You were like Sze-ma Shiang-ju, who kindled the heart of the beautiful widow by playing a song on a lyre, but I did not behave like Maiden Kao, who broke the teeth of the flirt by throwing a shuttle at him. How I was ashamed of myself for coming to you first! Yet when I recall the tenderness and affection we enjoyed together, I do not regret having this relation with you. I only feel it a pity that, loving each other as we do, we cannot formally be wed. My actions, far from the code of a virtuous woman, will remain a blemish through all my life. What I hope now is that we remain faithful to our love forever. If you, a perfect gentleman, can keep your promise and not disappoint me, I shall die with gratitude and joy. But if you believe that our affair will spoil your reputation and damage your career, and hence are ready to forget and forsake me, my soul shall love you still and follow you in wind or dew. That is all that I want to say in this short letter.

'Please take good care of yourself. I am sending you a jade ring which I have worn since my girlhood. I hope you will wear it as a remembrance of your old love. Also, I enclose a strand of tangled silk and a bamboo tea roller, which are things of little value. I select these objects because I hope your love for me will be as pure as the jade and as continuous as the ring. The bamboo tea roller bears the stain of my tears and the tangled silk represents my confused feelings when I think of you. I send all these to express my deep love. Though I am far away from you, my heart is near. And though we have no way to meet again, my spirit will come to you to seek reunion. Please take good care of yourself, for the spring wind is still cold at times. Eat well and rest properly. Keep our affair a secret and do not worry about me.'

Chang was deeply touched by Oriole's ardent letter, but he did not have the courage either to answer her or to return to her, for he had failed to pass the examination. Now he regretted entering into an illicit affair. He showed his lover's letter to many of his acquaintances, and it created a sensation in literary circles. Yang Chu-yuan, one of his intimate friends, composed a poem, 'Maiden Tsui,' in remembrance of the affair.

Jade is not as transparent as handsome Pan.
The snow has melted; fragrant is the grass in the courtyard;
The heart of the romantic is full of the sweetness of spring.
It breaks upon receiving the letter from his former sweetheart.

I also wrote a long poem as a continuation of Chang's own 'Rendezvous with a Fairy.'

News of the tragic end of Chang's romance spread quickly among his friends. Everyone was puzzled as to why he had changed his mind and abandoned Oriole. Since I am intimate with him, I once asked him his reason. He said: 'Too much beauty always brings ill fortune to others, if not to the possessor. There have been many examples in our history. Both Emperor Hsin of the Shang dynasty and Emperor Yu of the Chou dynasty lost their empires because they indulged in the company of beautiful women. Their kingdoms were destroyed, and they were killed and made laughing stocks for later generations. If Oriole happened to be espoused by an emperor, who knows but that, by taking advantage of her feminine charms, she might become as extravagant and cruel as the ancient court concubines. I am insignificant and do not possess enough merit to overcome the evil spirits. Therefore, I decided to control my passion and end my youthful folly.'

Those who were with me thought Chang was justified in his caprice.

MISS ORIOLE

A little more than a year later, Oriole became the wife of another man and Chang also married another girl. One day Chang happened to pass through the city where Oriole lived. He called on her husband and, introducing himself as Oriole's cousin, asked to see her. Oriole's husband asked her to come out, but she declined. Knowing that Chang must be bitterly hurt, she sent him a poem secretly.

Gone is the brightness from my face since we parted,
After thousands of tossings and languor, no desire to leave my bed;
Not embarrassed am I to get up and others meet,
But failing as I am, you I dare not see.

As Chang was leaving town, Oriole sent him another poem.

Forsaken, what more have I to say?
So dear to recollect the days we were together:
Remember forever our old true love,
And tenderly give it to the girl who now is with you.

There was no further communication between the lovers.

In the ninth month of the year of Cheng Yuan, an official named Li Kung-chiu, who was lodging in my house in Chingan Lane, talked with me about this love affair. Marveling at the girl's passion and sympathetic with her tragic end, he composed the 'Song of Oriole,' with the hope of making the story known to generations to come.

PART IV

BETROTHAL—
THE EDGE OF
WOMANHOOD

'Nine out of ten matchmakers are liars.'

The marriage rate for women in China has long been extremely high. Alternatives to becoming a wife traditionally were to be a concubine or second wife, a courtesan or singsong girl, a servant or nun. It was rare, however, that a girl would choose to enter a convent. Marriage was the norm.

Because there were more boys than girls in the population, a girl from a poor family could often marry up, although this could put pressure on her family to provide a dowry and on the girl herself in her new home. One excuse sometimes given for female infanticide was the exorbitant cost of a bride's dowry.

Some poor families, wishing to avoid the expense both of raising a daughter and a dowry, would sell their daughters to the families of their future husbands. These 'little daughters-in-law' worked in their future husband's homes before marrying after puberty. The groom's family acquired a helper and avoided the usual expensive gifts to the bride's family.

Among the elite, marriages were most successful if the two families were equal. The girl would garner more respect from her new family if her manners were polished, and she fitted in well.

A Mandarin sits in splendour with household females above

Balance between these families was displayed in the similar value of the bride's dowry and the groom's gifts. A wealthy bride might bring a personal servant to her new home, and this link with her past could smooth the transition.

One bright spot was that marriages between cousins of different surnames were permitted, often with felicitous results. Unlike the usual pattern, in which only the go-between might be acquainted with both families, relatives knew each other well and expectations were realistic.

The cost of maintaining secondary wives or concubines, and the domestic discord which could ensue, meant that they were much rarer than the literature in English might suggest. However, mandarins or government officials sent to the provinces, often left their primary wives at home to manage complex households, and would be accompanied by younger, comely concubines.

For most young women, marriage rituals were similar but varied according to circumstances. Once married, girls departed from their birth families where they had had only peripheral importance. Although there would be problems in the new home—most likely with the mother-in-law—the position of the new bride was central as the potential mother of sons. Thus, women's standing in society was designated by their birth family before marriage and by their in-laws afterwards.

43
IS SHE BETROTHED?
Arthur H. Smith
1899

Without a doubt, the most important act of a young Chinese woman's life was her betrothal. The relationship determined the family into which she would marry and for whom she would, it was hoped, bear male descendants. Hence the vital question about her future. However, missionary Arthur Smith felt that girls are betrothed too young.

A Chinese girl, as soon as she attains any considerable size, is exhibited in the inquiries which are made about her whenever she happens to be spoken of. These inquiries do not concern her character or her domestic accomplishments, much less her intellectual capacity—of which she has, theoretically, none to speak of—but they may all be summed up in the single phrase, 'Is she said?' meaning by the term 'said' 'betrothed.' If the reply should be in the negative, the intelligence is received in much the same way as we should receive the information that a foreign child had been allowed to grow to the age of sixteen without having been taught anything whatever out of books. 'Why?' we should say, 'what is the explanation for this strange neglect?' The instinctive feeling of a Chinese in regard to a girl is that she should be betrothed as soon as possible. This is one of the many points in regard to which it is almost impossible for the Chinese and the Anglo-Saxon to come to terms. To the latter the betrothal of a mere child, scarcely in her teens, is a piece of absolute barbarity.

As soon as a Chinese girl is betrothed, she is placed in different relations to the universe generally. She is no longer allowed such freedom as hitherto, although that may have been little enough. She cannot go anywhere, because it would be 'inconvenient.' She might be seen by some member of the family into which she is to marry, of which it is hardly possible to think of anything more horrible.

44
THE GO-BETWEEN
Adele Fielde
1894

The all-important go-between was usually most interested in her own fee. It was rarely in her interest to disclose all she learnt about prospective mates and their families, and so alliances were often formed without full disclosure.

Oppressive upon women as the marriage laws are, the common practices are harsher still; for if deception be used by the go-between, the matrimonial agent employed to negotiate the marriage, there is no redress except through a lawsuit, which is sure to be won by the litigant who can offer the magistrate the highest bribe. I have known a girl to be, unknown to herself and to her parents, legally bound, beyond help or recall, to a maniac; and I have known a girl, declared by the go-between to be sound and fair, to be discovered by her waiting mother-in-law and husband to be incurably maimed. Greed of lucre, and misjudgment as to what constitutes well-being, produce conjugal misery. There is redress for the man, soon after marriage, if he determines to put away his wife; but there is none for the woman, save by death.

45
A PROPOSAL OF MARRIAGE
ARTHUR H. SMITH
1899

Betrothal to a young man from another village meant both that the young woman was less likely to be seen before marriage, and that the go-between had more room to manoeuvre.

The imminent risk that the girl might in some unguarded moment be actually *seen* by the family of the future mother-in-law is a reason why so few engagements for girls are made in the town in which the girl lives, an arrangement which would seem to be for the convenience of all parties in a great variety of ways. It would put a stop to the constant deceptions practised by the middle-women, or professional match-makers, whose only object is to carry through whatever match has been proposed, in order to reap the percentage which will accrue to the agent. It would do away with the waste of time and money involved in transporting brides from one of their homes to the other, often at great inconvenience and loss. It would make the interchange of little courtesies between the families easy and frequent. But for all these advantages the Chinese do not seem to care, and the most frequent explanation of the neglect of them is that there would be the risk already mentioned. When these two families are such as would in the ordinary course of events be likely to meet, nothing is more amusing to a foreigner than to watch the struggles which are made to avert such a catastrophe. One is reminded of some of our childhood's games, in which one party is 'poison' and the other party is liable to be 'poisoned' and must at all hazards keep out of the way. The only difference between the cases is that in the Chinese game, *each party* is afraid of being 'poisoned,' and will struggle to prevent it. There is one set of circumstances, however, in which, despite their utmost efforts, Fate is too much both for the

A PROPOSAL OF MARRIAGE

poisoners and the poisoned. If during the betrothal a death of an older person takes place in the family of the mother-in-law, it is generally thought necessary that the girl (who is considered as already 'belonging' to that family) should be present and should perform the same reverence to the coffin of the deceased, as if to say: why should she not come and lament like the rest? If it is possible to arrange it, however, the marriage will be hastened, in the event of a death of a person belonging to an older generation, even if a later date had been previously set.

To a foreigner, the Chinese habit of early engagements appears to have no single redeeming feature. It hampers both families with no apparent corresponding advantages, if indeed there are advantages of any kind. It assumes, what is far from certain, and often not at all likely, that the relative position of the two families will continue to be the same. This assumption is contradicted by universal experience. Time and change happen to all, and the insecurity of human affairs is nowhere more manifest than in the tenure of Chinese property. Families are going up and coming down all the time. It is a well-settled principle in China that matches should be between those who are in the same general circumstances. Disregard of this rule is sure to bring trouble. But if early betrothals are the practice, the chances of material alteration in the condition of each of the families are greatly increased. When he is engaged, the character of the boy, upon which so much of a bride's happiness is to depend, has not perhaps been formed. Even if it has been formed, it is generally next to impossible for the girl's family to learn anything authentic as to what the character is, though to all appearances it would be so easy for them to ascertain by latent methods. But as a rule, it would appear that they do not concern themselves much about the matter after the engagement is proposed and accepted, and at no time do they give it a hundredth part of the investigation which it seems to us to warrant. If the boy becomes a gambler, a profligate, or dissipated in any other way, there is no retreat for the family of the girl, no matter to what extremities they may be driven. Chinese violation of the most ordinary rules of prudence and common sense in the matter of the betrothal of their daughters is, to a Westerner, previous to experience and observation, almost incredible.

A Chinese marriage engagement begins when the red cards have been interchanged, ratifying the agreement. These are in some districts formidable documents, almost as large as a crib-blanket, and are very important as evidence in case of future trouble. It is very rare to hear of the breaking of a marriage engagement in China, though such instances do doubtless occur. In a case of this sort the card of the boy's family had been delivered to the other family, at which point the transaction is considered to be definitely closed. But an uncle of the betrothed girl, although younger than the father of the girl, created a disturbance and refused to allow the engagement to stand. This made the matter very serious, but as the younger brother was inflexible, there was no help for it but to send the red acceptance card back by the middleman who brought it. This also was a delicate matter, but a Chinese is seldom at a loss for expedients when a disagreeable thing must be done. He selected a time when all the male members of the boy's family were in the wheatfield, and then threw the card declining the match into the yard of the family of the boy, and went his way. None of the women of the family could read, and it was not until the men returned that it was discovered what the document was. The result was a lawsuit of portentous proportions, in which an accusation was brought against both the father of the girl and against the middleman. This case was finally adjusted by a money payment.

The delivery of the red cards is, as we have remarked, the beginning of the engagement, the culmination being the arrival of the bride in her chair at the home of her husband. The date of this event is generally dependent upon the pleasure of the boy's family. Whatever accessories the wedding may have, the arrival of the bride is the *de facto* completion of the contract.

46
THE FATE OF FOUNDLING GIRLS
JUSTUS DOOLITTLE
1865

The Reverend Doolittle spent fourteen years as a missionary in Fuzhou, penning his book, Social Life of the Chinese. *He notes that unwanted baby girls were sometimes placed in asylums from which, if they lived, marriages were arranged for them. Where girls were sold as slaves, their employers were responsible for finding a spouse.*

The girls may not be taken out to be courtesans nor to be slaves, but only for wives—not for concubines, nor for inferior wives. When one makes application for a girl, the *tepaou*, or local constable of the district where the asylum is located, must make strict inquiries about the man, his object and circumstances, lest deception should be practised.

Very often the parents of a foundling make application for their child after she has been in the asylum for a few months or years. In case she is alive, and the records of the institution are properly kept, this is easily done, by mentioning its family or ancestral name, and the precise time of its birth.

Only girls are left at the asylum. In case, however, boys should be left there, they would be cared for, if they lived, for several years, and then bound out, as apprentices, to a useful trade, unless demanded by their parents. The rules of the institution would admit to raising boys as well as girls, but, in point of fact, boys are not thus deserted by their parents. They are always regarded as valuable acquisitions, even to poor families. With girls, however, the case is far different; they are usually regarded as unprofitable children in the family, and often are either drowned by their parents, or left to die by the roadside, or sold or given away to be the future wives of the sons of friends, or taken to the asylum.

The expenses of the asylum, comparatively speaking, must be large. The funds are obtained from the rent of buildings and landed property, and from contributions from rich men, the gentry, and mandarins, and anyone who is disposed to take part in this good or meritorious work of saving alive, and of raising those children who would otherwise be destroyed by their parents. It is commonly reported that those who have the management of its funds and of its business make considerable money by false entries in the books, and false reports in regard to the number of nurses and infants supported, etc., and it would be strange if they frequently did not thus take advantage of their position to defraud.

The number of infants who die in the asylum is said to be astonishingly large in proportion to those received, showing a great lack of proper attention and food; or, perhaps, a large proportion of the deaths may be fairly attributed to the exposure of the infants before they have been actually received into the care of the institution. A system of rewards has been adopted, the object of which is to stimulate the nurses to take good care of their charges. Small as these sums given as presents and rewards really are, they have a salutary influence upon the nurses. Still, it is estimated that many more than half of the foundlings die in the course of a few months after reception.

The foundlings are almost always betrothed and taken away long before they arrive at womanhood. Should, however, one be left unengaged on arriving at a marriageable age, and should an acceptable applicant for a wife present himself, she is led out to him, with her face and head closely veiled. The parties proceed to perform the worship of heaven and earth, after which they depart as husband and wife, she seated in the red sedan invariably used by a bride of respectable character while being conveyed to her husband's house. On arriving at her future home, the ceremonies are performed, and the festivities are enjoyed, usual at weddings. He who marries a foundling, of course, belongs to the lowest class of society as regards money and wealthy friends. While there is no positive disgrace attached to marrying such a wife, none do it who are able to procure a wife whose parents are known. It is much cheaper to get a wife from the asylum, if there happens to be a girl of adult age in it, than from a respectable family by the aid of a go-between. Usually, a successful applicant is required to pay to the managers of the institution only a few thousand cash for its benefit, while, were he to marry a respectable girl of known connections, she would cost him a much larger sum.

47
NEW CUSTOMS

RICHARD WILHEIM

1928

By the beginning of the twentieth century, betrothal rules showed signs of relaxing. These new attitudes had their roots in the Taiping Rebellion in the mid-nineteenth century in which women played a role, gaining respect. Change continued through the struggles against the Qing dynasty and the founding of the Women's Federation of China, affiliated with the Chinese Communist Party from the mid-1920s.

These old customs have been superseded. The women in China have long ago left: all the fetters of old prejudices behind them. Young girls are far freer in China today than, for instance, in Japan, where the old knightly ideal is kept up to a greater extent. Even freedom in the choice of a husband is proclaimed more and more and in connection with this movement the women of young China are making energetic attacks upon the comfortable practice which used to allow the husband, for his own pleasure, to have a number of servants or concubines who were included in the family. The free choice of the husband naturally removes the main reason for the existence of the concubines, because every man has to ascribe it to himself if he should find that his wife is less satisfactory than he had hoped. The question of the male succession alone will continue to play its part in marriage problems as long as the patriarchal family continues to exist in China, and, as long as this is the case, the possibility will always remain, if the wife does not provide male issue, that the husband can take a concubine, in case the marriage is not dissolved on that account—and he marries a new wife, which is permitted according to Chinese law. These new Chinese laws are, as far as divorce is concerned, far more free and easy than most of the corresponding European laws. On the one hand they are not burdened with considerations of the church, and on the other hand the question of providing for the children and their education is easily solved in divorce cases in China, because marriage is only a connection within the larger family and the children belong in any case rather to this family than to its particular parents.

From what has been said, it is evident that marriage is not so significant an epoch in the life of a man in China as it is in Europe, because it is not necessarily connected with the beginning of their own household. If the bride, by entering a new family and by her new social position, begins an entirely new chapter in her life, the position of the young man within his household remains more or less unchanged, for at most he is given a special building within the general family property for himself and his wife. The choice of his life-companion will have been made long ago by his parents. The date of the marriage is fixed, at a moment when, for instance, domestic affairs make an additional worker desirable to the mother of the youth. In that case the bridegroom, if he happens to live away from his home, would return for a few days. If he happens to attend a school in a different locality, one week's holiday suffices, whereupon the young husband comes back to the school as heretofore. This practice brings it about that the husband, as long as his parents are at the head of the household, is often away from his home for years with the exception of short intervals. His wife is looked after just as well as the children of the family, and for this reason it used to be a more important problem for a young wife how she got on with her mother-in-law than with her husband.

48
THE FACTS OF BETROTHAL
Encyclopedia Sinica
1917

The law pertaining to betrothal was detailed and specific. Girls were not free to sign a betrothal contract themselves.

The legal contractors of a betrothal may be (1) the paternal grandparents of the couple, (2) the parents of the couple, (3) the paternal uncle of the father, and his wife, (4) the paternal aunt, sister of the father, (5) the eldest brother, (6) the eldest sister, (7) the maternal grandparents. Failing these near relatives, those of more remote kin may arrange the contract. A married daughter may make a contract for female relatives of her father's family. If the contract be illegal or fraudulent, the parties arranging the contract are the ones punished. The consent of the couple to the contract is not required. If a widow wishes to remarry, her father-in-law, mother-in-law or other relative of her husband's family, signs the contract; failing these, a member of her father's family. If a widow has a daughter by her first marriage who has become an inmate of her second husband's home, the widow can sign her daughter's betrothal contract.

49
MARRIAGE SUPERSTITIONS
Adele Fielde
1894

Adele Fielde, who spent fifteen years in Guangdong Province, observes that rituals for a bride were steeped in superstition.

A girl who is partaking of the last meal she is to eat in her father's house previous to her marriage, sits at the table with her parents and brothers; but she must eat no more than half the bowl of rice set before her, else her departure will be followed by continual scarcity in the domicile she is leaving.

If a bride breaks the heel of her shoe in going from her father's to her husband's house, it is ominous of unhappiness in her new relations.

A piece of bacon and a parcel of sugar are hung on the back of a bride's sedan-chair as a sop to the demons who might molest her while on her journey. The 'Three Baneful Ones' are fond of salt and spices, and the 'White Tiger' likes sweets.

A bride may be brought home while a coffin is in her husband's house, but not within one hundred days after a coffin is carried out. Domestic troubles are sure to come upon one who is married within a hundred days after a funeral.

A bride, while putting on her wedding garments, stands in a round, shallow basket. This conduces to her leading a placid, well-rounded life in her future home. After her departure from her father's door, her mother puts the basket over the mouth of the oven, to stop the mouths of all who would make adverse comment on her daughter, and then sits down before the kitchen range, that her peace and leisure may be duplicated in her daughter's life.

A bride must not, for four months after her marriage, enter any house in which there has recently been a death or a birth; for if she does, there will surely be a quarrel between her and the groom. If a young mother goes to see a bride, the visitor is looked upon as the cause of any calamity that may follow.

50
A LUCKY DAY
Arthur H. Smith
1894

Even now, most Chinese families continue to marry on auspicious days and to pay inflated prices for wedding expenses to ensure good luck. An auspicious day was mandatory for marriage—more important even than the presence of the groom!

That the only essential feature of a Chinese wedding is the delivery of the bride at her husband's home, is strikingly shown in those not very uncommon instances in which a Chinese is married without himself being present at all. It is usually considered a very ill omen to change the date set for a wedding, especially to postpone it. Yet it sometimes happens that the young man is at a distance from home, and fails to return in time. Or the bridegroom may be a scholar, and find that the date of an important examination coincides with the day set for his wedding. In such a case he will probably choose 'business before pleasure' and the bride will be 'taken delivery of' by older members of his family, without disturbing his own literary ambitions.

* * *

The Chinese imperial calendar designates the days which are the most felicitous for weddings, and it constantly happens that on these particular days there will be what the Chinese term 'red festivities' in almost every village. This is one of the many instances in which Chinese superstitions are financially expensive. On 'lucky days' the hire of sedan-chairs rises with the great demand, while those who disregard luck are able to get better service at a lower price. There is a story of a winter in the early part of this century when on a 'fortunate day' many brides were being carried to their new homes during the progress of a tremendous snowstorm which blinded the bearers and obliterated the roads. Some of the brides were frozen to death, and many were taken to the wrong places. On the other hand in a blistering summer, cases have been known where the bride was found to be dead when the chair was deposited at the husband's home. The same bridal sedan-chair may be used many times. In regions where it is the custom to have all weddings in the forenoon, second marriages are put off until the afternoon, or even postponed until the evening, marking their minor importance.

51
MARRIAGE RITUALS
Charles Gutzlaff
1838

The Reverend Charles Gutzlaff, a Prussian by birth, was sent to China by the Netherlands Missionary Society. A talented linguist, Gutzlaff translated the Scriptures into Chinese and later served as Chinese secretary and translator for the British government. A bald, corpulent, red-faced man, he was an eccentric and somewhat shady figure whose many decades in China give credence to his observations of the Chinese.

The most common way, however, in forming the union, is to employ a go-between, who repairs to the parties and offers terms. The parents of the girl always demand a price for their child, which varies from six dollars to 5,000, according to the beauty or rank of the lady, and the circumstances of the other party. Sovereigns, and men in high office, frequently condescend to bestow their daughters upon favourites, who are then bound in sacred duty to behave as sons towards their benefactors, and to treat their partners as superiors.

The personal attractions of which a go-between makes the most careful inventory, are the lady's small feet, her pale complexion, and her slender waist. As soon as the bargain is concluded, the stipulated sum, with various presents, is delivered, and a lucky day for the wedding appointed; the bride weeps ten days with her sisters, because she is to leave the house of her parents. In the meantime, complimentary letters and presents pass between the parties, but the bride and the bridegroom are not permitted to see each other. This would be against all the established rules of decorum.

The only portion a bride receives from her parent is an outfit, which, on the wedding day, is sent with great pomp to the house of her future husband. Bridesmen and maids follow the sedan, sent

Wedding preparations at the home of a wealthy bride

by the bridegroom, in which the bride is locked up, accompanied with a train of musicians and people, bearing flags and other tinselled trophies. The key is carried by the mother of the bride, or by a near relation, who delivers it to his mother, on arriving at the gate of the bridegroom's house. She opens it, and he is then permitted to look at his intended; if she do not please him, he may instantly send her back, and he has only to lose the bargain money; but if she once alight at his threshold, she becomes irrevocably his wife. He introduces her with many bows and gallantries into the great hall. Here both prostrate themselves several times before the idol, and burn incense before the tablets of their ancestors, and then enter into the inner apartments, where the same ceremonies are performed by the parents. After this, the bride retires with the bridesmaid and her relations into the bedchamber, whilst the bridegroom returns to his companions. A rich repast is then spread, and all parties enjoy themselves. The marriage ceremony itself consists in drinking a cup of wine, which the bride and bridegroom exchange with each other to intimate their union. The congratulations follow a few days afterwards, when the new wife again becomes visible, and receives company. The ceremonies at these interviews are too numerous to be detailed. A month having elapsed, she revisits her parents, to perform once more, for several weeks, the duties of a daughter, and then to take a lasting farewell, being no longer considered the property of her parents.

Forced marriages often produce the most tragical results, if the females possess an independent spirit. They have generally recourse to poison, or shave their head to become nuns before they have joined in the matrimonial cup with the husband.

A man may divorce his wife if she be quarrelsome, disobedient, or afflicted with an incurable disease. In case of her elopement, he has a right to sell her. Adultery in the wife is punished very severely. In case the husband absents himself for three years, she is entitled to sue for a divorce. Such suits, however, are rare, for conjugal fidelity in the weaker sex, is a virtue to which the Chinese ladies may very justly lay claim. Public opinion and the doctrines of the sages contribute much to cement matrimonial union, and thus it may in general be said, that the ties of marriage are on the part of the female indissoluble. The husband, on the contrary, is permitted to take a concubine, if his wife be barren. She is treated like a servant, and if she has borne a son, is not unfrequently sent out of the house, the child being adopted by the rightful wife. Husbands however avail themselves of this privilege to a very great extent, and if they are rich enough they often keep a regular harem. The grandees show the example, and it is no wonder that the multitude should faithfully copy it. Beautiful and accomplished females, for which the country about Hang-choo and Soo-choo [Hangzhou and Suzhou] is celebrated, are extensively bought and sold. Horrible as this custom may be, it is not prohibited by government.

We find many things very praiseworthy in the state of matrimony, as maintained by the Chinese, especially amongst the middling classes, and the peasantry. Yet there are people who for the sake of filthy lucre prostitute their wives. If there were but few instances of this unparalleled vice on record, we might ascribe the atrocious fact of its occurrence to individual circumstances—either of desperate wickedness or want; but we shudder to say, that it is by no means the case. Their morals are more debased in the cities than in the country, and there is, in the former, no want of objects for inflaming the passions. Whatever produces profit is followed most eagerly by the Chinese, without the smallest regard to decency.

There is moreover another dark spot on their character, which it is loathsome to express in language, yet this abomination, so horrible in the sight of God, is committed with the utmost impudence.

It is very disrespectful in widows to marry again, yet, amongst the lower classes, it happens frequently. The government bestows, occasionally, rewards upon those who preserve their chastity after the first nuptials, but encourages a widower's second marriage. The number of barren women is comparatively very small.

52
SHICONG IS A CLEAR-THINKING GIRL
Tianjin Ribao
1981

This article from a Chinese newspaper, Tianjin Ribao, relates an admirable modern engagement.

The twenty-four-year-old girl Mao Shicong is the assistant company commander of the people's militia of the Tube brigade in Jinghai county. She is good-hearted, healthy, and a good worker. According to a proverb, if there is such a daughter in a family, one hundred families will ask for her. Naturally there were quite a few potential mates for a girl as good as Shicong. Through the introduction of the secretary of the production brigade's Party branch, Zhang Zhiming, Shicong met and fell in love with Liu Junbiao, the head of the people's militia of the Sanjianfang brigade of this county.

The custom in the countryside is that when a man and woman become a couple the woman must go to the man's family to eat an 'engagement meal'. Junbiao was of course no exception. He rushed to Shicong's house to arrange a date. He never expected that the moment he opened his mouth, Shicong would raise objections. Shicong said, 'If we want to be a couple, then let's just be a couple. Why do we have to do something fancy? Is it possible you are afraid I will fly off if you don't do it?'

Junbiao, embarrassed, said, 'But everybody in the village has this custom. Furthermore, everyone in my family wants to have a look at you.'

Shicong said, 'What family has that custom? We are both members of the Communist Party. Why don't we destroy the custom!' Ultimately she told Junbiao that she was willing to visit his home, but she would not set a date in advance and did not want any preparations made. 'I'll just pick a time to go myself and let your parents look me over. That will take care of it.'

Not long after that she went to their home. When Mother Liu saw Shicong, she looked her up and down. The more she looked at her the more she adored her, and she was as happy as if she had a jar of honey in her hand. She thought to herself, the first time a future daughter-in-law enters the door you must do something. She thought it over, and finally took out 300 yuan to give her as a 'meeting gift'. She insisted that Shicong accept it. After taking the money, Shicong said, 'You suffered great pain and endured hardship to raise Junbiao and his brothers. I am giving you this money back, to be considered an expression of my respect.'

'If she won't accept the "meeting present" then we must get Shicong two sets of clothes!' After a great deal of pressure was applied, Shicong reluctantly agreed to go with Junbiao to the department store. In the store were all kinds of things, and a wide variety of clothes, but Shicong was not in the mood to look. Junbiao said, 'Shicong, take a look and decide what you like.'

Shicong said, 'It seems to me that everything in the store is nice. You decide what to buy.'

He didn't know what he had done wrong. Finally Shicong got him out of his predicament by spending 2 yuan on a hat for him.

The next day Shicong wanted to return to her home. Mother Liu thought that she had not managed to give Shicong anything, so she secretly gave Junbiao 300 yuan and told him to find an opportunity to give it to Shicong. On the way home, there were several times when Junbiao thought he might raise the subject, but he was afraid of her reply. When they arrived at Shicong's home, Junbiao thought that if he took out the money, her parents would definitely refuse to take it; but if he took it home, he would have let down his mother. At the last minute he put the money under the quilt on the hearth. Despite his efforts, Shicong found the money. This made her think more deeply about the situation. She thought, 'Why is it that they are so determined to give me the gift? The main reason is that they still do not really understand me.'

A few days later she went to Junbiao's house again. She explained her views to him and he understood. He said, 'You are so broad minded. What could I possibly say?'

The two of them went to Mother Liu, and Shicong said, 'Junbiao and I are engaged because we share the same ideals. Why would we ever need your "down payment"?' She thereupon took the 300 yuan and returned it to Mother Liu.

53
MISUNDERSTANDINGS
Herbert Giles
1925

Some families betrothed their children when they were babies or even before they were born. The negotiations did not always go smoothly, however, as this humorous story shows.

A man who had a daughter, aged one, (i.e. newly born according to Chinese computation) was asked to betroth her to a boy, aged two (i.e. one). The father of the girl got angry at this, and said,

'What do you mean by trying to make a fool of me? My girl is one year old, and your boy is two, so that when she is ten years old your son would be twenty. What do I want with an old son-in-law like that?'

'Your calculation is all wrong', said the man's wife. 'Although our girl is only one now, next year she will be as old as the boy. Why not betroth her?'

PART V

MARRIAGE—
THE CURTAINED
SEDAN CHAIR

'In bed, husband and wife; out of bed, guests.'

Girls in modern China are no longer married off as early as possible. Delayed marriages are one solution to overpopulation, and the ideal marriage age for women is now considered to be mid-twenties. Women who previously might have borne many children are now limited by the one-child policy to a single offspring, but for most couples the preference is still for a boy.

Before the Communist Party came to power in 1949, marriages arranged between families precluded couples from even meeting before the ceremony. Girls seen chatting casually with boys were considered immoral and of less value on the marriage market. These attitudes which segregated young people continued to hold sway even after the Marriage Act of 1950, impeding the new legal freedoms for women. This act allowed women to initiate divorce for the first time—and they initiated the majority of cases! Most women now worked, especially in urban areas such as Shanghai's light industry. Financial independence gave them more freedom. Many men in the countryside, however, divorced their farm-bound wives from arranged marriages to marry more sophisticated city brides.

Free choice was reiterated in the new Marriage Law of 1981, but in the countryside, go-betweens continued to collect fees. As communes reverted to private farms, young people lost the opportunity to become acquainted. However, by the 1980s, about half the couples marrying had met without a go-between, but a new convention developed which combined a formal introduction with free choice. This has been followed by computerized dating agencies and personal columns, all allowing young women possibilities never before known.

54
THE FIRST DAYS OF MARRIAGE
Adele Fielde
1894

During her many years in China, Adele Fielde learnt a local south-eastern dialect and was at home in her Guangdong village. She presents a wealth of detail about the three-day wedding ceremony.

Early on the morning of the wedding, the bride is bathed in water in which twelve kinds of flowers have been steeped; has her hair stiffened with bandoline and wrought into a marvellous coiffure with many golden aigrettes; is attired in gorgeous apparel, which she puts on with an appearance of bitter unwillingness, and enters the red sedan-chair, weeping loudly. The marriage procession is headed by a man carrying a branch of a banyan-tree, whose local name is identical in sound with another word which means *completed* or *perfected*. It signifies the fact that all that is necessary to legal matrimony has been done in this case. This leader is followed by two men, each bearing a lantern on a stalk of sugar-cane, the former being a part of the bride's outfit, and the latter, rising stage by stage to a climax broad and flourishing, symbolizing the hope that the bride's life may likewise widen out. The next in the file is a man carrying over his shoulder a bamboo, the emblem of rapid increase, having a red bundle of foot-gear on one end of it, and a red coverlet on the other. After him come as many burden-bearers as are necessary to carry all the red boxes containing the trousseau.

On arriving at the door of the house, the bride sees her husband for the first time, and recognizes him, among those who await her, by his rich attire. By previous arrangement, she is first greeted by some woman reckoned lucky and prosperous, in the hope that she will be like the one who gives her earliest welcome in her new home. A mistress of ceremonies who has been engaged to see that

Reluctant bride with groom

during three days all is done according to established usage, throws upon the door-sill some burning straw, half extinguishes it, and leads the new-comer across it, saying:—

Now, fair young bride, the smoke bestride;
This year have joy, next year a boy.

This rite is supposed to disinfect the bride from any evil influence to which she may have been subjected by demons or white tigers along her route. She then immediately enters the room in which her red bedstead has been set up, and in which her possessions are all deposited. There she sits silent all the rest of the day, among her red boxes, no one speaking to her, nor noticing her in any way except by bringing her food. A feast is spread in the evening for male friends, who have been invited by card, and its preparation occupies the whole household. After the supper, the guests are permitted to see the bride, who is brought forward by

THE FIRST DAYS OF MARRIAGE

the duenna toward the door of the bedroom. In some cases only those who can offer a felicitous stanza are allowed to approach the bedroom door, and there is much rivalry in the composition of poetry to be recited. The stanzas usually contain allusions to posterity, as in the following translations from the vernacular: —

The bride is high-browed, fair and sweet;
Like awls her small and sharp-toed feet.
Brought home this year with honours meet,
Next year an infant son she'll greet.

Fresh twigs upon the pine, new sprouts on the bamboo;
The groom brings home the bride to rule his house: his field
To her a thousand-fold its annual crop shall yield,
And she will be a mother-in-law at thirty-two.

Practical jokes usually accompany the entertainment. Sometimes a guest enters, disguised as an aged man, and after persuading the duenna to bring the bride close to him by a plea that his sight is very dim, he suddenly tosses off his cap and spectacles and appears as a hilarious youth. This creates much merriment. Another popular joke is to leave a bundle of fire-crackers under the bedstead, with a slow match so placed as to explode them after midnight, and this is often accompanied by an artificial shower falling through the roof upon the bridal couch.

On the second day the young pair worship the images of the ancestors in the main room of the house, and make obeisance to each of the senior members of the family. In the afternoon the last presents are sent off from the groom's family to the bride's parents. They include pork, fish, cakes, and confectionery, according with the amount stipulated at the time of betrothal. During the second and third days all who choose may enter the house and view the bride, and the crowd of spectators is sometimes large. They say:—

We look at the new, and not at the old;
We all have, at home, old things to behold.

The third day is a busy one for the bride, as she must then formally begin her domestic duties. Early in the morning she washes clothes for herself and her husband, under the direction of the duenna. Then this mistress of ceremonies takes her hand, holds it upon the long handle of a ladle, and stirs up the food in a jar, from which she is to feed and fatten pigs. She meanwhile recites a rhyme, of which this is a close version:—

Stir up the swill, make the jar fume;
Raise hogs that are bigger than cows.
Stir deep and long, stir into spume;
Give thousand-weight swine to your spouse.

At the end of a month the bride's mother sends her a basket of artificial flowers, that she may make acceptable presents to her young neighbours. No bonnets nor other head-coverings are used by youthful ladies in China, and flowers are worn in the hair on all festive occasions.

At the end of four months, on a day selected as lucky by a wizard, the bride goes to pay her first visit to her mother, unless some event has made it mystically unsafe for her to leave her present domicile or to enter her old one. The length of the bride's stay in her former home varies in different villages. In some she remains a month in her mother's house, and in others it is considered very unlucky if she does not return the same day, before the smoke from the village chimneys indicates that supper is being cooked. But any circumstance that renders either of the families ceremonially unclean, and therefore unpropitious to luck, prevents the bride from having this outing. Uncleanness is of two sorts—that which results from a death, and that which follows the birth of a child.

They are distinguished as that of bad fortune and that of good fortune, the former continuing three years, and the latter one month. Were the bride to approach any unclean person, she would herself incur the danger of becoming an occult cause of calamity among her relatives. During the first few months after marriage she must carefully guard against exposure to any influence adverse to good luck.

A neighbour of a Chinese friend of mine had one daughter, an only child, of whom she was passionately fond. The girl was married off when sixteen years old. When the first four months were nearly past, her mother's neighbour died, and her visit to her old home had therefore to be delayed for a hundred days. Before this period had passed, the bride's mother-in-law died, and she had

THE FIRST DAYS OF MARRIAGE

to go into mourning for three years. Just before she put off mourning, she bore a son, and that made it necessary for her to again delay her first visit to her mother's house. Her mother, meanwhile, became subject to hallucinations, under which she frequently saw her child entering her door. She said she could distinctly perceive her face, could discern every detail in her dress, and could hear the jingle of her bangles. She would exclaim, 'O my child, you have come!' but, when she clasped the vision, she found only empty air in her arms. At last the daughter, who had all these years been but two miles away, really came to visit her mother. The two embraced each other and wept aloud; and thereafter the mother's hallucinations ceased.

After the first visit, a married daughter may go to the home of her parents at any time, and they, after the birth of her first child, may occasionally go to see her in her husband's house.

55
A CHINESE WEDDING
Marguerite Owen
1934

This lively description of a Chinese wedding is by a young American missionary in Anhui Province in 1934, and comes from one of her previously unpublished letters home.

My first Chinese wedding was a scene I'll never forget. I have been teaching a group of English students every afternoon. On a Monday one didn't appear and one of the others said he was to be married and I gasped. He seemed so young to me. The next day the three 'Chiao-so' received an invitation to come to the wedding and the feast following. It had rained for two days and we hoped it would clear for Wednesday, but it was still raining. At nine o'clock the oldest daughter in the groom's family told us to come at 12 noon, but at eleven the younger sister came running to tell us to come right away, as the bride was on her way. In a few minutes, we could hear the shrill pipes and drums making the weird music that accompanies the bridal chair, and with umbrellas and rain coats we gingerly threaded our way to the groom's house. (Note how many reversed from USA situations we saw.) We arrived at a most propitious moment—just as the bridal chair—closely covered and gaudily decorated stopped at the gate of the courtyard.

An awning had been stretched from the door to a wall about 25 feet away and in this square in the pouring rain under a terribly leaking awning, the ceremony took place. A path had been made of old boards & bamboo matting for the gayly dressed bride to walk on amidst the muck of a courtyard that was thronged with guests and curious onlookers. (Apparently anyone wandered in that felt curious!) As we were foreigners and arrived just behind, we were allowed to walk up the walk behind her. None of the bride's family

A CHINESE WEDDING

or friends were there, but the groom's family and his friends were exceedingly in evidence! There was this horrible din going on and the noise of falling rain, and I was so busy picking my footing in the mud, I didn't really see the moment of bride's actual arrival at the center of the spot, but in a moment or so—having located a secure foothold and adjusting my umbrella over me—beneath the dripping canopy, I began to take in the scene. Just at that time it began raining harder and it dripped so much—a hurry call was sent for the umbrellas. The groom and his friends were provided first and later-almost as if by afterthought—they gave the bride one.

There couldn't have been a more ludicrous setting for a wedding: The dripping canopy, the pushing, jostling noisy crowd in the commonest of everyday clothing. There was a small table facing the door and on one side stood the bride, and opposite the groom; she was looking down and he looked straight ahead! Their attire was another ludicrous sight—except that it was the only festive spot in the entire scene. There were no flowers, no bedecked attendants, and no decorations outside of the ornaments of the two about to be married. She wore a huge pink knot of silk draped over a head ornament of weird, colorful bangles which almost covered her face. From this knot two broad strips of pink silk floated down on each side forming a miniature tent over the bride. Her short blouse was of a lovely pink silk but just a shade different from the streamers so as to jar the eyes of the fastidious (I mean Occidental not oriental here) and the long heavily embroidered skirt was scarlet—vivid, vivid scarlet!! To our eyes it was a gorgeous monstrosity, but to the Chinese eyes, I'm sure it was lovely. She had on royal purple trousers—just glinting at the side, pale pink silk stockings and red satin slippers worked with brilliant flowers. The strangest feature of her attire was a pair of dark glasses—obviously not as a protection against the sun, but in lieu of a veil to hide her glances.

The bridegroom was completely eclipsed in splendor, but not in interest. He was wearing a long blue gown, typical Chinese fashion—but two wide scarlet sashes were tied across his chest and knotted into a huge red love knot right in the middle of the back! He also wore dark glasses and an American style grey felt hat with a gay red pompom right in the front. He wore it settled straight down on his ears, as it was a trifle too big.

The boy's (for he was no more than that) family are Christian so Pastor Wu and two of the deacons were there and a very short ceremony was performed—Scripture reading, admonition, prayer & hymn while the two looked fixedly down. There was no ring ceremony; no vows were said, and none of our lovely western ceremony. Then the announcer called off the names of those who should be honored—and at the mention of each name, he paused for the two to bow deeply three times. It sounded more like a 'ballyhoo' circus than a wedding. Then the bride was practically shoved into her room—where the poor girl stood for the rest of the day. This room was gay with her new furniture, and her gifts. She stood beside her bed looking down—never saying a word or showing the slightest trace of pleasure or displeasure. Except for the flickers of her eyes and an occasional shift of her poor tired feet (which weren't bound by the way) you would have thought she was a gaudy, ivory statue. Everyone pushed and stared and shoved and stared and made remarks and stared and just stared! I suppose she was prepared for it. She didn't even look nervous, but my heart ached so that there was not the slightest joy in seeing the new things or talking to two of our scholars who were present. I wondered where the groom was and a moment later saw him—minus all his trappings—in ordinary white trousers and flopping shirt—running here & there bringing tea, cigarettes for some guests at the beck and call of everyone. For two hours we sat waiting for the feast while everyone milled around examining all the bride's things and asking the price of everything. No one addressed a word to her. A hired serving woman stood fanning her as she performed the part of a sideshow for the curious crowd.

At a certain interval, she was led into the center room and seated in a red covered chair and the groom's mother and two other important relatives brought out her marriage ornaments—2 gold bracelets, 2 gold rings, earrings, and several hair ornaments.

She was arrayed in these while everyone looked on and then she was led back to take her lonely stand again. A crowd of the groom's friends filled the room and made all sorts of jesting remarks—then dragged him (the groom) in and forced him to kiss her. When they entered everyone else had left and the poor girl with her serving women were left at the mercy of that rude crowd! My fellow-workers said that was not usual, but my heart ached to see it.

A CHINESE WEDDING

THE BRIDAL FEAST.

In due time, we were called to eat—7 of us guests and one close friend of the family were at our table. We had the usual ten bowl feast beginning with sea-slugs and ending with 'hsi fan'—rice floating in glutinous mass. The bridegroom, again arrayed in his funny hat and gay bow, came to bow to us, and when we finished the groom's father & mother came to tell us good-bye! The bride was still standing and would be throughout the day—neither eating or drinking.

I walked away with a heavy heart for China's girl-brides and my heart's desire is to put the joy of the LORD in that girl's heart. Do pray for her and her boy husband who isn't cruel but young and thoughtless, and you who are women—give thanks to GOD for your Christian country & heritage.

56
A MUSLIM WEDDING
Huo Da
1992

Muslims in China, known as Hui, form a sizeable minority, currently over forty-five million. They first arrived in China as Arab merchants in the seventh century, later working as craftsmen, soldiers, and farmers. Intermarrying with Han Chinese and ethnic minorities, they retained their own religious and cultural identity while living within the wider Chinese community.

Today, fifty-six ethnic groups have been officially designated in China of which ten are Muslims, mostly residing in the north-west of the country. However, The Jade King, from which this passage is taken, is set in the small Muslim community in Beijing. The author, Huo Da, is a modern Chinese Muslim woman writing about the heritage of her own people. The novel, well worth reading in its entirety, follows the family of a skilled jade carver and includes this description of the wedding of Chinese Muslims in the period following the Cultural Revolution.

The *ahung* was invited to come. As the 'family *imam*' he was always present whenever there was a wedding or funeral in the Han family.

Under the canopy over the yard, the *ahung* began chanting the Peace Sura with melodious cadence. This is the opening rite of a Muslim wedding performed to renew the memory of the family's dear departed and to supplicate for peace in the household. Muslims always cherish the memory of their ancestors.

Also under the canopy was the devout Mrs Han on her knees. With a comingling of grief and joy, she recalled her late father Liang Yiqing: how he had struggled against poverty all his life, how he had lived and died for jade-carving; and her deceased mother—

A MUSLIM WEDDING

kind-hearted but weak and helpless—how she had come to an untimely end due to privations and sickness. Neither of them had ever enjoyed ease and prosperity, nor could they have expected that the Rare Gem Studio would one day revive and flourish. Although the studio no longer existed, the descendants of the Jadecraft-Master Liang were alive and well. And a rich trove of jade artifacts such as her parents had never dreamed of was right there in Bo Ya Mansion, where her parents never had had the good fortune to live. Now another generation of Liangs had grown to adulthood. Tianxing was getting married. And his children and his children's children would come into the world right there in that house. All these good tidings she reported to her parents and ancestors. Then she recalled her own wedding thirty-six years ago—a wedding in catastrophic circumstances, a wedding amidst dire poverty. No dowry, no banquet, no well-wishers. Absolutely nothing. Without a single earthly possession, she was married to Han Ziqi, or rather, Han Ziqi was married into her family, likewise empty-handed. Matters such as these Mrs Han had never mentioned to anyone, not even to her children or their aunt, though she herself could never forget them. To her, the wedding was a painful, shameful memory. That was why she had not attended a single wedding over the past few decades. Though she was now over fifty, the memory still rankled as much as it did when she was young, always bringing tears to her eyes. Over the years her greatest desire had been to make up for what she herself had missed. Of course, not for herself, but for her son when he got married. Now that day had come.

The chanting of the Sura over, Mrs Han got up, radiant with smiles. It was time for her to assume command in the grand show of the day.

The first thing the guests did on their arrival was to offer their congratulations: *Mubarak!* (the Muslim equivalent to gongxi used by the Hans). Then they were cordially entertained with tea and wedding sweets. Soon the rooms were packed with guests laughing and chatting.

In a brand-new Chinese tunic, Tianxing seemed less his natural self than in working clothes. In the presence of the guests he blushed and faltered, finding himself tongued-tied, awkward and 'tormented'. In striking contrast New Moon [her daughter] carried herself with perfect ease and grace, impressing the women guests so much that they buttonholed her just to have more of her company.

Meanwhile, the aunt and the chef specially hired for the occasion were bustling in the kitchen, giving full play to their culinary skills. By noon, the grand banquet was ready. On the tables in the canopied courtyard was an array of delicious dishes for which Nanlaishun Restaurant was noted. How else could one enjoy such pleasures of the table in those current 'hard times', had it not been for the residual prestige of the 'Jade King' and the desperate efforts of Mrs Han to show off at all costs?

With the boisterous feasting going on in the courtyard and the large number of cars and bicycles parked outside the gate, the affair was most spectacular, outshining the Jade 'Display' held years before.

In spite of all these things that claimed her attention, Mrs Han managed to do her mid-day worship. Later, at 3 p.m., in the company of New Moon and others, she headed the procession to bring the bride home. She and her daughter got into the 'bridal palanquin', now replaced by a car, which was bedecked with red silk and the red character Xi [meaning happiness]. Needless to say, the vehicle did not require carriers, but ran on wheels, swift as a gust of wind. Quite an experience to the riders—and in no way inferior to a real 'bridal palanquin.'

Outside the gate of the bride's home, which was likewise decorated with big red-character paper-cuts, was a large crowd awaiting the arrival of the wedding motorcade. It was headed by 'the mistress who would give away the bride', Chen Shuyan's mother, or Mrs Han's new sister-in-law.

Hardly had the car come to a halt than Mrs Chen stepped forward to greet Mrs Han, who returned the courtesy before getting out of the car, after which she exchanged greetings with the friends and relatives of the Chen family. New Moon, who knew little of the etiquette, tagged after her mother sheepishly, her face flushed, though she was secretly amused by the formalities.

Mrs Chen took the guests into the house and, after they were seated, produced a pair of satin shoes and presented them to Mrs Han, who took the gift with both hands. The presentation was only a formality; the shoes of such an elaborate antiquated style were certainly not meant to be worn by the bride. Then it was time for the men who came with Mrs Han to take their leave; only the females of the party stayed on. Then began the 'sitting at the fruit', which was in fact a meal of various dishes and soup served by Mrs Chen's two sons under her personal supervision. Mrs Han only went through the motions without really eating anything, this being also prescribed by custom.

After that, Mrs Han, accompanied by New Moon, went into Shuyan's 'boudoir'. Dressed in the new clothes given by the groom's family, the bride was sitting in a chair with her eyes downcast. Mrs Han went up to her, looped up a strand of her hair and tied it with a braid of coloured silk threads. Traditionally, a copper coin should be attached to each end of the braid and the new mother-in-law was to coil the bride's hair into a chignon and pluck off the fine hairs from her face. However, all these practices were now abandoned, as were certain items of the traditional bridal wear—the phoenix coronet, the embroidered cape and the red veil over the face. After tying the silk braid onto Shuyan's hair, Mrs Han put a diamond ring she had brought on the ring finger of the bride's right hand.

While the bride's mother watched all this in silence, she was unable to hold back her tears. 'Shuyan,' she said to her daughter, 'now you're going to a good family, to the place that will be your home hereafter, I can set my mind at ease.'

'Mother dear!' Looking up tearfully at her mother, with whom she was soon to part, the bride was the very image of sorrow. She hung on her mother's neck and the two of them wept their hearts out in each other's arms.

New Moon, who had expected to see nothing but happy faces on this red-letter day, was stunned at witnessing the scene. The heartbreaking sobbing of the mother and daughter so reluctant to part filled her with an irrepressible compassion so that tears began coursing down her cheeks. She kept drying them with a handkerchief but, inexplicably, they kept rolling down.

'What are you crying for?' whispered Mrs Han as she squeezed her daughter's hand. But inwardly she was grumbling, 'Oh, this girl. I told you not to come along but you insisted. And now you're crying away. The bride weeps because she can't bear to leave her mother. What are you getting so upset about?'

Finally New Moon fought back her tears. Not that she had wanted to cry, but the tearful bride was a heart-breaking sight.

Holding her daughter in her arms, the mother bade her a most heart-rending farewell, 'Dear girl, your mother owes you so much. In your twenty-one years of life with us, you haven't had one single day of ease and comfort. You've had to look after the elders and the little ones. Now your brothers are grown up, but you're leaving home. I've no dowry of any kind for you. Not that I don't love you, but it's beyond my means. Shuyan, please don't blame your mother. She hopes from the bottom of her heart that you'll be happy in your new home.'

'Oh, mother, please don't say any more.' Chen Shuyan wiped away the tears from her mother's face but her own dropped onto her mother's shoulder.

'Come, come! To be sure, you two have much, much more to say. But then, you can always visit each other later. So please don't feel so bad.' Mrs Han interposed affably. 'My dear sister, you can trust your daughter to me without worry. I'll treat her as my own, the way I do New Moon.'

'Thanks to Allah's blessing! Thanks to Him, my daughter has found such a kind mother-in-law,' said Mrs Chen. 'From now on, Shuyan, you are to love your mother-in-law as you love me. Come, call her Mother!'

'Mother!' Shuyan uttered in an affectionate voice as she plunged into Mrs Han's arms.

That plunged New Moon into tears again, tears of joy this time. From now on she would have a most congenial sister-in-law, a dear sister, and her family would always be good to Shuyan.

It was time for the bride to get on the 'palanquin'. Supported by New Moon and another girl, Chen Shuyan walked out of her 'boudoir' and her parents' house. And accompanied by her mother, who was, by tradition, 'the mistress who would give away the bride,' she stepped into the car.

Honking their horns, the motorcade started off and drove out of the lane onto the thoroughfare. The day was clear and bright, the air crisp, and the autumnal breeze invigorating. The cars with their red streamers fluttering and their riders laughing and chatting merrily drew the attention of the people along the way, who looked on with wide-eyed admiration.

In the car New Moon felt a bit chilly from the air coming in through the open windows, but she was extremely happy. She looked sideways at the bride beside her and found no more traces of tears on the latter's face.

A MUSLIM WEDDING

The cars did not have a long way to go from the Chens' house to the Hans'. But Mrs Han had told the drivers to make a detour slowly round the Mosque. The roundabout route was taken purposely to give everybody in the neighbourhood a chance to witness the grand procession whether they knew her family or not. When they were nearing the Hans', she asked the driver of her own car to speed up and the other cars to slow down so that she would be home ahead of the rest to direct the reception of the bride.

There was an enormous crowd of onlookers at the gate of Bo Ya Mansion when the rest of the cars pulled up.

As the 'usher' announced the arrival of the bride at the top of his voice, Mrs Han, who had come home a few minutes earlier, came out of the house, followed by a group of well-wishers, and stepped quickly up to the car to greet Mrs Chen, who returned the courtesy before alighting. Then Mrs Chen was ushered into the yard under the canopy where she was greeted by female relatives of the Hans before being shown to a seat in front of a prayer mat. The bride herself was accompanied by New Moon and women guests direct to the bridal chamber.

The white-bearded *ahung*, in a long robe and wearing a turban, was conducted by Han Ziqi to the seat of honour at the *nikah* (sura-chanting) table, where sat also the match-maker and the Hans' new in-laws. Friends and relatives of the groom's family occupied other tables, except the foremost one. On this table three censers had been placed in a row with spiralling wisps of burning rue and sandalwood, and just before the censers was a large red folder, together with the 'four treasures for writing' (i.e. writing-paper, writing-brush, inkcake and inkstone). There was also a wooden box containing *kebin* (courtesy money), a tray of 'fruit of happiness'— longans, red dates, peanuts and ginkgo nuts—as well as several bunches of flowers. The canopied courtyard was both splendid and dignified.

Everything ready, the ceremony commenced.

First of all, the exchange of greetings between the fathers of the bride and groom, which consisted of grasping each other's hands while they recited in unison 'There is no god but Allah; Mohammed is His messenger.' As the two men of the same trade but with different fates clasped hands, Shuyan's father wept, stirred by a rush of sentiment. The salutation was followed by the presentation of the courtesy money by the groom's father to the father of the bride. After this the guests of the bride's family paid their respects to the groom's father while the *ahung* wrote out the marriage contract in the red folder. This done, he began chanting the marriage *sura*, as Tianxing knelt on the mat listening:

'The union of man and woman is a holy and immaculate act. It is by the mandate of heaven. This woman is handsome and virtuous. Take her and treat her kindly. Your union is lawful.'

When the 'usher' sang out, 'Arise, the groom!' Mrs Han, who had all the while been in the east apartment together with New Moon and the women guests to keep the bride company, knew it was time for the announcement of the marriage contract. She told the ladies to take Shuyan to the designated seat to listen to the document. The benediction and the eight-clause marriage contract incanted by the *ahung* were in Arabic, which not everyone present could understand. Nevertheless, the incantation enhanced the solemnity of the ceremony, giving those present to understand that the happy marriage was sanctioned by Allah, approved by the parents of both parties and willed by the couple themselves, and that courtesy money had been presented and accepted, and the ceremony presided over by an imam and attended by well-wishers and, therefore, the newly-weds would have Allah's blessings.

In a solemn tone the *ahung* asked in Arabic the groom and bride in turn: 'Will you have her as wife?' and 'Will you have him as husband?' The young couple, like all those without experience, were at a loss as to what to say in reply. In the east apartment, Mrs Han told the bride, 'Say *Dadan*!' while the groom under the canopy was prompted to reply with *Gaibiltu*. With blushes they repeated the words in their turn, voicing their assents. Thus the sacred marriage was sealed. Earlier on, the young couple had obtained the government-issued marriage licence from the neighbourhood committee. However, for Muslims in China, the marriage contract is just as indispensable, for marriage must be protected by law *and* sanctioned by Allah.

After the reading of the marriage contract, the audience repeated the *duaki* after the *ahung*, and the two fathers once again clasped hands to signify that the marriage was successfully sealed, and unbreakable.

The 'usher', who had taken his place beside the groom, now helped the kneeling Tianxing up to his feet. While Tianxing bowed his thanks to the guests, the 'usher' sang out, 'Today bow twice.

Tomorrow visit the other house!' which was in fact a reminder for the bride's parents that the wedding ritual had come to a close and that the newly-weds would visit them early the next morning. Then came the climax of the wedding when the guests showered the groom with sweets from the tables, sending him scurrying off amidst hilarious laughter. Soon the party turned their attention to the delicious dishes served one after another, in no time at all making a clean sweep of everything.

Late that night when all guests had left, the newlywed couple retired to the bridal chamber.

Mrs Han was completely exhausted from the day's events, but inwardly happy and gratified. At the nightly prayer, she knelt before Allah, murmuring with tears of joy as if under the influence of alcohol, 'Oh, Lord! . . .'

The aunt, who had performed so demanding and important a service, was completely worn out. After clearing the tables, she felt as if her very bones were falling apart. The moment she got into bed, she began snoring as loud as rumbling thunder.

Mr Han laid himself on the sofa in his study. Now another debt he owed to his children was discharged. He felt drained and thought himself entitled to a good, long rest. The wedding had proved to be even more demanding than the three-day 'Jade Display'. Maybe I'm really getting on in years, he reflected. Ah, time spares no one!

In the west apartment New Moon could not fall asleep, she was so excited by all that had happened that day.

The wedding had been a new experience for her. At the same time there was immense gratification in having taken part in bringing to fruition the happy union between her brother and her bosom friend, whom she must now address as sister-in-law. Coming from different families, the couple were now bonded tightly together by their mutual love and from then on would be sharing a common life. They would not be lonely travellers on the journey of life. This was the will of God. The Creator had made man and woman, and had bestowed upon them the most sacred of sentiments—love. It was love that made a man and a woman trust each other, understand each other, rely on each other and help each other. It was love that brought about a doubling of one's flesh and blood, of one's wisdom and strength. Love was sacred. But love perplexed her too. She was after all too young, inexperienced in love and, hence, unable to know exactly what it felt like. Did it stir one's soul as the melody of the violin concerto 'The Butterfly Romance'? Or did it move one as the lines from Byron's poetry that flow and ripple like a pristine mountain stream?

> *Haidee spoke not of scruples, ask'd no vows,*
>   *Nor offer' d any; she had never heard*
> *Of plight and promises to be a spouse,*
>   *Or perils by a loving maid incurr'd;*
> *She was all which pure ignorance allows,*
>   *And flew to her young mate like a young bird,*
> *And never having dreamt of falsehood, she*
>   *Had not one word to say of constancy.*

She now seemed to understand what love was. It was something pure and true. Something steadfast and enduring. Something that germinated in the heart and would take root there forever.

In the depth of the night, New Moon tossed and turned in her bed, kept awake by her musings. From now on Shuyan would not keep her company in the west room. Shuyan now belonged to her brother—'He' as Ophelia sings, 'let in the maid, that out a maid never departed more.' She prayed for Shuyan while inexplicably regretting her 'loss'.

Very early the next morning, one of the bride's brothers came, in keeping with the custom, to present the 'open door' gifts and greet the family. He was warmly received by the Hans headed by the mistress of the house.

When Shuyan finished her morning toilet she came into the canopied yard and served tea in lidded bowls, first to her parents-in-law, then to the aunt and finally to her sister-in-law, New Moon. After this she presented to the family the various gifts she had brought in her 'dowry chest', again in the order of seniority—a pen to her father-in-law, a pair of stockings to her mother-in-law, a handkerchief to the aunt and a cake of scented soap to New Moon.

The presentation of gifts over, the newly-wed couple were ready to go on the 'return visit' to the bride's maiden home. The gifts for this courtesy call had long been prepared by Mrs Han. They included live fish, live chickens, tremelas, persimmon preserves, dried dates, chestnuts, fried cakes, moon cakes, tea, beef, mutton, steamed rolls, uncooked noodles and much more. When asked to take these to his parents-in-law, Tianxing grumbled, 'Is there no end to this business?'

The bride stole a glance at her husband, who cringed at every etiquette. She blushed for him and smiled thinly.

'Elder brother, what are you worried about?' New Moon was a little impatient with him though she said smilingly, 'Are you so bashful and timid? Don't let it bother you. I'll go with you. Shuyan, I mean, sister-in-law, what do you think?'

'Fine!' replied Shuyan. 'If you come, it won't be so boring. But we don't have a car today; we've got to go on foot. Can you make it?'

'I don't see why not,' said the girl excitedly. 'You talk as if I'd never walked.'

'Enough. That's enough from you, young lady.' Mrs Han interrupted in irritation. 'She's visiting her maiden home as a newly married daughter. Where do you fit in? What business have you in this?'

'Oh?' New Moon looked foolish.

After seeing off the young couple, Mrs Han returned to her seat under the canopy, smiling from ear to ear. As though to derive greater pleasure from the occasion, she took up the cup of tea just served by her daughter-in-law, lifted the lid to whisk aside the tea leaves on the surface and took a sip with relish before she released a long sigh of gratification. Thank Allah. The wedding has come off so beautifully. No more worries for me.'

57
THE MOST HAZARDOUS GAMBLE OF ALL
George Kates
1930s

In his book, The Years That Were Fat, *gentleman scholar George Kates describes a neighbourhood wedding in 1930s Beijing.*

How different things were in the Wax Storehouse! Here activity was unceasing from before dawn until late at night; the sheer continuity of it rang in my ears. Here was argument, laughter, anger, noisy quarreling—every emotion constantly finding its expression. I was immersed in the life of my own neighborhood, of my own alley. Next door, a young bride, dressed in red like a little idol, might mount her embroidered sedan chair, moved to uncontrollable tears in the last moment of parting from her family.

One never saw the bride, since the embroidered curtains of the phoenix chair—hers for that single day of her life—were always tightly closed (and everyone wondered how she felt inside). Certain female relatives of maturer years in charge of matters, however, were customarily carried home from the ceremonies, later in the day, in chairs that were partly open in front. Their uncovered glossy hair was invariably dressed with precision; they were in their immaculate best silks; and everyone looked on, realizing that they had been upon serious business.

After I had been invited to a few weddings, I learned what happened indoors. It was long and complicated. The bride, that very day presented for the first time to her husband, was always unbelievably modest and respectful. Tradition demanded that she keep her head down, from humility, when spoken to; but she usually let it droop, literally, under its elaborate phoenix

THE MOST HAZARDOUS GAMBLE OF ALL

Bride behind veil of pearls

headdress. These days the headdress is usually of chemically dyed crimson chenille, an intense color, cheaply trimmed with glass pearls. In all her finery, the bride makes herself as self-effacing as possible. I never saw one who did not seem painfully weary from fullness of emotion.

In my lane, I heard of course constant talk of weddings and of matchmaking in general. Criticisms of suitability, and blunt and unabashed curiosity about the outcome, were perennial matters for gossip. A wedding, like a funeral, was definitely one of life's 'big affairs,' as the Chinese classify them; and other people's destinies always made good material by which to appraise one's own. Was not traditional Chinese marriage, further, the most hazardous gamble of all—even to a people deeply fond of gambling?

58
POSTHUMOUS MARRIAGE
Encyclopedia Sinica
1917

It's not essential that both parties be present for a Chinese wedding. Sometimes the bride or groom—or both—are not even alive. However, the parents wish to see the families united, and they believe a ghost will rest more peacefully, if joined posthumously in marriage.

Posthumous marriages (*ming hun*) are not uncommon among better-class families. If a son dies unmarried and before adult age, the parents seek by go-betweens a family that has lost a daughter of about the same age and at about the same time. Betrothal and wedding ceremonies are duly carried out, the tablets taking the places of the pair. The bride's coffin is then laid in the grave side by side with the bridegroom's, and she is thenceforward a deceased daughter-in-law in the family.

Such marriages are prohibited in the *Chou Li*, yet have been common from the earliest history down to modern times.

There is also marriage which is posthumous for only one of the pair. If one of a betrothed couple dies before marriage, the wedding may still take place, the tablet representing the dead. Or if a girl dies unbetrothed a living husband may still be found for her; both betrothal and wedding ceremonies being performed with her tablet.

59
THE CHINESE NEVER KISS
CHARLES TAYLOR
1860

The details of the marriage traditions differ from region to region, but are always elaborate and colourful. The medical missionary Charles Taylor reveled in the particulars of the ceremony.

Marriages are contracted by parents for their children during infancy; nor, according to the usage of the country, can the parents of the one child negotiate directly with those of the other. An indispensable actor in the transaction, is a 'middle person'—commonly called in English a 'go-between.' This individual may be either a man or a woman, and is generally an intimate friend of one family or the other. Supposing it a woman—she ascertains upon inquiry among families of the same social position, if a matrimonial alliance between them would be agreeable, giving to each all the information desired respecting the other. If there be no objection, she inquires of them the precise date of the birth of the two children—the boy generally being, at least, a year or two the elder—and consults a fortune-teller or an astrologer, who, by comparing their horoscopes, pronounces whether a marriage between them will be fortunate or otherwise. If the response is favorable, it is so announced to the parents of both, and presents of greater or less value, according to their station in life, are exchanged between the families as a ratification of the betrothal. If the girl dies before marriage, another is sought for the youth in the same manner as at first. But if he dies, it is far more reputable for his betrothed to live single—she sometimes becomes a nun. Presents are sent annually, and communication is kept up by messages, or writing, or both, during the years that elapse till the marriage; but the affianced pair do not see each other until the hour of their nuptials. When both become of suitable age—say from fifteen to twenty-one, one of the 'lucky days' is selected for this event, which is always consummated at the house of the bridegroom, whose parents provide a sumptuous feast on the occasion. The bride is arrayed in her costliest attire—has a gaudy head-dress projecting several inches over her face, glittering with strings of pendent beads, while from its square front hangs the veil which hides her face. A 'flowery sedan,' with four bearers, is hired to convey her to the residence of her future husband. This vehicle is of much larger dimensions than those used for ordinary purposes—is covered with flaming red cloth, gaily embroidered, and has long, heavy, silken tassels hanging from the four corners of its projecting top. On leaving her home, and taking her seat in the bridal sedan, she breaks out into the most violent lamentations, which must be continued, according to 'custom,' throughout the whole progress of the procession, till she reaches the entrance of her future abode; for the newly-married pair always live for some time with the parents of the husband, to whom the wife becomes a servant. Especially does his mother often exercise over her a most tyrannical and exacting authority. So much so, that the cruelty of a mother-in-law has passed into a proverb. The bride is aware of this, and hence her wailing on leaving the home of her childhood for a new one, where she may be treated with a rigorous harshness. The sedan is preceded by men and boys carrying gay flags and lighted lanterns, even in the daytime; and then comes a band of musicians, consisting of twelve boys in uniform, walking in pairs, and wearing long drab gowns, black or claret-colored velvet jackets, and red-tasselled caps. Prominent among their instruments is the gong, of course; then cymbals, horns, trumpets, and several others, which for want of any other name in English, I shall call clarionets, fifes, flageolets, and flutes, because they bear some resemblance to those instruments. Next comes a long train of well-grown boys, also walking two and two in holiday costume, which differs from that worn by the musicians, only in that the gowns are of light-blue, figured silk, and the jackets of dark-blue broadcloth. When the procession arrives at the place of its destination, packs of fire-crackers are let off, and strings of gilt paper burned near the entrance at which the sedan is set down. The 'go-between' opens its door, leads out the veiled bride, and conducts her into the reception-room, or 'ancestral hall,' where the guests are already assembled. At its further end, stands a table, on which are burning red wax candles and sticks of incense, in honor of the ancestors, whose pictorial representations hang over it against the wall. Here the groom is waiting, and receives his bride with a simple bow; then both kneel reverently, and bow three times to the pictures of their ancestors. The 'go-between' then takes two pieces of narrow, thin silk—each about a yard in length—the one green and the other red, and tying an end of each together, puts the other end of the green silk into his right hand, and the red into hers. They then kneel face to face, and bow to each other three times; then, rising to their feet, turn and worship their ancestors again in the same manner. Repeating these alternate genuflections several times, the ceremony is completed, and the groom leads his bride into an adjoining apartment, where he takes off the veil, and beholds her face for the first time in his life. He then comes out, expressing in his looks satisfaction or disappointment, and receives the congratulations or condolence of his friends; while the females present enter the room he has left, and salute the bride simply in words—the Chinese never kiss. The tables laden with luxuries next receive due attention—the males eating in one apartment, and the females in another. So the remainder of the day, with several more in succession, are passed in festivities, consisting of dinner parties, given by relatives and friends, amusements, and general hilarity. The dowry of the bride consists in part, and often entirely, in the furniture for her apartment—all of red—and her wardrobe, in red trunks and boxes, borne along by coolies in the wedding-procession. As yellow is the imperial, so red is the festive color, among the Chinese.

60
POOR LITTLE CHINESE BRIDE
Susan Townley
1904

Lady Susan Townley, part of the foreign diplomatic community, gives her more personal view of the wedding process during her visit to Shanghai.

One day as we were driving along the Bubbling Well Road we met a long procession of coolies carrying on their shoulders what looked like the complete furniture of a Chinese house, and case upon case of red lacquer containing we knew not what. We turned and followed the procession and eventually found ourselves in the courtyard of a gaily decorated house, built in a style that was partly European and partly Chinese. Bright banners and lanterns floated overhead, and in one corner were massed a band of boy-musicians each armed with a different native musical instrument. The courtyard when we entered it seemed full of shoddy retainers (the retainers of great men in China always are shoddy), and the appearance of the first of the furniture-bearing procession evidently was the signal for the commencement of the rejoicings, for immediately the musicians struck up, and countless crackers were let off, the candles in the lanterns being also lighted. With a good deal of pushing and screaming, the bearers shoved their way through the crowd into the house, presently emerging without their loads. We stood just within the entrance gates curiously watching the scene and catching occasional glimpses of gorgeously arrayed Mandarins on the doorstep, and of equally gorgeous Chinese ladies peeping over the balcony, when suddenly to our surprise we were beckoned to by an attendant who made us signs to advance. Nothing loath, we followed the man and presently found ourselves inside the house, being made welcome by a quaint little Chinese lady in brightly embroidered trousers and coat, who told us in very fair English that

she was the wife of a British subject in Shanghai, she herself being closely related to the late Li Hung Chang, whose nephew was to be married in the house we were in on the following day. The rejoicings we saw were occasioned by the arrival of the bride's trousseau and furniture! Whilst we sat and talked the furniture was still being brought in and distributed over the various apartments, and as the coolies passed with their loads our new friend explained to us their various uses. Two square tables exactly like each other were covered with lovely Chinese embroidery. Those she said were the dining-tables of bride and bridegroom respectively. On them rested glass cases containing sets of chopsticks, one set being of coral, another of ivory, a third of silver, bride and bridegroom also had a silver spoon and silver cup and saucer each. Whilst we chatted we sipped green tea out of delicate little China cups. Presently we were conducted through a door, to a sort of inner court with a glazed roof, round which at the top ran a verandah opening into the rooms of the upper storey. Under this verandah against the walls were stacked the mass of personal effects we had seen carried in. Several Mandarins and people of high degree were engaged in a most businesslike way in checking the things from a list in a book, and whilst so employed we had leisure to admire the magnificent sable coats they wore, and to hear from our little friend of all the wonders of silks and jewels enclosed in the red lacquer cases before us. The bride's parents she said were very rich, and had spent a small fortune on the young lady's outfit, and seeing how interested we were she invited us to return on the following day but one (we were unfortunately not allowed to see the actual marriage ceremonies which took place on the next day) promising to introduce us then to the bride and to show us the contents of the cases. . . .

We returned two days later according to our promise, to be introduced to the bride and bridegroom. We were evidently expected, for a servant was waiting and immediately ushered us into the house. He took us to the foot of the staircase leading to the upper floor (the house was built in a mixed style half-English, half-Chinese), and there left us to find our own way to the room we had seen two days before and knew to be set apart for the bride. At the door we were met by the bridegroom who at first sight appeared anything but prepossessing. He was short, and inclined to embonpoint, an inclination exaggerated by the thickness of his heavily wadded winter garments. He had cataract in one eye and his neck was seamed from ear to ear with old scars, as though someone had begun to cut off his head, and on thinking better of it had sewn him up again! Besides this, he had a lame leg and walked with a limp. I pitied the bride in spite of the riches, fine clothes and fine house of her husband. But he spoke English quite tolerably, and we soon found him in spite of his physical defects a kindly, well-mannered youth. He was arrayed in a magnificent mandarin coat of satin, embroidered with Chinese emblems, amongst which figured chiefly the dragon worked in gold. On his head he wore a red-buttoned hat turned back with sable, a peacock's feather hanging down behind secured in a jade holder. A red silk sash was draped around his shoulders and crossed over his breast, and this was evidently part of the bridal array as the same sash was worn by all the attendants waiting upon the bride. The bridegroom was very proud of his fine clothes. When we first arrived he invited us to sit down and himself took a seat, then the women with the red sashes came and removed his hat, his heavy jade necklaces and his outer coat.

Refreshments were laid out upon a square table, a mass of different kinds of sweetmeats arranged in separate little saucers of fine porcelain, cups of green tea being served with them. Whilst we sipped our tea and ate bonbons the bridegroom talked freely of himself, his upbringing and his marriage. He promised us that we should presently see the bride, and described to us how on the previous day he had gone in state in a green sedan chair to fetch her from her parents' house, she returning in a chair of scarlet cloth embroidered all over in gold.

At this moment one of the bride's attendants came and whispered something to him, and immediately he rose and offered to take us to see her. He conducted us to the room we had been in on our previous visit, and knew to be her sleeping-room, and pushed aside the silk draperies of a sort of alcove formed by the wall of the red-lacquer bed and a screen. There, in a dark corner was propped the heroine of the day! She was apparently seated on a stool, and red-sashed female attendants stood on either side ready to assist her should she wish to rise, for her very tiny feet made it impossible for her to do so unassisted. She was arrayed in a gorgeous red robe of stiffly embroidered material reaching to her feet, the long sleeves of which covered her hands which were crossed upon her lap. On her head she wore a thing resembling a cocked hat put on crosswise and outlined with red silk pompons, and from over each ear hung down to her waist long red silk tassels. From the front of this curious head-dress depended a curtain of real pearl chains which reached almost to her waist, and completely veiled her face, unless curiosity compelled one to push them aside as I did and peer between them at the pretty little face they concealed.

She looked very young and sweet, but there was a scared expression in her soft long brown eyes, and I fancied she might have been pale but for her white and red paint. Sitting there in the angle formed by the bed and the wall, propped up, her face concealed, her hands folded in her lap and her rich robes falling stiffly to the ground around her, she looked like one of those little images one sees in the temples. Her husband seemed pleased with our evident admiration of her. I asked him what she was called, and was amused when he promptly responded, 'Miss Wang.' 'But,' I insisted, 'hasn't she some beautiful name such as 'Lotus Flower' or 'Pearl Blossom' by which you familiarly call her,' whereat the young swain blushed and answered, 'I have not asked her yet!'

However, to return to my bride: she seemed very silent; I never heard her voice all the time I was there, but the husband explained to me that Chinese etiquette forbids a bride to speak for the first three days after her marriage, during which time it is the privilege of her friends to tease her and provoke her though she may not retaliate. Altogether the role of a Chinese bride did not appear to me to be an enviable one. Whilst I still stood chatting with the bridegroom, my first friend, Mrs Canning, appeared upon the scene with a wedding gift for the bride. It was a little gold-chased box with a mirror in the lid. The bride was evidently much pleased, and slipping noiselessly from her seat to her knees touched the ground with her forehead in token of her gratitude.

I was told that the wedding festivities would last three days. Each day the bride is arrayed in a different and more gorgeous dress and these dresses are never worn again, the bridegroom on the other hand as he told me with pride can wear his robes again should he contract a second alliance! On the first day the bridegroom fetches the bride home and together they worship the ancestors' tablets by kotowing before them and pouring libations, which constitutes the legal act of marriage, after which the bride kotows to her new parents and to her husband. On the second day the bride receives her husband's friends and family or rather as we have seen she is 'on view' to them, for she may not speak, and on the third day the newly married couple return together to her family where he goes through similar ceremonies to those performed by her in his house. During these three days the bride is treated as a new and valuable possession of the husband's, and is shown off, admired and criticised freely without having even the privilege of speech. Poor little Chinese bride!

61
MARRIAGE LAWS
Lord Macartney
1798

Lord Macartney arrived in China in 1793 as an emissary from George III to the Chinese Qian Long emperor, requesting a relaxation of the restrictions on trade. Although viewed as a subservient foreigner offering tribute, Macartney was exempted from the required kowtow—after considerable negotiation. However Britain's requests were ignored, and the emperor issued edicts ordering the British not to disobey Chinese customs and laws.

The laws respecting marriage in China are remarkable, as being widely different from the customs of other eastern nations, and bearing more of the genuine marks of the patriarchal age than those of any other country.

A Chinese is restricted to one lawful wife, but then he may keep several concubines under the same roof, who are deemed wives of the second rank, and their children are regarded as legitimate.

Though divorces are allowed, yet they are not common, and are never granted but in the cases of adultery, mutual dislike, bad tempers, sterility, jealousy, impudence, disobedience, or dangerous disorders.

He who looks into the early history of man-kind will see a strong coincidence between the primitive institution of marriage and these regulations.

62
A BRIDE AND HER MOTHER
Arthur H. Smith
1899

A bride still maintains strong ties to her original home.

Every Chinese wife came by no choice of her own from some other family, being suddenly and irrevocably grafted as a wild stock upon the family tree of her husband. As we have already seen, she is not received with enthusiasm, much less with affection (the very idea of which in such a connection never enters any Chinese mind) but at best with mild toleration, and not infrequently with aggressive criticism. She forms a link with another set of interests from which by disruption she has indeed been dissevered, but where her attachments are centred. The affection of most Chinese children for their mothers is very real and lasting. The death of the mother is for a daughter especially the greatest of earthly calamities. Filial piety in its cruder and more practical aspects constantly leads the married daughter to wish to transfer some of the property of the husband's family to that of her mother. The temptation to do so is often irresistible, and sometimes continues through life, albeit with many dramatic checks. The Chinese speak of this habit in metaphorical phrase as 'a leak at the bottom' which is proverbially hard to stop. It is a current saying that of ten married daughters, nine pilfer more or less. It is not uncommon to hear this practice assigned as one of the means by which a family is reduced to the verge of poverty. The writer once had occasion to acquaint a Chinese friend with the fact that a connection by marriage had recently died. He replied thoughtfully: 'It is well she is dead; she was gluttonous, she was lazy; and besides, she stole things for her mother!'

Visits to the mother's family constitute by far the most substantial joys in the life of a young Chinese married woman. It is her constant effort to make them as numerous as possible, and it is the desire of her husband's family to restrict them, since her services are thus partially lost to them. To prevent them from being wholly so, she is frequently loaded down with twice as much sewing as she could do in the time allowed, and sent off with a troop of accompanying children, if she has reached so advanced a stage as to be a mother of a flock. An invasion of this kind is often regarded with open dissatisfaction by her father and brothers, and what could be more natural than her desire to appease them by the spoils which she may have wrested from the Philistines?

After the death of her mother the situation has materially altered. The sisters-in-law have now no restraint on their criticisms upon her appearance with her hungry brood, and her whole stay may not improbably be a struggle to maintain what she regards as her rights. It is one of the many pathetic sights with which Chinese society abounds to witness the effort to seem to keep alive a spark of fire in coals which have visibly gone out. Not to have any 'mother's family' to which to go is regarded as the depth of misery for a married woman, since it is a proclamation that she has no one to stand up for her in case she should be abused. To discontinue altogether the visits thither is to some extent a loss of face, which every Chinese feels keenly. We have known an old woman left absolutely alone in the world, obliged at the age of ninety-four to gather her own fuel and do whatever she wanted done for herself, except draw water, which was furnished her by a distant relative as an act of special grace. Her poverty was so abject that she was driven to mix fine earth with the little meal that sufficed for her scanty food, that it might last the longer. Yet this poor creature would sometimes be missed from her place, when it was reported that she had gone on a visit to her 'mother's family' consisting of the great-grandchildren of those whom she had known in youth!

By the time a married woman had reached middle life her interest in her original home may have greatly weakened. There are now young marriageable girls of her own growing up, each of whom in turn repeats the experience of her mother. To their fathers and also to their brothers these girls are at once a problem and a menace. Could the birth-rate of girls be determined by ballot of all the males of full age, it is probable that in a few generations the Chinese race would become extinct. The expression 'commodity-on-which-money-has-been-lost,' is a common periphrasis for a girl. They no sooner learn a little sewing, cooking, etc., than they are exported, and it is proverbial that water spilled on the ground is a synonym for a daughter. 'Darnel will not do for the grain-tax, and daughters will never support their mothers.' These modes of speech represent modes of thought, and the prevailing thought, although happily not the only thought of the Chinese people.

Girls as a rule have next to no opportunities for cultivating friendships with one another. The readiness with which under favourable condition such attachments are formed and perpetuated, shows how great a loss is their persistent absence. When it is considered that each Chinese family consists not of a man and his wife and their children, but of married sons, and of their several wives, each one introduced into the circle in the same compulsory way, each with a strong and an uncurbed will, yet powerless to assert herself except by harsh speeches and bad temper, it is evident that the result is not likely to be unity.

63
DIVORCE

J. Dyer Ball
1912

Laws governing marriage long favoured men, with a specific list of reasons for which wives could be divorced or resold. It was not until the Marriage Act of 1951 that the rights of women were considered.

Divorce is allowed in China for seven reasons: Barrenness (though in this case the difficulty may be obviated by the taking of a secondary wife), lasciviousness, jealousy, talkativeness, thieving, disobedience towards her husband's parents, and leprosy. But the author scarcely remembers coming across a case of divorce during his long residence in China; and the requirements in the resort to it are sufficient to prevent its being often carried out in real life, as far as regards a first wife.

To begin with, her parents must be alive to receive the discarded wife. Moreover, there is a high standard of morality amongst respectable and well-to-do families in China; so that the second reason is not likely to occur. As to jealousy, the author has seen a great deal of it in China. As regards this and talkativeness, the Chinese husband apparently thinks that 'what cannot be cured must be endured.' Thieving is not worthy of attention as a reason amongst respectable people. As to her husband's parents, a wife is married as much, if not sometimes more, to be a daughter-in-law as to be a wife; and, with the ingrained respect the Chinese have for the aged, transgression is not likely to be more than venial, except in a few cases. The last reason, leprosy, is a more serious matter, [but] the contigency of its occuring is small. With concubines the matter is very different; and, if she have no relations to make it unpleasant to her so-called husband, she has no redress. Divorce in China, if acted on, is quite one-sided; no wife could think of divorcing her husband—the king does no wrong, can do no wrong.

64
THE FRENCH BRIDE
Jane Tracy
1930

Jane Tracy travelled to India and China in the 1920s to view the work of the YMCA and missionaries in China. Like many others, she seized the opportunity to publish her fresh reactions to the country in her book, See China With Me. *While journeying along the Yangtze River from Shanghai one of her fellow travellers gave cause for concern.*

The French lady proved to be the wife of a Chinese, a Mr. Feng, who had been a resident of France for fourteen years connected with the Chinese Embassy, and at the time of his marriage had no expectations of ever being recalled to his native land to live. . . .

It was too cold and stormy to sit on deck, but fine for taking exercise, which we did many times a day; otherwise the warm salon was occupied. Madame Feng could speak English better than we French, so she spent all her time with us and we found her charming. Her husband had told her of his country, but nothing of the manners and customs of Chinese homes, the position of women, nor what her position would be in his family. We all knew she would be simply a menial, to do the bidding of his mother and grandmother and that they would look down with scorn and derision on her if she failed to have a family, particularly a son. We shuddered for her awakening should she be obliged to remain permanently in China after she became acquainted with these facts.

To our great relief, the husband of the French lady, met her at Hankau [Hankou], bringing smiles to her anxious face, and a feeling of thankfulness to us, for everyone, particularly Bishop Roots, seemed to sense the dangers for Madame, thinking her husband might have deserted her, as he had left her alone and unprotected in a hotel at Shanghai for many days. He probably realized the difficulty of introducing a foreign wife into a Chinese home.

65
THE INJURED WIFE

Arthur H. Smith
1899

If a bride were treated badly, her birth family might attack the problem directly.

It is not the ignorant and the uneducated only who thus take the law into their own hands on behalf of injured daughters. We have heard of a case in which the father of the girl who drowned herself was a literary graduate. He raised a band of men, went to the home of his son-in-law, and pulled down the gate-house to the premises, and some of the buildings. In the resulting lawsuit he was severely reproved by the District Magistrate, who told him that he had no right to assume to avenge his own wrongs, and that he was only saved from a beating in court by his literary degree.

A still more striking example was offered by an official of the third rank, whose daughter's wrongs moved him to raise an armed band and make an attack upon the house of the son-in-law. This proved to be strong and not easily taken, upon which the angry *Tao-t'ai* contented himself with reviling the whole family at the top of his voice, exactly as a coolie would have done. Wrongs which can only be met with such acts as this, on the part of those who are the most conservative members of Chinese society, must be very real and very grievous. In the very numerous cases in which a daughter-in-law is driven to suicide by the treatment which she receives, the subsequent proceedings will depend mainly upon the number and standing of her relatives. The first thing is to notify the family of the deceased that she has died, for without their presence the funeral cannot take place, or if it should take place the body would have to be exhumed, to satisfy her friends that the death was a natural one, and not due to violence, which is always likely to be suspected. A Chinese in the employ of the writer, was summoned one day to see his married daughter in another village, who was said to be 'not very well.' When the father arrived, he found her hanging by her girdle to a beam!

In *cases of this sort, a lawsuit is exceptional.* There are several powerful considerations which act as deterrents from such a step as sending in an accusation. It is almost always next to impossible to prove the case of the girl's family, for the reason that the opposite party can always so represent the matter as to throw the blame on the girl. In one such instance, the husband brought into court a very small woman's shoe, explaining that he had scolded his wife for wearing so small a one, which unfitted her for work. He alleged that she then reviled him, for which he struck her (of which there were marks), whereupon she drowned herself. To a defence like this, it is impossible for the girl's family to make any reply whatever. The accusation is not brought against the husband, but against the father-in-law, for practically the law does not interfere between husband and wife. It is only necessary for the husband to admit the fact of having beaten his wife, alleging as a reason that she was 'unfilial' to his parents, to screen himself completely. We have heard of a suit where in reply to a claim of this sort, the brother of the girl testified that she had been beaten previous to the alleged 'unfilial' conduct. This seemed to make the magistrate angry, and he ordered the brother to receive several hundred blows for his testimony, and decided that the husband's family should only be required to provide a cheap willow-wood coffin for the deceased.

66
ATTEMPTED SUICIDE
George Morrison
1895

Today, China continues to have the highest female suicide rate in the world. Previously, suicide of young brides was the ultimate protest and was not a rare occurrence. It was the only way a girl could absolutely refuse a forced marriage. New relatives feared the wrath of a ghost and would try to placate a bride if her threats were considered serious.

I went to two opium-poisoning cases in Tali; both being cases of attempted suicide. [One] was that of a young bride; a girl of unusual personal attraction, only ten days married, who thus early had become weary of the pock-marked husband her parents had sold her to. She was dressed still in her bridal attire, which had not been removed since marriage; she was dressed in red—the colour of happiness. 'She was dressed in her best, all ready for the journey,' and was determined to die, because dead she could repay fourfold the injuries which she had received while living. In this case many neighbours were present, and, as all were anxious to prevent the liberation of the girl's evil spirit, I proved to them how skilful are the barbarian doctors. The bride was induced to drink hot water till it was, she declared, on a level with her neck, then I gave her a hypodermic injection of that wonderful emetic apomorphia. The effect was very gratifying to all but the patient.

67
THE USEFUL CONCUBINE
George Kates
1930s

Concubines did exist but not in large numbers. If a wife were unable to bear a son, the husband might take a concubine. If the concubine had a son, the child would address the wife as 'Mother'. The wife often preferred to choose the concubine herself because it gave her 'face' and increased her control. A concubine who had been purchased as a slave commanded less respect in her new home than one who had never been sold. When a new concubine came into a home, she served tea to the senior women as a sign of subservience. Although the wife held tremendous power within the home, the status of a concubine soared after the birth of a son. In this excerpt the role of concubine offers a resolution to a problem. A fazi *is an ingenious solution.*

'What is to be done?' The answer is invariably the same: 'We must think of a good *fa-tzù*!'

Perhaps a few homely examples will illustrate how such arrangements work. In my time there was a young girl, quite poor, employed in the American hospital in Peking, who suddenly developed symptoms of tuberculosis. She therefore found herself in a critical situation, overnight, and unexpectedly falling into peril of destitution—or so it might have been in the West. Further, her parents depended upon her; some *fa-tzù* had to be invented without delay.

Now it so happened that someone who knew her was acquainted also with a wealthy Chinese banker, recently widowed, who urgently needed a well-trained person to act as a substitute mother for his young children, but who also did not wish to acquire another wife in thus providing for them.

The *fa-tzù* was promptly devised: 'No perfect solution is now possible. She can, however, become a secondary wife or concubine.' So off she went to a sanatorium, as soon as arrangements had been made; the banker was willing to take a risk. Her parents were also supported by the new agreement. Since her tuberculosis was only incipient, once anxiety had been removed and she was given proper care, she did soon become better again. The problem of her future husband, who wanted not so much full marriage as care and training for his children, and her own, were thus both solved together. This most un-Western arrangement is a typical *fa-tzù*.

I knew of another similar case. Three extremely dashing and attractive young married women in Tientsin had a widowed father who pined alone after they had all left home to make fashionable marriages. He felt indeed solitary. What could be done? They had an inspiration: 'Why not all club together and buy papa, for his birthday, a really excellent concubine!' She must be both nurse and charming companion, to care for, cajole, and distract him. This was arranged, doubtless by the choice of someone of proper qualification, for whom it became in its turn also a good *fa-tzù*. The West would find it difficult, I believe, to cope so easily with similar situations.

These two cases may perhaps be thought a little garish; but they illustrate their principle. *Fa-tzù*, however, are also applied to find solutions for minor matters. I remember so well, when we found ourselves at a temporary loss in some small household difficulty—changing to a new sewing woman; or even having an old suit altered at the tailor's—how my servants would come to announce that a *fa-tzù* was going to be necessary, and then go back to the kitchen to 'think-arise-arrive' it. This might take a while; but a smiling face usually appeared at my door in due course, a solution was propounded, and some ingenious dovetailing of matters, impossible to reconcile completely, but better thus resolved than if allowed to run their course, would finally bring content to all concerned.

68
THE STATUS OF CONCUBINES
Adele Fielde
1894

In other cases, some concubines were easy to spot—by their feet.

Poor men, and men of the middle classes, rarely have more than one wife, because of the cost of a large household, and the objections usually made by a chief wife to the taking of concubines. Even when no children are born to the first wife, attempts are usually made to obtain these in some other way than by the taking of an inferior wife. As adopted children stand in precisely the same legal relationship to their adopted parents as do own children to their progenitors, and as the adoption of children is usually feasible, those who have no children generally supply themselves with posterity by the expenditure of a few scores of dollars in the purchase of a young son.

Polygamy is, however, common among the wealthy and in families of rank. The chief wife is always a woman with dwarfed feet, while the inferior wives are usually natural-footed. The chief wife is wedded with elaborate formalities, while the concubines are taken without other ceremony than the transfer of a sum of money to their parents. The children of concubines are reckoned as the issue of the wife; they call her mother, and after her death make at her grave the same offerings that they make at their father's tomb. The children of the chief wife do not address a concubine as mother, nor do they ever make offerings at her grave.

PART VI

THE YOUNG BRIDE AND THE MOTHER-IN-LAW

'The seats in the great hall all come in rotation: the daughter-in-law will some day be the mother-in-law.'

Foreigners might assume that the centre of a Chinese bride's universe is her new husband. Instead, she has married a family, and her new focus is likely to be a demanding mother-in-law whom she is expected to serve until finally she steps into that powerful role herself.

Beyond her household work and management, children are added responsibilities, and the relations between the couple are rarely of paramount importance.

In modern China, instead of a large extended family, households often contain a nuclear family including a grandmother or unmarried sibling, or a parent or both mothers of the couple. Either the husband or wife might be transferred elsewhere for a period for work or military service, and the additional resident females are expected to aid in child care.

69
ON THE REVERENCE DUE TO FATHER- AND MOTHER-IN-LAW

BAN ZHAO
c. 100 AD

Married at fourteen, Ban Zhao knew something about being a proper daughter-in-law. In addition to her scholarly work and advice to the empress, she accompanied her magistrate son to a distant posting after she beame a widow. A section from her ode, 'Journey to the East', is included here.

Father and mother-in-law
   Are your husband's family.
   When you arrive at their threshold
You become a new woman;
Reverence and serve them
As your own parents.
Honour *greatly* your father-in-law;
Before him, let neither gladness nor sorrow
Show forth in your face.
Dare not even to *walk* behind him;
Stand not before him when you speak,
But to one side or behind him,
And hasten his every command to obey.
When your mother-in-law sits
You should respectfully stand;
Obey quickly her commands.
In the morning early rise
And quietly open the doors,
Making no noise to waken her;
Her toilet articles hasten to prepare;
Her washbowl and towel,
Her toothbrush and powder
All bring together.

Let not the water be too cold or too hot.
When the mother-in-law wakens,
All these things respectfully present to her,
Then immediately retire to one side,
Until her toilet is completed.
Then approach and present the morning salutations;
Again retire and prepare her tea.
Quickly and cheerfully carry it to her;
After which the breakfast table arrange;
Place the spoons and chopsticks straight.
The rice cook soft, and
Let the meat be thoroughly done.
From ancient days until now,
Old people have had *sick* teeth;
Therefore, let not the food be so dry
That your mother-in-law
With labour vainly eats.
Daily the three meals
Thus carefully prepare.
When darkness comes,
And your great one desires to sleep,
Carefully for her spread the bed,
When she may peacefully rest,
And you may retire to your room.
Following these instructions,
All your superiors will praise you,
All that know you will esteem you as good.
Do not imitate that other class
Who care not for woman's duties.
Loudly they talk before their superiors;
When told to do anything,
They ever answer, 'My body is tired,'
When truly they are only lazy.
They obey not their superiors,
Nor care whether they are hungry or cold;
The reputation of such is wholly bad;
Heaven and earth have no patience with them!
Thunder and lightning are angry with them!
When their punishment comes
Their repentance is too late,
There is then left no road of escape.

70
THE CRUEL MOTHER-IN-LAW

Arthur H. Smith
1899

In his twenty-two years as a missionary, Arthur Smith often observed that the Chinese mother-in-law had tremendous power over a young bride.

A Chinese married woman must address her mother-in-law as 'mother,' but for precision is allowed to refer to her as 'mother-in-law mother.' A Chinese woman calling on a foreign lady asked the latter (in the presence of her husband) about her family in the homeland. The lady mentioned that she had 'a mother-in-law,' upon which the Chinese woman in an awed whisper pointing to the foreign gentleman, inquired: *'Won't he beat you for saying that?'*

A great deal is heard of the tyranny and cruelty of these mothers-in-law, and there is a firm basis of fact for all that is so often said upon that point. But it must at the same time be borne in mind that without her the Chinese family would go to utter ruin. The father-in-law is not only unfitted to take the control which belongs to his wife, even were he at home all the time which would seldom be the case, but propriety forbids him to do any such thing, even were he able. In families where a mother-in-law is lacking, there are not unlikely to be much greater evils than the worst mother-in-law. Abuse of the daughter-in-law is so common a circumstance, that unless it be especially flagrant, it attracts very little attention.

It would be wholly incorrect to represent this as the normal or the inevitable condition to which Chinese brides are reduced, but it is not too much to affirm that no bride has any adequate security against such abuse. It assumes all varieties of forms, from incessant scolding up to the most cruel treatment. If it is carried to an extreme pitch, the mother's family will interfere, not legally, for that they cannot do, but by brute force. In a typical case of this sort, where the daughter-in-law had been repeatedly and shamefully abused by the family of her husband, which had been remonstrated with in vain by the family of the girl, the latter family mustered a large force, went to the house of the mother-in-law, destroyed the furniture, beat the other family severely, and dragged the old mother-in-law out into the street, where she was left screaming with what strength remained to her, and covered with blood, in which condition she was seen by foreigners. These proceedings are designed as a practical protest against tyranny and an intimation that sauce for a young goose may be in like manner sauce for an older one also. One would suppose that the only outcome of such a disturbance as this would be a long and bitter lawsuit, wasting the property of each of the parties, and perhaps reducing them to ruin. But with that eminent practicality which characterizes the Chinese, the girl was carried off to the home of her parents, 'peace-talkers' intervened, and the girl was returned to her husband's home upon the promise of better treatment. This would probably be secured, just in proportion to the ability of the girl's family to enforce it.

In another case reported to the writer, similar in its nature to the one just mentioned, the girl was sent to her husband, after 'peace-talkers' had adjusted the affair, and was locked up by the mother-in-law in a small room with only one meal a day. Within a year she had hanged herself.

71
THE STORY OF A CRUEL DAUGHTER-IN-LAW

Adele Fielde

1894

Instructional tales abound in China's oral and written traditions, underscoring the importance of social rules in Chinese society. Here, when the husband is stuck between his wife's hard-heartedness and a loving mother, the heavens provide the correct solution.

The first duty of every married woman is believed to be that of taking care of her husband's mother, and many bright examples of self-sacrifice are kept before the feminine mind in illustrative folk-stories. A popular book tells of one poverty-stricken woman who gave the natural food of her babe to its grandam; and of another who sold herself as a slave that she might get the means of buying a coffin for her dead mother-in-law.

On the contrary, one who fails in devotion to the parents of her husband is sure to come to a bad end, as in the following instructive instance.

An unfilial son had a wife who hated his old mother. He was an only child, and had been the idol of his mother's heart, the object of her constant care. In her old age she was wholly dependent upon him; and, as she had become bedridden, she needed much attention from his wife. The wife was selfish and hard-hearted, but her husband was fond of her; and when she declared that she would no longer endure his mother's presence in the house, but would leave him and marry some other man, he told her he would carry his mother away, and cast her into a pit. So he deceitfully took his aged parent on his back, telling her it was long since she had been out to take the country air, and that she would be the better for a little change of scene. They started toward the woods, and, as they went, the old woman told her son that he had gladdened her heart ten times. The first was when he was born, and when, after much sorrow, she knew that she had a living boy; the second was when she first saw him smile, and she knew that he was comfortable in her arms; the third was when he first held a thing in his hand, and she knew, by his grasp upon it, that he was strong; the fourth was when he began to walk, and she knew that he would learn to take care of himself and to help her; the fifth was when he first went off with other boys to gather fuel, and she thought that, having him, she could keep the house, and make a home; the sixth was when she first gave him some money, and he started off without her to buy their food in the market; the seventh was when she could afford to let him go to school, and he came back at nightfall, and told her what the teacher had taught him; the eighth was when he put on the garb of an adult, and she knew that she had a man to depend on at last; the ninth was when she got a wife for him, had paid all the wedding expenses, and made him able to establish a household of his own; the tenth was when he just now took her on his back, to carry her out to get sight of the sky and the fields, that she might be refreshed, and live the longer.

As she talked thus, her son's heart was softened, and he could not cast away the mother who had loved him so well. He therefore turned about and went homeward, but he did not dare take the old woman back to the house in which his wife was; and so he put her down in a shed, where ashes were heaped, and straw was stored. He made a bed for her upon and behind some straw, and told her he would bring her food at meal-time. When he went into the house, his wife asked him what he had done with the old woman, and he said he had thrown her into the pit. The wife was satisfied, and became very pleasant toward her husband. The hours passed, the meal-times came and went, and the man could not make up his mind to take food to the shed, through fear that his wife would thus discover that his mother was there.

The old woman got hungry, and at last crawled out from behind the straw toward the door, to see if her son was not coming to bring food to her. Just at that moment the wife came to empty a pan of ashes in the shed, and as she opened the door she saw the old woman, with dishevelled hair, pallid face, and wild eyes, staring out at her. Stricken with terror at the sight of what she believed to be the ghost of her mother-in-law, she fell backwards, struck her head on a stone, and instantly died. The son afterwards brought his old mother back into his house, and took good care of her.

72
THE MANCHU BRIDE
Dorothea Hosie
c. 1912

Lady Dorothea Hosie, the daughter of a China scholar from Britain, spoke fluent Mandarin. She chose to live with a Chinese family and observed customs on a daily basis.

Flower next inveighed against Manchu customs. A Manchu friend of hers, a girl of sixteen, told her she refused outright to wear the heavy wooden butterfly-shaped headdress of ceremony, as it made her head ache. She said that it was in Manchu families, rather than Chinese, that the daughter-in-law is oppressed, that in some houses she might never sit in the presence of her mother-in-law, even if she were on the eve of motherhood. 'She is treated just like an amah!' said Flower scornfully.

But to return to Flower. Having thanked Heaven she was not born a Manchu, she told me of Li Cheng. He was not engaged, because their mother had not yet seen a girl worthy of him. There were three or four, however, she was thinking over. When her daughters married and left the home, Aunt Kung would want someone to manage the house and be a companion and daughter to her, for she would be getting old. For—and this seems a remarkable state of affairs to us—the mother of the house, on her son's marriage, hands over the purse-strings to her daughter-in-law, whose duty it then becomes to see to the housekeeping.

Not that the mother-in-law derogates her dignity or suffers, for she expects, out of the sum allowed by the head of the house for housekeeping, to be provided by the daughter-in-law for all her *menus plaisirs*, and a reckless mother-in-law can drive the younger woman to financial distraction. Flower told me of a friend of hers whose mother-in-law had taken to opium-smoking, another to gambling, when she usually lost heavily, and yet a third who was driven by the desire to go to theatricals any and every day. The extra sums needed for these inconveniently expensive follies had to be squeezed out somehow by the son's wife. At times she failed to do it, contrive how she might, and was then put in the unpleasant position of having to ask her father-in-law for more money for the house, and being obliged to listen while he expatiated on her extravagant housekeeping and uttered encomiums on his wife's economical methods before she appeared on the scene. One might ask why she did not tell him the truth. Whatever may be their faults, Chinese are intensely loyal to each other and detest tale-bearing. Their code of honour is very rigid in the matter and they have to be goaded beyond endurance by the offender before they will speak. Also, to them, gambling, opium-smoking, and kindred vices, seem to be almost of the nature of madness, which cannot be helped: so why struggle? And, in any case, a daughter-in-law must obey her mother-in-law, said Flower, in every way.

So I told Flower in return of an acquaintance of mine, a slender young Manchu princess, as pretty or prettier than the paint with which her soft smooth cheeks were liberally besmeared, and as neat as a new pin. I met her at a function in the Legation with her mother-in-law, and she begged me to go and see her. She came out to the furthest court permissible to greet me, and we went through quite half a dozen before we reached her own sanctum, wherein she and her young husband and her fine little boy of two lived. This opened off her mother-in-law's, and the two ladies had their meals together, at which they were joined by the father-in-law and the husband, for they were modern folk.

'What a big place this house is!' I exclaimed. 'Do you have to look after all the inmates?'

'I do, indeed,' she said with bitterness. 'There are no less than thirty-two people inside the walls of our home, counting amahs and grooms. Far too many! I have to manage them all, their food and wages, and make them keep the place clean. And, oh, dear, some are so lazy, and others are so quarrelsome! My poor father-in-law never has any money, because he has so many to keep. It is most tiresome!'

She almost wrung her hands, and I felt with her, for I should not have liked her task, and she was a mere chit of twenty.

73
THE PREGNANT WOMAN AND THE COW

Tie Ning

1990s

Translated by Li Ziliang

Tie Ning's fascination with the details of human nature surfaces in this pastoral story of a naïve mountain village woman who marries a man from the comparatively sophisticated plains. Ah, Fragrant Snow, *Tie Ning's most famous work, examines people's impatience with the narrowness of others. In the following story, the main character contemplates her own limitations.*

Taking her leave of the country fair, a pregnant woman made her way home along a dirt track, with a cow in tow. It was late autumn and the sun was shining over the smooth expanse of open land, brushing it clean with its warmth.

The pregnant woman let go her hold of the cow to set it free for a while. Freeing herself in this way, she began to feel more comfortable. Her two strong arms, enjoying their liberty, swayed as she walked. The roundness of her belly, protruding beneath the thin, flower-patterned cotton coat that covered it, clearly indicated her condition. It gave her the air of a valiant general as she walked.

The pregnant woman and the cow rambled on, an arm's length apart. When the cow turned to the wheat field to eat the seedlings, the pregnant woman shouted: 'Black! Get out of there!'

The cow's name was Black, although it was yellow, and it was reluctant to leave the field. The pregnant woman became annoyed. 'Black!' she shouted at it, her voice echoing over the tranquil land as if she was greeting an old friend in the distance. As there was not another soul in sight for the pregnant woman to be addressing,

THE PREGNANT WOMAN AND THE COW

Black was compelled to acknowledge the call. It hurriedly snatched a couple more of mouthfuls before leaving the field and returning to the proper path.

A decorated, white marble archway was clearly visible in the distance. Once past it, the pregnant woman would almost be home. The landscape was vast and empty in all directions. The archway stood abruptly erect in the space, as if it had dropped straight down from the heavens. In this expanse of bare land, its awe-inspiring magnificence was beyond description. The sight of its dazzling facade constantly fueled this awe, even in the local elders who had been acquainted with the archway all their lives.

As she contemplated the archway, the pregnant woman told herself how fortunate she was to have been married into this place: indeed, without exception, every time she saw the archway she couldn't help but sigh with gratitude for her lucky match.

The pregnant woman was a native of the mountain area and life there was harder than on the plain that lay before her eyes. However, the pregnant woman was beautiful, and beauty offered the possibility of wealth and hope to those trapped in a poor existence. Her parents could not afford to send their daughter to school, yet they never asked her to do hard work and saved the best food for her as if they were nurturing a treasure to be offered when the right suitor came along. Their only wish was to send the treasure to the plain to enjoy the kind of life that was not afforded to them in the mountain area.

At last there came a day when the pearl of the parents' hearts was married to the plain. Arriving on the flatlands, her mother-in-law proudly told her about the fortuitous geomantic orientation of the place, saying that it used to be the burial site of a certain imperial kinsman of the Qing Dynasty, the tomb of this imperial kinsman lying, in fact, just to the north of the village. It was to his memory that the decorated archway had been erected. The pregnant woman had no idea what official rank an imperial kinsman held, nor what span of time had elapsed between the Qing Dynasty and the present. The tomb had been robbed and it was now an empty pit containing nothing but broken bricks and wild grass. As she stood beside the pit, the pregnant woman looked at the weather-beaten bricks and thought to herself once again: 'How lucky I am to be married to this place!' The tomb used to be a symbol of wealth before the treasures it contained were stolen away. But the pit and the archway enriched this place. This was exactly due to its favourable geomancy.

As she settled into her new life, the accent of the mountain people that she bore slowly softened into acceptability, and the happy life the pregnant woman led in this place increased her natural beauty. Her parents-in-law were very kind to her and her husband often told her he'd like to do the kind of work that would make more money for her, for their family. When he was free from farm work he would go to the city with the construction team to build buildings. In his absence from home, his mother would come to keep his wife company and serve her with brown-sugar water. With her lips fresh and red from the brown-sugar water she became even more charming and lovely. Her mother-in-law would tell everyone she met that her son's wife was really a beauty.

Pregnancy only increased her beauty. Feeling the need to have regular exercise, she took to walking. She loved to go to country fairs, not to buy anything in particular, but just to take a look. Before she set out, her mother-in-law would always bring the cow out for her, asking that she ride it so she might not tire herself out. She loved to have Black as companion on the empty paths across the plain, so she would happily take the reins from her mother-in-law. Black was pregnant too, the pregnant woman thought to herself. As both she and the cow were carrying babies she felt they had a common bond. They were both proud of themselves. Thus they set off together, their bellies protruding. The pregnant woman never rode Black, and she always followed the pace set by this gentle beast.

When she first arrived on the plain, the pregnant woman felt her vision broaden widely. After living there for some time, a sense of loneliness gradually descended upon her. When she was in the mountains it wasn't possible to see very far in any direction; thus there wasn't room to contemplate what lay ahead. But what lay at the end of the plain? she thought as she walked. It seemed to her that in all her life she would never be able to walk to the end of this stretch of flat land. When she could no longer bear the loneliness she shouted: 'Bla-c-k!' Her voice startled Black who was as ever absorbed by the motion of walking. The cow stopped and waited for the woman to catch up, looking at her gently. The pregnant woman who had fallen far behind, was quick to overtake it. There was no one in sight as far as the eye could see. Stretching its neck, the cow then hurried to catch her up, soon to leave her behind

THE PREGNANT WOMAN AND THE COW

again. The pregnant woman smiled silently to herself, enjoying the sense of movement on the plain; liveliness that she herself had created. Thus, it suddenly seemed to her that she and Black were not alone, for the plain was filled with her voice, the stirring life in her belly, and the clumsy motion of the cow.

The pregnant woman and the cow were now approaching the archway. Unblinkingly the pregnant woman faced the glow of the evening sun. Her nose glistened with beads of sweat. In twos and threes, black spots appeared moving in the distance; children going home from school. The pregnant woman felt tired. Each time she saw the jumping children she would feel tired. She held her stomach and headed towards the stone tablet lying by the road, to have a rest. As the pregnant woman sat on the stone, Black turned to the wheat field again.

This huge stone tablet belonged to the imperial kinsman too. It used to stand on the back of an equally huge stone tortoise opposite the decorated archway. The stone tablet was pulled down by some rude young men from the city. Her mother-in-law told her that these young men had tried to pull down the magnificent archway too. Failing this, they then decided to blow it up with explosive. Mother-in-law's father led the villagers to kneel before these young men in a plea not to blow it away, an action that saved the ancient structure. The fallen stone tablet had lain there by the road ever since.

The stone tablet gradually became a seat for people passing by. The corners and edges of the block were worn smooth and round. Engraved on the surface were some big characters that now faced the sky, unknown to the pregnant woman who was illiterate. She had asked her husband about the meaning of these words but he didn't know either for he had had only three years' schooling. He added: 'What's the use of knowing them? The tablet is nothing but an old stone.'

Sitting on it, the pregnant woman regarded the big characters once again. She positioned herself on one of the characters, then, suddenly and unconsciously, she moved to the edge of the stone. She did not know the reason why. Before, when she paused here to rest awhile, she had never cared whether she sat on the characters or not. She cared this time because of the baby she was carrying. This baby gave her hope which was embodied in the approaching black dots of the children tumbling out of school. She dared not ignore them because for her these young ones were associated with the characters. Ignoring them meant ignoring her own child, or so she thought.

The pregnant woman knew that one day her child would be among the group of children going to and from school, that her child, like them, would be sure to learn many characters and ask her a lot of questions as she had asked her mother when she was a child. If she took her child to the country fair, he or she would certainly see the stone tablet and ask about the meaning of the characters on it as she had asked her husband. It occurred to her that she did not want to admit to her child that she didn't know. But the fact was that she really did not know their meaning. She felt uneasy as if her baby were pushing her into a corner.

The children returning home from school came by the stone tablet and chorused their greetings. The pregnant woman stopped one of them, a relative of hers, and asked for a piece of paper and a pencil. Holding the paper in one hand and the pencil in the other, she then waited until the children had left her a distance behind. It seemed to her that she had waited for quite a long time, which made her feel as if she were going to do something shameful.

When the plain was restored to its original quietude, she put the paper on the stone tablet and started her work. She wanted to trace these big characters onto the paper, to take the tracing back to the village and ask the man of letters how to read them and what they meant. She paused even as she began; it promised to be a difficult task. Though she was clever with her hands, the pencil struggled against her attempts to control it. She stared hard at these strange hieroglyphs. The more she looked at them, the more confusing they became. Turning her eyes away, she looked into the distant sky and the mountains on the horizon. A small tree rose perpendicular over the vast plain, clouds flowed across the sky, and crows hovered over the archway. These things distracted her attention from the tablet and yet at the same time, focussed her energy upon the characters. She looked at the carved forms on the stone once again and then, timidly but with determination, made the first stroke on the paper.

Once the first stroke was completed, nothing could stop her. She drew the characters carefully, and as she followed each line, she began to imagine their meaning. Though she could not be sure, she guessed that they must mean something good, because every character appeared beautiful to her, just as she appeared beautiful in the eyes of other people. When this thought occurred to her, she felt a close association with the characters and her heart filled with a modest joy. She considered how appropriate the word 'beauty' was to describe the characters appearing slowly under her pencil. 'How nice characters are!' she exclaimed with a sigh.

The sun was setting. The pregnant woman had been bending over the stone tablet for quite some time, and the intensity of concentration on her labour had caused her to perspire heavily. Sweat now dampened the collar of her blouse, even running from the collar to her breast. Her face glowed crimson and from time to time her strong wrists trembled. But still she could not stop, for her heart would not allow her to. She had never come across such an absorbing, albeit painstaking, occupation as this. Yet as it absorbed her, this task drained all her mental and physical energy.

Black had long since returned from the wheat field and was lying by her side. The pregnant woman hadn't noticed the cow's reappearance. Black lay there offering companionship and encouragement to the pregnant woman, gazing at her, its face pale and obedient.

Finally the pregnant woman finished her work. In the shade of dusk she counted the characters carefully. There were seventeen:

'Tablet in Honour of Prince the Faithful, Respectable, Honest, True, Assiduous, Discreet, Pure, Peaceful, Joyful, and Virtuous.'

The pregnant woman counted the characters on her paper. They numbered seventeen too:

'Tablet in Honour of Prince the Faithful, Respectable, Honest, True, Assiduous, Discreet, Pure, Peaceful, Joyful, and Virtuous.'

The characters on the paper were distorted and queer, like a row of deranged insects or disordered coils of hemp rope. In spite of this, they were obviously characters. The evidence of her having written these on the paper gave the pregnant woman a new sense of value; the achievement seemed to have stirred in her a true inner beauty. She felt she had obtained the courage to cope with the child which would be born soon. The copying of these characters was in preparation to give this child a satisfactory answer should the mother be asked about the meaning of these markings. Her child would certainly grow up learning to write beautiful characters such as these. This child would surely have a lot of expectations of its mother, and this mother was ready and willing to try and live up to her child's expectations. Sooner or later the baby would leave the pregnant woman's womb, but the stone tablet with the characters would remain in her mind forever, her own claim to the hopes and dreams that everybody harbours. As a gesture for the future of her child, she was drawn to the stone tablet, which, having sparked her own interest in learning, she took as her own sign of good geomantic fortune.

The pregnant woman put the piece of paper in her pocket and, ready to resume her journey, called Black. Cooking smoke was rising above the village beyond the archway.

Black was reluctant to stand up and adopted a kneeling position as if to let the pregnant woman climb onto its back.

'Black . . .' she cooed at the cow with compassion, urging it to stand up. She instinctively stretched out her hand to touch the cow's clumsy, rounded belly, which reminded her that Black too, was to give birth soon, and that maybe her baby and Black's calf would come into the world on the same day. Black rose to its feet.

The pregnant woman and the cow walked across the plain like two beings who depended upon each other for survival. The warm, reliable odour of the cow filled the pregnant woman's nostrils. She retained her hand on its back and it reacted by rubbing its face against her. The two walked on across the plain, regarding each other from time to time, but mostly like two generals surveying the land. It was getting dark, but the archway still glistened with a hazy whiteness. Soon, the couple had left even the archway behind. As she walked along, the pregnant woman contemplated the plain, the starred sky, the distant mountains, the trees nearby with the birds' nests they wore like black hats on their boughs, the noisy country fair, the pregnant cow, the strange but beautiful characters, and she considered her future child, and the future of this child . . . She could not imagine life without one of these things; yet these few things were all she needed, all her life.

A warm sensation flowed over the pregnant woman's body and flooded her heart. She had a strong desire to tell someone about this sudden warmth she felt, to share what she was experiencing in her heart. But even should there have been someone around, she would have been unable to do so, for it was really beyond description. All she could do was to enjoy the emotions, washing over her.

'Black,' the pregnant woman whispered in the darkness, her voice trembling wildly with happiness.

74
ETIQUETTE
CHARLES TAYLOR
1860

Chinese culture relies on a series of polite verbal exchanges which are often self-deprecating. Whether a husband means it or not, form requires that he belittle his wife.

Etiquette requires that in conversation, each should compliment the other and everything belonging to him, in the most laudatory style; and depreciate himself with all pertaining to him, to the lowest possible point. The following is no exaggeration, though not the precise words:
'What is your honorable name?'
'My insignificant appellation is Wong.'
'Where is your magnificent palace?'
'My contemptible hut is at Suchan.'
'How many are your illustrious children?'
'My vile, worthless brats are five.'
'How is the health of your distinguished spouse?'
'My mean, good-for-nothing old woman is well.'
In leaving his house you must back along out, bowing to the host and shaking your hands all the way. He follows you, doing the same, and repeating, 'Slowly go, slowly, slowly go.' This is to signify his reluctance at your departure.

75
MISTRUST AND SUSPICION

Arthur H. Smith
1894

Women, admittedly, have few advantages in Chinese society, and so some may squirrel away any personal funds—just in case.

Despite their disadvantages wives may contrive to conceal from their husbands the fact that they have a little property in the hands of some member of the wife's family. The writer is acquainted with a Chinese almost sixty years of age, who has a flock of grandchildren, but who will have nothing to do with his wife, nor she with him. During all their married life, between thirty and forty years, he has cherished the suspicion that she has somewhere at interest a considerable sum of money which she will not share with him. It is certainly not true that all Chinese deceive one another, but it is surely true that there is always danger of it, which everywhere begets unrest and suspicion. It is also an allied phenomenon that the principals in a matter may be totally unable to ascertain the real facts with which every one else is perfectly acquainted, but which no one will tell.

76
HAWKING
W. Scarborough
1888

This passage comes from A Collection of Chinese Proverbs *by the Reverend W. Scarborough.*

When a husband and wife find it impossible to get enough to eat at home, they sometimes go out to 'hawk,' at a great distance from home, where they are quite unknown. The woman then becomes the man's 'sister,' and is eligible for marriage on moderate terms. She is no sooner established in her new home, than she takes occasion to elope, carrying with her as many of the valuables of her new husband as she can lay her hands upon, rejoining her real husband at some place agreed upon.

A Manchu sweetmeat-seller

ON THE INSTRUCTION OF CHILDREN
Ban Zhao
c. 100 AD

Ban Zhao, a poet and China's first female historian, taught and advised the empress. This excerpt comes from her ode written for her daughter, 'Admonitions for Women'.

Families generally have both boys and girls.
    When they are three or four years old
    It is important to begin their instruction.
This work is truly the mother's.

78
PROTECTING WOMEN
John Thomson
1909

Not only was John Stuart Thomson an eminent photographer travelling in China in the late nineteenth and early twentieth centuries, he also wrote sympathetically about Chinese at all levels of society.

'How is your wife?' Wife and daughters must remain unmentioned; their privacy is like their honor, inviolate; they live only in the husband's and father's eye. Mixed social gatherings never occur. There are no women on the Chinese stage. Among the better class, the boys and girls of the family are entirely separated after the age of six. There is nothing among their middle class of that curse of American and European cities, 'a street education' after school hours. Whatever may be the result of the Chinese system in individual development; however narrow the wife's social sphere may be by reigning alone in a feminine world, the intent is sincere, and based upon the lofty desire not to soil women even so much as with the opportunity for temptation.

79
MOTHERHOOD
Hiram Parkes Wilkinson
1882

Hiram Parkes Wilkinson wrote a book on the family tradition in China.

As usual, numbers of women crowded round the *shendzle*. Bright and pleasant they looked. We had a nice little chat with some of them after dinner. One bright young mother placed her baby, of whom she was evidently very proud, in my lap, and said, 'Now you can have him.' The little fellow smiled up in my face, not in the least afraid. How beautiful motherhood is!

The one thought of that young Chinese mother was that precious baby, and this was a little trick to get him into notice. I patted and praised him, and the mother blushed, and beamed with perfect sunshine on her face. The women were all exceedingly friendly, and one and another, as I passed out, said, 'When will you come back again? When will you come back? Come soon.'

80
THE POWER OF MOTHERS
George Morrison
1895

George Morrison observes that in some cases mothers could be extremely powerful.

A mother in China is given, both by law and custom, extreme power over her sons whatever their age or rank. The Sacred Edict says, 'Parents are like heaven. Heaven produces a blade of grass. Spring causes it to germinate. Autumn kills it with frost. Both are by the will of heaven. In like manner the power of life and death over the body which they have begotten is with the parents.'

And it is this law giving such power to a mother in China which tends, it is believed, to nullify that other law whereby a husband in China is given extreme power over his wife, even to the power in some cases of life and death.

81
EIGHT STRINGS OF CASH
Arthur H. Smith
1894

Money has always been extremely important among Chinese peasants because they had so little. However the risks taken here seem excessive.

While this chapter was in preparation a Chinese friend called to ask advice. He had a nephew thirty-six years of age, who until recently had never been married. He is a dull-witted man, with very little property, and had never been regarded as a desirable match. About five months previous to the recent occurrence which led to the request for advice, a girl aged sixteen was found who had a deformity in one limb preventing her from making a match. A go-between proposed her for this bachelor and it was arranged that he should pay her family eight strings of cash for a 'bridal outfit,' and in due time the marriage took place. As might have been expected it was a conspicuously infelicitous one. On the twenty-sixth day of the first moon of the current year, the husband ate a bowl of millet which seemed to him to have a singular taste, but he did not suspect poison until he had taken it all, when he saw arsenic at the bottom. After violent retching he was somewhat relieved. The next day but one the same thing occurred, the symptoms being graver. He vigorously remonstrated, and his bride left for her home some miles away. The husband was now very ill, and was waited on for some days by his uncle, at the times of whose visit for advice the nephew's life was supposed to be out of danger. The uncle wanted to know what should be done about it. In an empire where 'talkativeness' is a legal ground for divorce, it naturally appeared to an Occidental that repeated, albeit clumsy attempts at poisoning might be equally so. But the uncle explained that there was a sister-in-law who objected. Why? Apparently because having invested eight strings of cash in a wife it was a pity to lose her for a mere trifle like this! The matter was put into the hands of peace-talkers, who arranged that the relative who had brought the bride the arsenic should kotow to the man poisoned by the arsenic, and that the family of the bride should pay the injured husband fifteen strings of cash wherewith to recruit his depleted vitality. Meantime the bride remained at her mother's home, where one of the women was said to have beaten her a little. She is not divorced, her husband being reluctant to proceed to such extremities, in part on account of the large investment originally made, and in part for fear of ridicule. In due time she will probably be sent back to his home to resume her experiments in the art of making home happy.

A blind singing girl and duenna

82
SUNDRY SUPERSTITIONS
Adele Fielde
1894

During her years in Swatow (Shantou) in eastern Guangdong, Adele Fielde became aware of numerous Chinese superstitions.

The superstitious beliefs and observances of the Chinese are numberless, and they occupy more or less the time and mind of every individual in the nation. Those here recorded are common among the people near Swatow. I am unable to say how many of them are purely local.

When a child is just one month old, the mother, carrying it in a scarf on her back, induces it to look down into a well. This is supposed to have a mentally invigorating effect, producing courage and deepening the understanding.

SUNDRY SUPERSTITIONS

A mother feeds her young infant from a cup rather than from a bowl or plate, because a bowl, being capacious, has an occult influence in making the child a large eater; while a plate, being shallow, causes him to throw up his food on slight provocation. The cup, being small and deep, insures his taking but little food, and keeping it for assimilation.

When a child becomes ill, the mother gathers thorns from twelve species of plants and makes an infusion in which she washes the child, hoping to wash the disease, with the demon that produces it, into the water. She then carries the water to an open space where many people go to and fro, and there throws it upon the ground. As she goes from her own house, the inhabitants of the streets she traverses shut their doors, to prevent the disease from entering their abodes. A woman of my acquaintance recently told me that, having no fear of demons, she did not shut her door when a neighbour passed her house carrying water in which a child having fever and ague had just been washed, and the very next day she herself had chills!

If a child falls from a high place to the ground, spirit-money is immediately burned upon the spot by the mother, to propitiate the demon who is trying to pull the child down to destruction.

When a child has fallen, there is danger that he may have left his twelve wits in the earth on which he fell, so the mother at once makes with her empty hand the motion of dipping from the ground to the child's chest. Thus she replaces in the child what might otherwise be permanently lost in the soil.

During the month succeeding the birth of a child the mother must not cross the threshold of another person's room. Should she do this, she will endanger the welfare of the occupants, and in her next life she will perpetually scrub the floor of the room entered.

83
MULTIPLE WIVES
George Morrison
1895

Dr George Morrison worked with the Chinese community in Sichuan Province and saw at close quarters how illness affected the family.

Li, it may be said at once, is a man of no common virtue. He is the father of seven sons and four daughters; he can die in peace; in his family there is no fear of the early extinction of male descendants, for the succession is as well provided against as it is in the most fertile Royal family in Europe. His family is far spreading, and it is worth noting as an instance of the patriarchal nature of the family in China, that Li is regarded as the father of a family, whose members dependent upon him for entire or partial support number eighty persons. He has had three wives. His number one wife still lives at the family seat in Changsha; another secondary wife is dead; his present number two wife lives with him in Yunnan. This is his favourite wife, and her story is worth a passing note. She was not a 'funded houri [secondary wife],' but a poor *yatow*, a 'forked head' or slave girl, whom he purchased on a lucky day, and, smitten with her charms, made her his wife. It was a case of love at first sight. Her conduct since marriage has more than justified the choice of her master. Still a young woman, she has already presented her lord with nine children, on the last occasion surpassing herself by giving birth to twins. She has a most pleasant face, and really charming children; but the chief attraction of a Chinese lady is absent in her case. Her feet are of natural size, and not even in the exaggerated murmurings of love could her husband describe them as 'three-inch gold lilies.'

In the families of the poor there is no margin of any kind for sickness, but sickness comes impartially to every grade of life. When the bread-winner is laid aside, when the mother of a little flock is no longer able to keep the simple domestic machinery in motion, then indeed trouble has arrived. If a young married woman is sick, the first step is to send for her mother; for ordinarily no one in the family into which she has married has the time or disposition to take care of her, least of all the husband, who regards himself as aggrieved by her disability, and who is often far more inclined to expect the family of his wife to bear all the resultant expenses, than to meet them himself. One of the legal occasions for divorce is chronic illness, although we have never heard of a single instance where formal steps were taken for that reason. It is a current saying that in the presence of a long continued sickness there is no filial son. How great the family strain often is, there are many things to prove. In the midst of it all one is sometimes agreeably surprised to find an amount of tenderness and forbearance worthy of all praise. But in the constitution of Chinese society these exhibitions are and must be in a great minority. A man well known to the writer in speaking of the serious symptoms of a disease of his wife, remarked that he had asked her how long she expected to keep up the groans called forth by the intolerable agonies of terrible and incurable ulcers, and that for his part he had offered to provide her with a rope that she might relieve him of his inconvenience, and herself of her miseries, though upon being remonstrated with for such an inhuman view of the case, he frankly admitted that his troubles had made him 'stupid.'

PART VII

WORKING WITH ONE'S HANDS

'If she rises early, she offends her husband; if late, his father and mother.'

Literature about China describes women as *nei ren* or 'inside people' noting their primary roles as keepers of the home. In truth, most Chinese women have always worked at some form of income-producing manual labour such as spinning, planting rice, caring for silk worms, hauling stones, and sometimes even stopping to give birth in the fields. Only the wealthy minority could afford multiple servants. This provided work for poor women and kept their own women inside. Many women who toiled as servants or even slaves in private homes might be abused by the reigning household women, but channels for complaint were almost non-existent.

Unlike men, all women were expected to work with their hands. Female peasants worked long, hard hours in the fields or home in order to live, but among the wealthy, women played plucked instruments, painted, and embroidered. If they were literate, they practised calligraphy and wrote poetry, often expressing their emotions and longings for the inaccessible.

84
WORK IN A WESTERN HOME
CHARLES TAYLOR
1860

Doctor and missionary, Charles Taylor published his memoirs of China after his return to the United States. In China, both Western and Chinese families who could afford to do so would hire 'baby-amahs' or nannies to help with or even raise their children. Western children often learnt a Chinese dialect before learning English.

Our little boy also seems to breathe new life, and prattles Chinese with increased vivacity, as you would soon be convinced if you were sitting with me in my study at this moment and listening while the little fellow trives to repeat the sounds which his nurse is trying to teach him. She is highly delighted to find that he understands and pronounces her native tongue with greater facility than ours, and diligently improves the advantage she has gained, by giving him lessons every day. She is remarkably fond of him, and her affection is so warmly reciprocated, that his mother pretends to be quite jealous, and often says the child loves his 'sung-sung' (nurse) better than he does herself.

85
IRRESISTIBLE BABIES

C<small>HARLES</small> T<small>AYLOR</small>

1860

Among transient beggars, children learn to 'work with their hands' at an early age.

There is a class who correspond to the character and habits of gipsies in Europe, and who flock to Shanghai in winter, and disappear with the return of warm weather. With these, also, as with a vast number of constant residents here, beggary is a regular business, and they in particular, seem to thrive on it, for a fatter, healthier looking set of people than many of these gipsy-beggars you never saw. They come among the rest, to avail themselves of the bounty of the foreigners, and it is often quite an interesting, not to say an affecting sight, to see a mother with a fat, chubby, smiling, naked babe, suspended in her bosom by a band of rags passing over her shoulders. This little nursling is taught, as soon as it can direct its tiny arms, to hold out its hand to every passer-by for a cash or two. It is impossible to resist the mute pleading of these pretty gipsy babies, and if you go out with a pocket full of copper cash, you will find it empty when you return, if many of these beggars have crossed your path.

* * *

There is many a capable woman in China, and when such a one is married to an incompetent man, or a confirmed gambler, or an opium sot, she is compelled, if in poor circumstances, to be the bread-winner of the family. Amongst the poor both husband and wife support the family by their labours, and the children add their mites as soon as able, beginning by scouring the streets and water's edge for every scrap of wood or shaving, to keep the pot boiling at home. They soon learn to mind a street stall, or to do any other thing to help. The baby is strapped on their backs when they are little more than infants themselves, and thus baby is out in the open air nearly all day long, and kept out of mischief's way, while the little brother or sister is picking up chips or doing some other light toil to add to the means of the house.

86
WOMEN'S WORK
Arthur H. Smith
1899

In nineteenth-century China, almost everything was made, cleaned, or gathered by hand. Young girls were expected to work in any way possible.

The observations which may be made with regard to the industry of Chinese boys, are equally applicable—*mutatis mutandis*—to Chinese girls. In all lands and in all climes, 'woman's work is never done,' and this is most especially true of China, where machinery has not yet expelled the primitive processes of what is literally manufacture, or work by the hand. The

Boiling silk and spinning worms as part of silk preparation

care of silk-worms, and the picking, spinning, and weaving of cotton, are largely the labour of women, to which the girls are introduced at a very early age. The sewing for a Chinese family is a serious matter, especially as the number of families who can afford to hire help in this line is a very trifling proportion. But aside from this employment, in which a Chinese girl who expects to be acceptable to the family of her mother-in-law must be expert, girls can also be made useful in almost any line of home work to which the father may be devoted. In the country districts all over the empire, boys and girls alike are sent out to scratch together as much fuel as possible, for the preparation of the food, and this continues in the case of the girls until they are too large to go to any distance from home. It is not an unmeaning appellation, which is given to girls generally, that of *ya-y'ou*, or 'slave-girl,' used just as we should say 'daughter.' To a foreigner, this sounds much like the term 'nigger' applied to black men, but to the Chinese there is a fitness in the designation, which they refuse to surrender.

TOIL

ROYAL ASIATIC SOCIETY
1871

This is an excerpt from an article published by the North China branch of the Royal Asiatic Society, entitled 'Journal of a Mission to Lewchew'.

Sept. 14th. Whenever I have gone abroad, I have always seen many sordid-looking women at the roadside making clothes most diligently. To-day I asked about them, and first learned fully from the attendants how very indolent the men here are, and how the women toil. They use no beams to carry burdens, work at weaving and mending even in the markets, collect fuel, and bring water; they carry most things on their heads. Their dress has no buttons or girdle, and neither sex wear trowers; the lappel is tucked over under the arm, and the dress is longer than the men's, doubled and very long, so that the wind never blows it open. Their head dress is pushed down so as to rest burdens on the crown, and let their hands be free to take care of the dress. They practice this from girlhood, and will walk steadily up hill with a hundred catties and drop nothing,—which is the most dextrous thing I have seen done in this land. They roll up the sleeves to the shoulder while at work and tie them behind. The hair is washed when dirty with the help of a clay, and they strip to the waists out of doors when doing these ablutions. They carry their children astride on the hip, thus keeping the dress close to the person.

88
WORKING ON A BOAT
George Staunton
1799

Peasant women have long toiled on boats and some also doubled as prostitutes. George Staunton, who travelled to Beijing with Lord Macartney's expedition, seems here to be writing about the city of Chaozhou in Hebei Province, close to the capital.

The boats which ply from one part of the city to another are chiefly managed by females, who are generally young and neatly dressed, with an evident intent of attracting the attention of passengers. A similar custom had been observed before on the Tai-hoo lake, where men absent from their own families abounded. At Chau choo-foo, the commerce of two navigable rivers occasioned a concourse of male strangers. The frail females in the boats had not embraced this double occupation, after having quited their parents, or on being abandoned by them on account of their misconduct; but the parents themselves, taking no other interest in the chastity of their daughters, than as it might contribute to an advantageous disposal of them to wealthy husbands, feel little reluctance, when no such prospect offers, to devote them to one employment, with a view to the profits of another.

89
LIFE ON A BOAT
Annie Brassey
1879

Annie Brassey was one of those intrepid Victorian ladies who lacked neither courage nor funds. Her journal is a detailed, lively record of her eleven-month voyage—until it was cut short by her death aboard her boat. Here she describes one of the small multi-purpose boats in which Chinese women rowed people ashore from vessels at anchor.

I never shall forget my astonishment when, going ashore very early one morning in one of these strange craft, the proprietor lifted up what I had thought was the bottom of the boat, and disclosed three or four children, packed away as tight as herrings, while under the seats were half a dozen people of larger growth. The young mother of the small family generally rows with the smallest baby strapped on to her back, and the next-sized one in her arms, whom she is also teaching to row. The children begin to row by themselves when they are about two years old. The boys have a gourd, intended for a life-preserver, tied round their necks as soon as they are born. The girls are left to their fate, Chinamen thinking it rather an advantage to lose a daughter or two occasionally.

90
MEDIUMS
JUSTUS DOOTITTLE
1865

During his fourteen years with the American Mission Board in Fuzhou, the Reverend Doolittle observed many aspects of women's daily life and beliefs which he later published in his book, Social Life of the Chinese.

Women frequently employ female mediums. The object of their doing so is to ascertain the news from a deceased relative or friend, or the kind of medicine a certain sick person should use in order to recover from illness, etc. There are two classes of these female mediums.

One class profess to obtain and transmit the news required by means of a very diminutive image, made of the wood of the willow-tree. The image is first exposed to the dew for forty-nine nights, when, after the performance of a superstitious ceremony relating to it, it is believed to have the *power of speaking*. The image is laid upon the stomach of the woman to whom it belongs. She, by means of it, pretends to be the medium of communication between the living and the dead. She sometimes professes to send the image into the world of spirits to find the person about whom intelligence is sought. It then changes into an elf or sprite, and departs on its errand. The spirit of the person enters the image, and gives the information sought after by the surviving relative. The woman is supposed not to utter a word, the message seeming to proceed from the image. The questions are addressed to the medium; the replies appear to come from her stomach. This is called 'Finding or seeking for the thread'. There is probably a kind of *ventriloquism* employed. The fact that the voice proceeds professedly from the stomach of the medium doubtless helps to delude. The medium makes use of no incense or candles in the performance of this method. Widows who desire information in regard to their deceased husbands, or childless married women who wish to learn in regard to the future, not unfrequently call upon this class of spiritualists or mediums. The expense is but small, generally about two and one half cents for obtaining the news from the spirit world. Sometimes the willow image is held to the ear of the inquirer, in order that she may understand more readily what is said on the subject of inquiry.

Another class of women who pretend to be able to obtain information from or about the dead proceed in a very different manner. The medium sits by a table. Having inquired in regard to the name and surname of the deceased, and the precise time of death, she bows her head and rests it upon the table, her face being concealed from view. On the table are three sticks of lighted incense placed upright, sometimes in a censer, as usual; sometimes they are put in a horizontal position upon a vessel containing a small quantity of boiled rice. Two lighted candles are also placed upon the table. The woman who seeks information, and perhaps one or two of her acquaintances, gather near in profound silence. After a short time, the medium raises her head from the table with her eyes closed, and begins to address the applicant. She is now supposed to be possessed by the spirit of the dead individual in regard to whom information is desired; *in other words, the dead has come into her body, using her organs of speech to communicate with the living.* A conversation ensues between the living and the dead, mutually giving and receiving information. At the close of the interview the medium places her head down on the table, and after a few minutes she oftentimes begins to retch or vomit. After drinking some tea she soon becomes herself again, the spirit of the dead having retired.

The medium sometimes professes to become, by the use of similar means, possessed of the spirit of a specified god or goddess, and while thus possessed she prescribes for the sick who may have applied for medicine. In such cases it is believed that the medicine is really ordered by the divinity invoked. The god or goddess *casts himself or herself into the medium* for the time being, and dictates the medicine which the sick person must use in order to recover health. Occasionally the applicant is also directed to propitiate a particular divinity before using the medicine.

91
DESPERATE MEASURES
J. Dyer Ball
1912

Judging from his numerous publications, such as Things Chinese, *James Dyer Ball was possibly more intrigued by Chinese culture than by his job as a British civil servant in Hong Kong.*

One woman, not knowing that I discovered it, was pinching her infant child, and thus forcing it to scream as we passed along, thinking thereby to obtain alms from us. Another was sitting by her child as he lay stretched out on the side of the street, apparently very ill with the small pox. I did not stop to examine it at that time, but supposed it was really the case, until I was informed by another missionary that he had seen the same child in apparently the same stage of the disease for the last two years. She puts drops of flour paste on its face to resemble the pustules of small pox. In Canton it is a very common practice to put out the eyes of the children, in order to insure greater success in begging. I recollect, while in that city, meeting a man, woman, and several children, apparently all of one family, and all blind.

92
IDLE MEN
Lord Macartney
1798

When Lord Macartney visited Beijing on an official mission to the Emperor to request a relaxation of the restrictions on trade, he also observed the lives of ordinary, working people.

In some villages women were seen at their doors with rocks and reels spinning cotton. Some were employed in harvest work. The general appearance of these was very ordinary; their heads being large and round, and their stature low. Their dresses were loose, completely hiding the shape, with wide trowsers, and their feet and ankles wrapped round with bandages. The wives of the peasants have not only the care of domestic concerns, but work at every trade that can be carried on within doors. They rear silkworms, spin the cotton, and afterwards weave it into cloth. Yet even these injure their health, by the preposterous fashion of crippling and disfiguring their feet.

Though the women are of such service to their husbands, the latter hold them in the most abject submission, obliging them to wait at table as servants. This authority, however, is meliorated by the rules of gentleness inculcated from infancy among the very lowest orders of society. The elder branches always reside with the young ones of the family, and thereby serve to restrain them within the bounds of moderation. Still indolence is the principal characteristic of the men, who sit idle at home, while their wives and daughters go barefoot up the mountains to cut fuel, to sell at Funchal. Their food, which consists chiefly of pumpkin and salt-fish, together with the hardships they endure, makes them look old even in the younger part of life.

IDLE MEN

LADIES OF THE TEAHOUSE
Richard Wilheim
1928

Richard Wilheim spent twenty-five years in China, covering the collapse of the Qing and the emerging new order. He wrote numerous books on Chinese economics, psychology, literature, and folktales, many of which have been translated from the original German. He visited a Chinese teahouse in the 1920s where he met 'sing-song girls'—a different kind of working woman.

After a survey of the clubs and restaurants, we must throw a glance into the tea-houses. We have seen already that Chinese society is on the whole male society. This fact brings with it, as it did in ancient Greece, the custom of allowing little ladies who sing to appear while the men are united over their meal. Originally these girls were young artists, they had knowledge of literature, they usually made verses themselves, they played the zithern and sang to its accompaniment. They were used to intercourse with men and whereas the society lady became dumb and blushed, or if there were two of them, giggled into her handkerchief when confronted by a strange man, these little ladies were free and *spirituelle* in their conversation at such cheerful gatherings of young men. They are the pride and tradition of their profession: 'We sell our voices but not our person.'

For the protection of their virtue they were always accompanied by an old servant and usually by their music teacher, who accompanied the songs of his pupils on the lute or the violin. But as is often the case, this kind of free and intellectual companionship leads easily to erotic associations. The men found in their intercourse with these artists what was denied to them in their married lives, which was hardly ever preceded by a period of wild oats. Chinese lyric poetry is full of verses about these girls and tradition has handed down many stories of faithful love, the pangs of separation and of anguished longing which has ended in death. In fact, all the pathos and tragedy of love not protected and hallowed by social sanction existed in these relationships.

In the course of time, this state of affairs did of course change somewhat. The houses in which the little artists live are mostly owned by brothel proprietors. The servants who are supposed to protect the virtue of these girls, usually have a financial interest in a form of conduct on the part of their charges far removed from innocence and purity. Appearances are nevertheless well preserved and the girls live in tea-houses where you can visit them and talk to them and form friendships. You drink a cup of tea, eat a few melon seeds or sweets, smoke a cigarette and pay a fixed sum, a quarter of which goes to the girl with whom you converse. Another quarter is received by her 'aunt'—this is what the old ladies in whose care the girls are, are called—and the remaining half is the due of the owner of the place. The proceedings are conducted in a perfectly decent way. For instance, after dinner you meet a few friends, then you chatter a while and go home without any further intimacy. When you go for the first time to a tea-house in which you do not know any of the girls, they are introduced to you one by one and you give the name of the young beauty with whom you want to converse to the servant.

The girls are always dressed in charming clothes which are usually made in Shanghai or Suchou. The girls are gay and friendly and they know very well how to turn away any blunt attempt to approach them. A really clever girl will manage to converse with several guests whom she has accommodated in different rooms at the same time. She talks to the first one a little, flits away almost unnoticed to converse, with a second and so on and so forth. If a guest shows impatience at her absence, she is back on the instant with the most innocent expression and manages to convey the impression to every one that he is the only guest she cares for; she takes all his orders and accompanies him to the door when he goes. The conversation usually turns on the artistic and literary life of the day and politics are also discussed. Many a serious man feels the need for forgetting the worries of the day in harmless conversation with his little friend. The girls are on the whole most discreet. It is part of their education never to speak with a man about another guest.

In the course of time such a relationship may also become more intimate. But such intimacy is by no means the most important factor. Even then the mutual relation retains its delicacy and is far removed from the brutalities associated with prostitution in Europe. The man has always to continue to woo for the girl's favour and if she grants it to her lover, the fiction of a prolonged or short marriage is always maintained. It is for instance absolutely impossible that a guest in a tea-house carries on even a purely friendly relationship with two girls, as such a proceeding would be an offence against good taste.

In one respect a remnant of liberty is left to the poor little girls, in spite of the unhappy fate which falls to their lot. They are usually very young when they enter a tea-house and frequently spend many years which are devoted to the study of music and conversation with the guests. No young girl is compelled to sell her innocence. She gives herself to a man for the first time of her own free will. It has happened too that such delicate bands have proved themselves sufficiently strong to induce the lover to purchase the liberty of his beloved by payment of money and that he has made her his concubine or even his wife. Generally these girls are by no means the worst companions and they frequently make his life as peaceable and pleasant as possible owing to the gratitude and affection they feel for him as their deliverer. It can of course happen that one of these exquisite children develops into an intriguing female who is capable of bringing chaos into the whole family. There, as everywhere else, good and evil are found side by side.

Although these things are veiled by a certain poetry, which makes them appear to foreigners in a far more charming light than similar circumstances elsewhere, the lot of these tea-house girls is usually infinitely sad as the following story shows.

Little Siu Ying was the child of a simple merchant of Shanghai. She spent her innocent childhood in Honkew, the harbour quarter of the town. The hope of happiness and duty filled the child's dreams. A fortune-teller had once prophesied a fair future and said that her destiny would be no ordinary one. She would either be educated in a school or make a name for herself as an artist. Siu Ying was a shy, gentle child and played in the streets like other children. A small brother came into the world and she was entrusted with the care of this little squealing object. Life took a grave turn for her. The little brother was a tyrant and his sister had a hard time in looking after him and satisfying all his wants.

The father died suddenly just as she was beginning to mature from being a child into womanhood. It appeared that the father not only failed to leave an inheritance, but that his business owed considerable debts. One day a lady friend came on a visit, she looked good-natured and kindly. She talked with the mother about little Siu Ying. Such girls had often made the fortune of the whole family. She promised to have the little girl educated as an artist and to take her with her to the capital. There she would earn a lot of money, so that she would be able to feed the whole family and in time she would no doubt be able to repay the debt of her dead father and thus cleanse his memory before the world. The kind lady was even prepared to pay a few hundred dollars at once.

Merely for the sake of form a contract was made: the girl was handed over to the kind lady as a pledge for the borrowed money which was to bear interest at four per cent. per month and the little girl was to be free as soon as capital and interest were repaid.

Siu Ying was in the seventh heaven when she heard of the journey and all the golden things at the other end. Beautiful silk clothes were bought for her and she looked very pretty in them in the mirror. Before long, the journey started over the sea to Peking. Her mother gave her a ring of green chrysoprase when she said farewell. The girl took the little brother with her to relieve the mother of her anxiety for his education. Another aunt who had also lent a little money went with her. The first aunt had a small daughter and so there was quite a family, when, filled with high hope, she waved good-bye to her mother.

She had said good-bye to youth and happiness. A small dark room was rented in Peking and a place was reserved for her in a first-class tea-house. The furnishing of the room cost another few hundred dollars. A teacher was engaged to teach the little Siu Ying the rudiments of singing. She had to learn a great number of songs by heart and to sing them mechanically to the accompaniment of the shrill tones of the violin of the teacher. Another master gave her and her brother lessons in reading and writing and all these tasks meant wearisome and hard labour. It was not singing like the free and happy song of the birds. It was a tortured imitation of notes played to her and her heart was not in her work. The writing too was very difficult for her little unpracticed fingers.

The best of it was the clothes. They were made after the latest fashion and she was pleased to look pretty when she made up her little face in front of the mirror. She had to entertain the guests and that was terrible. On one or two occasions a few young men had chosen her for fun as hostess. They said such strange things and looked at her in so strange a way. It was awful even when they laughed. She did not know what they wanted. She became frightened and more shy than ever, while at night she was homesick and cried bitterly.

It was hard for her. Owing to her shyness she had to be content with low earnings. Out of these she was expected to support all those people who had attached themselves to her, and, on top of that, she was to pay the interest on the advances which had been paid. She could not make enough money, and her debts, instead of being reduced continued to grow. . . .

Then a student came from the Yang Tse district. He seemed to care for her and was wretched when she did not return his love immediately. He swore that he would persuade his mother to let him marry her. Every day the aunt persuaded her more and more. Eventually she gave in. Then followed a few brief weeks of sweet love during which the girl matured into her full beauty and profundity of spirit. The student returned home and promised to write immediately.

He has never shown any signs of life.

Siu Ying awaited his return with anxiety. She felt something strange within her body. The aunt consoled her and said it was no doubt due to the spirits which sometimes torture girls. She told her that perhaps she would bring forth a mouse and that would not be terrible. At the same time she gave her all sorts of medicines, but she did not bring a mouse into the world. Wherever she went people began to whisper and to giggle. Several of her friends laughed spitefully at the misfortune that had befallen her; others were sorry for her, but no one could help her. She had to disappear out of the tea-house and hide somewhere. Whatever may have become of her?

In this way tragic events take place behind the bright exterior of the festive illuminations in the eight alleys in which night after night the motors throng and distinguished guests visit the little girls in the tea-houses.

94
UNLAWFUL PLEASURES
Marco Polo
c. 1300

During his travels, Marco Polo visited the east coasts ports of Ningbo and Hangzhou, but spent most of his time in Beijing. The following passage describes a range of women.

There are within the city ten principal squares or marketplaces, besides which, numberless shops run along the streets. . . . In the several streets connected with the squares are numerous baths, attended by servants of both sexes, to perform the ablutions for the male and female visitors, who from their childhood are accustomed to bathe in cold water, as being highly conducive to health. . . . All are in the daily habit of washing their persons, especially before meals.

In the streets reside the females of bad character, who are extremely numerous; and not only in the streets near the squares, which are specially appropriated to them, but in every other quarter they appear, highly dressed out and perfumed, in well furnished houses, and with a train of domestics. They are perfectly trained in all the arts of seduction, which they can adapt to persons of every description: so that strangers who have once yielded to their fascination are said to be like men bewitched, and can never get rid of the impression. Intoxicated with these unlawful pleasures, even after returning home, they always long to revisit the place where they were seduced. . . .

In their domestic relations, they (citizens) show no jealousy or suspicion of their wives, but treat them with great respect. Any one would be held as infamous that should address indecent expressions to married women.

95
HARD AND TIRESOME WORK
Arthur H. Smith
1899

The American missionary Reverend Arthur Smith explains how very hard country women worked.

The severe labour entailed upon Chinese women in the drudgery of caring for large families, assisting in gathering the crops, and other outside toils, and the great drafts made upon their physical vitality by bearing and nursing so many children, amply suffice to account for the nearly universally observed fact that these women grow old rapidly. A Chinese bride, handsome at the age of eighteen, will be faded at thirty, and at fifty wrinkled and ugly.

It has been already remarked that the life of the Chinese village woman is an apt illustration of the inherent impossibility that woman's work should ever be *done*. Before her own children have ceased to be a constant care by day and by night, grandchildren have not improbably made their appearance, giving the grandmother little peace or rest. The mere preparation of the food for so many in the single kettle which must serve for everything, is a heavy task incessantly repeated. All articles of apparel, including shoes, are literally manufactured or done by hand, and so likewise is the supply of bedding or wadded quilts which like the wadded garments must be ripped open from time to time, cleaned and renewed. Women and girls take their share of watching the orchards and the melon patches, etc., by day, and sometimes by night as well. When the wheat harvest comes on, all the available women of the family are helping to gather it, and in the autumn harvest likewise every threshing-floor abounds with them, and their countless children. In cotton growing districts the women and girls are busy a large part of the time in the fields, and often earn the

HARD AND TIRESOME WORK

only pin-money which they ever see by picking cotton for others.

The preparation of this indispensable staple for use occupies the hands of millions of Chinese women, from its collection in the field—a most laborious work since the plant grows so low—to its appearance as garments, and its final disappearance as flat padding to be used in shoe-soles. The ginning, the 'scutching' or separation of fibres, the spinning, the cording, the winding and starching, and especially the weaving are all hard and tiresome work, and that too without end in sight while life lasts. In some regions every family owns a loom (one of the clumsy machines exiled from the West a century ago) and it is not uncommon for the members of a family to take turns, the husband weaving until midnight, when the wife takes up the task till daylight, (often in cellars two-thirds underground, damp, unventilated, and unwholesome). Even so it is frequently difficult to keep the wolf away from the door. Within the past few years the competition of machine twisted cotton yarns is severely felt in the cotton regions of China, and many who just managed to exist in former days are now perpetually on the edge of starvation. This is the 'seamy side' of 'progress.'

96
NEW YEAR FUN
Arthur H. Smith
1899

Chinese New Year is the most important annual celebration in China. Here women are observed doing something other than work with their busy hands.

But the remarkable thing is that at New Year's time all restrictions seem to be removed, and both men and women give themselves up to the absorbing excitement of cards, dominoes, etc., with money stakes of varying amount, and with no fear or even thought of future evil harvests. In the abstract, gambling is of course recognized as wrong and not to be indulged, as likely to lead to trouble. But at New Year's time 'everybody does it'.

Old women and young women squatted on their mats or their *k'angs* feverishly shuffle their cards and pay their little stakes, and all are having a good time.

97
POLICEWOMEN
Hiram Parkes Wilkinson
1882

In this passage, one alternative to the traditional forms of women's work is suggested.

In this inn-yard I saw two women police. The Chinese have at all their magistrates' offices women who assist in the duties of the court. In rural districts they have women who are entrusted with the duty of helping to keep the peace, and who have a right to interfere in the cause of justice. Western lands have thought of many places that women might fill to advantage. Has any one suggested women police? These 'Ya-Men' women are easily known. They are generally in the prime of life—from thirty-five to forty-five—usually of a tall and strong build, and very loud-voiced. When they come into an inn-yard they salute the landlord or the muleteers. They are women of good character, but their position is not envied. I should have said they are always widows, and are in this service with consent of the parents of their late husbands. Recognized by law, there are also lady doctors.

98
THE TICKET SELLER
Chinese Profiles
1980s

These are real-life conversations with a variety of ordinary Chinese people. The following piece contains a few inconsistencies, but this is the way our young lady talks, as she describes her job in Beijing.

I've been working for the bus company for more than a year now. My mother was a ticket seller too. She started working in 1958, during the Big Leap Forward. When she retired at the age of 50, I took over her job for her.

In general now, the bus company doesn't recruit new workers from the outside. That's one way of providing jobs for the children of the people who work for the bus company. My father was a bus driver. He was born in Beijing and never left.

My mother didn't like the idea of me working for the bus company, so when I graduated from senior middle school I signed up for the university entrance examinations. At that time there was a rumour going around that they were going to revise the policy about kids taking their parents' jobs, so I changed my mind and signed up for a job. In those days I wanted to study engineering. What did I want to be? I would have been happy with any kind of work. I probably wouldn't have got in. But still . . .

I started working for the bus company when I graduated from junior middle school. I've been here four years now. I started out on the Number One route, one of the busiest in the whole city. It stops at Xidan, Tiananmen Square, and Wangfujing. It's so crowded all the time you can hardly breathe. On that line we used to change shifts in the middle of the route, and those buses were always so packed that it was almost impossible to get on, not to mention get over to the ticket counter. When I got off work at eleven o'clock, my older brother and sister had to take turns coming to meet me, since the *hutong* [alley] we live in is in a pretty out-of-the-way place.

You can always tell who's copping a ride by just looking. When they get on the bus, they always head for the crowded places, and when they get off they try to get away quickly, or don't get off until you're just about to close the door and the bus is about to start. People from out of town are honest and buy their tickets, but there are some soldiers who don't, so you've got to say something to them. Maybe they do it because they don't have any money. Then there are all those young housekeeper types from Anhui who get on the bus and try to play dumb, and those guys who sell stuff in the free market. They're so cheap they'll do anything to save a few pennies. We can pick them out just by looking; never miss, you know.

I earn about seventy *yuan* a month. That includes my basic salary, bonus, and bathing and bicycle subsidies. I give it all to my mother, and ask her for money when I need it. But it's not enough for me. Who am I closest to? My mother and father, of course! At work? Well, there's this ticket seller in our bus crew.

I handle my own money. I manage to save about twenty *yuan* each month. Is that for my dowry? Are you kidding?

The best thing is to get a promotion and become a driver or a dispatcher. A lot of drivers start out as ticket sellers. Sometimes you can move up after a year, but sometimes you can go on selling tickets for years without getting promoted. How would I describe my ideal mate? I think I'm, too young . . .

I want to marry someone who I can look up to, someone who doesn't work for the bus company. I don't care if his job's worse than mine, but I really think he's got to be someone better than me. We can't help getting dirty. If you look at your shoulders after just one run, you'll see a layer of dust. There's no way we can take a bath at work. The hours at the bathhouse are the same as ours. By the time we get off work, they're all locked up. That's why they give us a five *yuan* fifty bathing subsidy.

Five fifty isn't even enough for one trip to the Silian Bath House and Beauty Parlour, but it's all right if you go to a cheaper place.

Getting a permanent's out of the question. You can't even use hair cream on this job. Otherwise you'd end up with your hair all dried out and full of dust. It's bad all year round. It's hot as hell in the summer. This bus's like an oven; and it gets worse when people start squeezing in next to each other. There's a ton of dust in the springtime, and you freeze to death in the winter. Aren't your feet cold? I bought this overcoat with my own money. The bus company gives out uniforms you can wear in spring and fall. There always seem to be a lot more people riding the buses in late spring and early summer. A lot of guys like to take their girlfriends for rides around the city then. They've got monthly passes.

Look how beautiful Beijing can be. It's a completely different scene every season. . . .

I've never made any friends on the bus. People get on, people get off. . . .

PART VIII

WIDOWS AND THE LATER YEARS

'The rouged beauty cannot regain the bloom of youth.'

CHINESE WOMEN

Girls became brides as teenagers in traditional China, and so widowhood could descend at an early age. During the Ming dynasty, the ideal was to commit suicide after the death of one's husband, but continued life was considered preferable by the early Qing. Even so, a widow was sometimes referred to as 'one who has not yet died'.

Monumental arches honouring chaste widows could be erected for women whose husbands' had died before their wives turned thirty and who remained single until they were fifty, and no longer considered marriageable. This custom began in the Yuan dynasty (1276–1368 AD).

When a woman reached the age of fifty (forty-nine by Western reckoning), her husband threw a banquet for her. She was often presented with a scroll containing a painting of Ma Gu, a Taoist goddess, portrayed with a deer for longevity and a pine tree representing immortality.

Older women who could afford the luxury of not working were able to explore their spiritual interests. Meat was considered polluting, and some women became vegetarians in a move toward spiritual purity. A few elderly women withdrew from family life altogether in their quest for Buddhist enlightenment and inner contentment.

Most convents in China served as refuges for women and places of prayer and spiritual exploration. Nuns often came from very poor families grateful to dispose of daughters, while others were abandoned female babies. Buddhist nuns severed family ties and often chanted sutras at funerals to support themselves.

In some provinces, 'irregular convents' existed which doubled as inns in which young nuns offered companionship and sexual favours in exchange for gifts and monetary contributions to the convent. After nuns turned thirty, they shaved their heads and concentrated on religion. Sometimes a new magistrate would restrict the activities of these convents—usually with temporary results.

99
HONG TAITAI

Cheng Naishan
1980s

Translated by Janice Wickeri

Cheng Naishan explores the effects of the Cultural Revolution on Shanghai capitalists and their families. Born in 1946 in Shanghai, she first taught English at a local middle school before publishing enough to become a full-time professional writer. 'Taitai' was the traditional bourgeoise name for 'Mrs' used before 1949, and denotes an old-fashioned, often lively, pre-Communist lady. Although it continues to be used in capitalist Hong Kong, in mainland China it is usually replaced with the person's full name and, if used, is considered quaint.

Everybody called her Hong Taitai. Fifty years ago that name was celebrated throughout Shanghai society. A party marking a baby's first month of life, a wedding banquet or a birthday all fell short of perfection if Hong Taitai was not in attendance. There was a period after 1949 when the words 'Hong Taitai' seemed redolent of mothballs, as if they had been shaken from a camphorwood chest. But within the circle of the few rich families in Shanghai, for example, they still carried a good deal of weight right up until the 'great proletarian cultural revolution' of the 1960s. In Shanghai, one had one's own little circle of happiness. And no matter how the storms raged outside, as long as one had three meals a day and stuck to one's own affairs, and thanks to the government policy of buying out the bourgeoisie, one could rest assured of eating at the Park Hotel today, the 'Maison Rouge' or Jade Buddha Temple tomorrow. No one would interfere. It was a very active period for Hong Taitai. The managers of both the public and private sections of the big restaurants and hotels all knew her; she was a very warm person. If Hong Taitai came forward to do the honours for a banquet on some special occasion, it would be reasonably priced but ample. And the food would be something special, quite out of the ordinary.

My first impression of her dates from my tenth birthday.

I was the ninth child in the family, nicknamed 'Jiujiu', or 'Little Ninth'. My parents were in America. When they left they had been afraid that I was too small to make such a long trip and would be in the way. Then the situation had changed, unexpectedly and so greatly, and I was left behind in Shanghai for good to live with my eldest brother and his wife. My brother was 21 years older than I and often joked that he could have fathered a child my age. He did spoil me as if I were his own daughter. Fatherliness in an eldest brother has always been the Chinese way.

The day of my tenth birthday they did things up a bit on my account, though it was nothing more than noodles and a few dishes. In those days my brother and sister-in-law were rather careful of appearances. They couldn't have competed with Hong Taitai at any rate; she was the wife of a bourgeois. Brother and his wife, no matter what, were subject to their work units, and they had to be careful. So they did no more than invite the brothers and sisters still in Shanghai over for an ordinary family dinner.

We had just sat down—we hadn't even got around to pouring the wine—when there was a knock at the door, and a voice, vivacious and sweet, was heard, 'I've come to beg a bowl of birthday noodles.'

'It's Hong Taitai!' My sister-in-law gasped, startled, and pushing back her chair she fled into her room to change her dress.

'That's how thoughtful she is.' My brother hastened to open the door; sisters and sisters-in-law busied themselves getting an extra bowl and chopsticks, bustling and rushing about. Thinking back on it now, this Hong Taitai's entrance into my life was strangely like that of the domineering Wang Xifeng in *A Dream of Red Mansions*, who always announced her arrival on the scene with some arresting remark like: 'So sorry I'm late welcoming visitors from afar!' The exact words were different, but the effect was the same. Her voice was so confident and hearty; she had an air of being completely at home.

'Hong Taitai!' The family stood to greet her.

HONG TAITAI

'Ah, I made it on time,' Hong Taitai said, removing her white kid gloves. She wore a square of checked wool on her head, the ends so long they fluttered with her every movement, adding immensely to her charm. When she took off her full-length cashmere coat, she was wearing a claret-coloured *qipao* [traditional dress] underneath, a phoenix embroidered in gold thread down the front, dazzling in its brilliance. In the 1950s such elegance had become a rare sight for anyone, let alone a child such as myself who had as yet seen nothing of the world. This sudden manifestation of such a gorgeously dressed beauty took my breath away.

She sat down next to me and pressed a red envelope into my hand. There was a shining golden character glued to the envelope—longevity—but because it was in the traditional, complicated form, it took me a moment to recognize it. At that time such red envelopes, used for giving presents of money to children on special occasions, were no longer on sale. Hong Taitai said she had glued it together herself of red paper; the character was also her own handiwork.

'Hong Taitai, really, you shouldn't put yourself out of pocket over Jiujiu's birthday. She's a child.' My sister-in-law had changed and come back out, and though she was much younger than Hong Taitai, she looked faded beside her. The only thing one noticed in that whole room was that brilliant combination of red and gold: dazzling, but pleasingly so!

'Mr Hong and I are old friends of your parents. I went to see Jiujiu at the hospital the day she was born. She was so alert and bright-eyed, such personality, not like most babies. When the nurse brought you in you were as pink as a glutinous rice dumpling.' She described it vividly, and I was enthralled.

'At first your parents planned to come for you after a while, but now look. . . . They must miss you terribly. I pity you that your mother isn't here. So though I pay no attention when one of your brothers or sisters has a birthday, Jiujiu is different; I have to come to celebrate your tenth birthday, to stand in for your mother and raise a glass to you, wishing you long life!' Her words warmed my heart.

After the meal, my brothers and sisters put on some music, *A Rose for You*, a Xinjiang folk song quite popular at the time, and the brothers and brothers-in-law all surged toward Hong Taitai. But she frowned, and with a graceful flick of the hand in which she held a cigarette, said, 'Put on Bing Crosby. We old folks like the old songs.' When that bewitching voice was heard, she laid aside her cigarette and began, tripping lightly, to dance. As she danced, the side slits in that claret qipao rose and fell, now hiding, now revealing her graceful legs. I really hoped I might grow up a bit faster and be all that she was: full of life, charming, beautiful.

When all the guests had gone, I took out the red envelope she had given me and counted: forty yuan! Forty yuan in those days!

'A grand gesture. Mr Hong is the only one who could afford her,' Sister-in-law said, pouting her lower lip. 'What a memory she has. How could she remember Jiujiu's birthday, let alone that it was her tenth!'

'That's her stock-in-trade.' Having said that, brother added sympathetically, 'Her lot is a hard one, too. If she'd been born into a good family and got an education, she'd certainly have done well, an intelligent person like that.'

Only later did I find out that Mr Hong was in the raw silk business and when Mrs Hong took up with him, he was already quite successful. He had a wife and family, but he rented a small house in the western district of Shanghai and lived there with Hong Taitai. She it was he took everywhere with him, thus in everybody's mind, she was 'Hong Taitai'. But there was talk, both out in the open and on the sly, some of it not very complimentary. As for the true facts of Hong Taitai's background, no one was able to find out. Even the Hongs' housemaid, Aju, knew only that one night, carrying a white leather bag, she had arrived with Mr Hong and had been there ever since. It was said that Hong Taitai was a good cook, and Mr Hong had grown pink and stout under her care. Almost overnight she became well known; Mei Lanfang [an opera singer] and Zhou Xuan [a film star] both were guests in the Hong family parlour. For a time, the house was filled with important guests every day. It seemed that this Hong Taitai had 'arrived' in society the same way—a white leather bag in hand. And with her arrival, Mr Hong's business expanded.

My second meeting with Hong Taitai occurred while I was in senior middle school, at Mr Hong's memorial service. Elder Brother was the natural representative of our family and took me along on the strength of my having been the recipient of Mr Hong's forty-yuan birthday gift. The service was held at the International Funeral Home. There were leading comrades from both the Chinese

People's Political Consultative Conference and the Association of Industry and Commerce present. As we entered, I saw Hong Taitai dressed in a black taffeta *qipao* with close-fitting sleeves, wearing a pair of the black leather pointed-toe shoes that were extremely popular in the sixties. Though there were indications that she was putting on weight, her graceful waist made her appear as lovely as ever. She walked composedly among those who had come to pay their condolences, greeting those who ought to be greeted, nodding to those who needed nodding to. The grief weighing on her made her seem even more dignified and noble. On the hairnet holding the thick tresses was a spray of pure white orchids, giving her a very refined air. As soon as her glance fell on us, she hurried to greet us.

'Jiujiu, you've become a young lady.' Her gentle voice dispelled the dread I felt in this venue of eternal parting. 'You're the next generation. Wear a yellow flower [a symbol of mourning].' Her soft white hand fastened the yellow bloom to my blouse. She began to speak of all Mr Hong's good qualities, and as she spoke she grew sad and dabbed at the tears in the corners of her eyes with a linen handkerchief. By comparison with the main wife, weeping and wailing to one side, she appeared to be more highly bred, more worthy of the title Mrs. Yet in the end it was mere similitude, for when the formalities began, she conscientiously peeled off to one side, a mourner who knew her place.

'Hong Taitai will suffer now! This is really difficult for her!' The other mourners commented surreptitiously among themselves.

'Yes, Mr Hong was a man among men. But was he willing to entrust the family property to Hong Taitai? Naturally, it was safer with his wife. With him gone, Hong Taitai is left with nothing, not even a last word. It's hard for her.'

Hearing such talk, looking at the lovely black-garbed Hong Taitai, I thought of Chen Bailu in Cao Yu's play *Sunrise*.

Once Mr Hong died, we saw little of Hong Taitai. In the adults' eyes, she was, after all, a woman of uncertain past!

In a twinkling, I was twenty years old. The celebration was still a family affair. Recalling the gaiety of ten years ago, I couldn't help thinking of Hong Taitai. I accused Elder Brother of being a snob, but he said I was naive. As we locked horns, there was a soft knocking at the door. It was Hong Taitai's maid, Aju, a woman about thirty years old from Shaoxing. She was carrying a red-lacquered tray, which held a specially prepared duck. Attached to the duck was a glittering gold *shou* character—longevity—exactly like the one I had received ten years before.

'Hong Taitai's indisposed, so she sent me to convey her best wishes to Jiujiu. She prepared the duck herself,' Aju rattled off as instructed. One could see she had learned it off by heart before she came. Everyone asked after Hong Taitai, and Aju stammered, 'The house has been let out. Hong Taitai has a second-floor room with a balcony and a room on the first floor for me and the kitchen. It's enough for the two of us; it's fine, just fine. Goodbye now.' With that she made her escape.

Everybody began to inspect the duck. It lacked nothing in appearance, fragrance or flavour. It was then the three hard years of natural calamities. A duck such as this one would cost at least ten yuan on the black market. At the same time that we were saying what a crime it was to eat Hong Taitai's food, we were all scrutinizing the duck. It was lean. It was quite possible that it was one Aju had stood in line all night to buy, in which case it wouldn't have cost much more than two yuan. Since it had been personally cooked and sent over specially, it seemed to be worth much more than that. But the gift was small after all, so she didn't appear in person. 'She's a very capable woman!' everyone agreed.

Not long after, the tempest [cultural revolution] blew up in 1966, and people could hardly fend for themselves, much less worry about Hong Taitai.

Two years passed, and things became relatively quiet. I happened to be walking by Hong Taitai's one day, and looking up at her balcony without thinking, I suddenly discovered the old familiar curtain fabric. Spurred by this, I headed upstairs. A young man wearing a work overall with 'work safely' printed on it barred my way and asked in a rough manner, 'Who are you? Who are you looking for?' 'I'm looking for Hong Taitai,' I stammered out. I regretted that as soon as it was out. To call someone 'taitai' in those days was to invite criticism.

Unexpectedly, he sang out, 'Hong Taitai, someone to see you,' and led me upstairs.

'Jiujiu!' Hong Taitai welcomed me with surprise and pleasure and wiped away tears, moved. How rare in those days, a genuine sigh and embrace. I leaned against her bosom and cried.

The room was still furnished with French-style furniture. The mirror was covered with pictures of leaders, the best method of protecting mirrors in those days. Aju brought tea, and I had just said, 'Thank you, Aju,' when Hong Taitai corrected me softly, 'Call her Sister Aju. I've adopted her.' That guy on the stairs was Aju's husband.

Hong Taitai was wearing a blue Chinese-style cotton jacket. With her hair cut short, in revolutionary fashion, she looked much like someone who would be principal of an elementary school.

'Thanks to their moving in with me, no one dares bother me. The house was ransacked till there was not even one yuan left and I was half-dead myself. As I was crying over it, Aju came and said we should bring her man to live with us; he was a worker and no one would dare bully me then. I said I didn't want to involve them in my troubles, but she said, 'Anyway I'm a servant. Even if worst came to worst I'd still be a servant. I'm not afraid.' I'm so grateful to Aju and her family!'

'Hong Taitai,' Sister Aju cut her short, embarrassed.

'I've told you before, don't call me Hong Taitai. Call me mother.'

'Ah,' Aju laughed ingenuously. 'I can't do it. I'm not used to it.'

'I get only 18 yuan a month for living expenses, so I have to depend on the two of them to take care of me, and they have two children of their own.' Hong Taitai sighed deeply. 'Ai, how could I have come to this! If I had only gone out to work earlier on, I wouldn't have got into this predicament, no income all!'

Hong Taitai kept me on to dinner. She hadn't been able to break that habit. With Aju, her husband and their two lovely, innocent daughters, plus Hong Taitai and myself, there were six gathered round the square table. It was a home-style meal of two dishes and a soup with an additional plate of scrambled eggs in my honour. The bluish glow of the eight-watt fluorescent tube shone gently on us. Hong Taitai now and again put some food into the children's bowls with her chopsticks, very grandmotherly. I thought I heard them call her 'Nanna', and I found it very strange.

'They mean mother's mother,' Hong Taitai explained. 'I like them to call me that.' The children, seeing their opportunity, purposely raised a chorus of 'Nanna', and Hong Taitai beamed. I sensed that she had never before laughed so contentedly. Her son-in-law stolidly scooped in his food without saying a word. But when I was taking my leave he dashed ahead turning on the stairway lights all the way down. 'My son-in-law hasn't any education; he's a bit rough, but he's a very good man,' Hong Taitai told me softly. 'There's no need to be afraid of him.'

When I got back and told my brother and sister-in-law what had happened, they expressed great admiration for Hong Taitai. 'That Hong Taitai, she can take the bad with the good. What an incredibly capable woman!'

Later I got married. Tied down to housework and child, I hardly made the effort to see my brother and sister-in-law, let alone Hong Taitai.

In 1982, my parents made their first visit back to Shanghai from the US. All the old friends gathered, and of course Hong Taitai was invited as well. During the 'cultural revolution' many of them had lost touch with each other, and they were glad to renew relationships, but though it grew quite late, Hong Taitai still didn't appear.

'Where's Hong Taitai? We're waiting for her reappearance in society.'

'Ah, didn't you know, she's a famous slowpoke.'

Just as we were really growing anxious, she arrived, accompanied by Aju. She was wearing a downy mohair coat over a close-fitting black satin jacket, and though her hair was raven black, you could tell it had been dyed. Yes, she had aged some, but she was as graceful and refined as ever. The company rose to greet her, but she pushed Aju forward, 'My adopted daughter.'

When it came time to eat, no place had been set for Aju.

'Aju, go out and have a bowl of noodles and come back for Hong Taitai in two hours,' we suggested.

'Just squeeze together a bit,' said Hong Taitai, pulling Aju to the table and asked the waiter to bring another bowl and chopsticks. The others were rather startled; the atmosphere grew somewhat embarrassed. Though society as a whole had changed, such circles still clung to iron-clad rules. Before all the hot dishes had been served, Hong Taitai got up to leave, saying she had something to do.

The gathering fell to discussing her.

'How could she take a servant into the family? She must be crazy!'

'Well, it's not so surprising. Her own background is more or less the same.'

'That's what happens when one lives with servants. You become petty and overlook etiquette.'

These dreadful comments, served up with the food and drink, dropped airily from their mouths. I hastily gathered up my child and left.

HONG TAITAI

A few days ago, a woman friend of mine moved by chance to a place in Hong Taitai's lane, and I dropped by to see her, since I was in the neighbourhood.

She welcomed me happily, 'Jiujiu's come!' Her silver hair made her look kinder than ever. She said she no longer dyed it. 'I'm getting old, and it doesn't turn out well anymore,' she said, patting her hair. Sister Aju politely brought tea and sweets for me.

'Jiujiu thinks of me. Of the old crowd, you're the only one who thinks of coming to see me. How big is your son now?'

'Ten.' As I said it, I remembered my own tenth birthday and told her how struck I had been by her beauty.

She smiled wanly. 'That's past.'

She told me that in the beginning a few old friends still came to see her. Now everything was back to normal after the 'cultural revolution'. There were even mahjong parties and dancing, but she was done with it all, because her stiff old legs couldn't manage it now.

'Actually it's all a waste of money and time. Aju is so busy. I can't do much to help her, but I can knit a few sweaters, to thank her for being so good to me. They're extremely frugal themselves, but they know my delicate appetite, and there's always one dish especially for me at each meal. There aren't many daughters—even natural-born ones—like that.' She touched my sleeve, speaking emotionally, while her hands never ceased their work on the small sweater she was knitting.

'Mother Hong, what are you making?' A passing neighbour stopped in.

'My granddaughter's having her baby any day now. I'm knitting it a little sweater.'

'Well! The fourth generation! You're very lucky, Mother Hong!'

'Yes, I am,' Hong Taitai replied contentedly, and she smiled.

100
LI QINGZHAO
To the Tune of
'A Lonely Flute on the Phoenix Terrace'
Twelfth century

Li Qingzhao (Li Ch'ing Chao),1083–1149, remains China's most renowned poet. Educated by her scholar parents, she continued her intellectual activities with her husband, writing a history and preserving manuscripts. Best known for her ci (poems to set tunes with fixed tonal and rhyme patterns), her verses range from rousing and patriotic to longing and amorous. Many of her poems are titled only by the name of the familiar tune to which they are sung.

LI QINGZHAO

I let the incense grow cold
In the burner. My brocade
Bed covers are tumbled as
The waves of the sea. Idle
Since I got up, I neglect
My hair. My toilet table
Is unopened. I leave the
Curtains down until the sun shines
Over the curtain rings.
This separation prostrates me.
The distance terrifies me.
I long to talk to him once more.
Down the years there will be only
Silence between us forever now.
I am emaciated, but
Not with sickness, not with wine,
Not with Autumn.
It is all over now forever.
I sing over and over
The song, 'Goodbye Forever.'
I keep forgetting the words.
My mind is far off in Wu Ling.
My body is a prisoner
In this room above the misty
River, the jade green river,
That is the only companion
Of my endless days. I stare
Down the river, far off, into
The distance. I stare far away.
My eyes find only my own sorrow.

101
THE GREATEST HONOUR
George Morrison
1895

In addition to the multitude of difficulties facing women, the highest honour a woman could garner was a refusal to live after the death of her husband.

Fu-to-kuan four miles from Chungking is a powerful hill-fort that guards the isthmus where the Yangtse and the Little River come nearly together before encircling Chungking. Set in the face of the cliff is a gigantic image of Buddha. Massive stone portals, elaborately carved, and huge commemorative tablets cut from single blocks of stone and deeply engraved, here adorn the highway. The archways have been erected by command of the Emperor, but at the expense of their relatives, to the memory of virtuous widows who have refused to remarry, or who have sacrificed their lives on the death of their husbands. Happy are those whose names are thus recorded, for not only do they obtain ten thousand merits in heaven, as well as the Imperial recognition of the Son of Heaven on earth; but as an additional reward their souls may, on entering the world a second time, enjoy the indescribable felicity of inhabiting the bodies of men.

Cases where the widow has thus brought honour to the family are constantly recorded in the pages of the *Peking Gazette*. One of more than usual merit is described in the *Peking Gazette* of June 10th, 1892. The story runs: —

'The Governor of Shansi narrates the story of a virtuous wife who destroyed herself after the death of her husband. The lady was a native of T'ienmen, in Hupeh, and both her father and grandfather were officials who attained the rank of Taotai. When she was little more than ten years old her mother fell ill. The child cut flesh from her body and mixed it with the medicines and thus

THE GREATEST HONOUR

An arch to honour a virtuous widow

cured her parent. The year before last she was married to an expectant magistrate. Last autumn, just after he had obtained an appointment, he was taken violently ill. She mixed her flesh with the medicine but it was in vain, and he died shortly afterwards. Overcome with grief, and without parents or children to demand her care, she determined that she would not live. Only waiting till she had completed the arrangements for her husband's interment, she swallowed gold and powder of lead. She handed her trousseau to her relatives to defray her funeral expenses, and made presents to the younger members of the family and the servants, after which, draped in her state robes, she sat waiting her end. The poison began to work and soon all was over.

102
THE AUTUMN FAN
The Lady Pan
First century BC

Romantic poems penned in elegant calligraphy on fans were one of the few ways the rare literate lady could express herself. Herbert Giles translated this ancient work.

O fair white silk, fresh from the weaver's loom,
   Clear as the frost, bright as the winter snow—
   See! friendship fashions out of thee a fan,
Round as the round moon shines in heaven above;
At home, abroad, a close companion thou,
Stirring at every move the grateful gale;
And yet I fear, ah me! that autumn chills,
Cooling the dying summer's torrid rage,
Will see thee laid neglected on the shelf,
All thought of by-gone days, like them by-gone.

103
THE MANCHU LADY
Dorothea Hosie
c. 1912

The Revolution of 1911 toppled the weakened and corrupt Qing Dynasty, opening the way for the Republic of China and more democratic ideals. Since Lady Hosie lived with a Chinese family, she understood when a Western friend proposed sharing quarters with a Manchu lady who yearned for the Confucian values of the hierarchical empire.

It is now some years since the Revolution and it would be perfectly safe today to seek a domicile in the Imperial City, for the great Manchu walls, so forbidding and such a formidable barrier to us, have been pierced with numerous archways. Those gates, which we feared on the night of our flight might be shut upon us, are left open now, unguarded day or night; and carriages, rickshaws, even motor-cars run in and out at will. But it has taken years to achieve this result; and what were we to do in the meanwhile?

Miss Bowden-Smith solved the problem for herself. She had a friend, who was also her teacher. A Manchu lady, not only noble in birth but in character, she was a woman of decision, unmarried, and with a remarkable record of devotion to filial duty to her father, now dead. A staunch Confucianist, she had started a school for girls where the only moral instruction given was the teaching of Confucius. Most pathetically, she bewailed the prevailing neglect of the Master which, she affirmed, was the sole cause of the present social unrest. China's only hope, to her mind, was to repent and return to the study of the Master's principles. She spent all her own means on her school. In her robe of blue cotton, clean, severe, straight to her feet, and with her austerity of life, early rising, simple diet, and unbending manners, she was a fitting exponent of the ideals of a past age.

This teacher acknowledged that there was scant chance of China turning back to Confucius, so far had the nation gone the primrose path to destruction. She tried to win back a portion that should be saved, by starting a Confucian tent at the annual fairs held outside Peking, though the noise of the cheapjacks and jugglers and the smell of cooked food were repugnant to her fastidious taste. Alas, her only visitors were kind-hearted foreign ladies from the crowded Mission tents next door and she knew it was only kindness that sent them—or pity. She believed, however, that one way was left for earnest Confucianists, men and women, to rouse the country to its parlous conditions. Her idea was that these should publicly announce their intentions and their reasons, and then, with equal publicity, commit suicide.

The teacher was but some five feet two in height, but her spirit was in inverse proportions to her size. One had only to look upon her worn, lined, dead-white face framed in its smooth black hair, her firm-set unsmiling mouth, and her dark tragic eyes, to know that she was capable of carrying out her premature demise with unswerving fidelity to every grim and forceful detail she had previously planned. She could point to precedent. Some five years earlier a mandarin's widow, driven by the manifest need for the education of Chinese girls, had been impelled to start a school. When those who could would not send their daughters, she gathered together orphans. A few friends helped her with a little money, but it was mainly her own she spent, till all her property was gone. She then sent a memorial to the magistrate begging help from the provincial treasury; but she received no satisfactory reply. Finally, she announced to the authorities that, unless funds were forthcoming by a given date, she should commit suicide as a protest against the neglect of girls' education by the State. She kept her word. She took a dose of opium, surrounded by her weeping orphans—history does not relate their subsequent fate. She sat herself in her sedan-chair and was carried through the streets in a dying condition. Her object was to expire on the magistrate's threshold, thereby causing him a vast amount of trouble, and thus taking the surest revenge on him. Not merely would Chinese law consider that he was responsible for her death, almost her murderer, but he would also have to pay her funeral expenses. Unfortunately, the lady died before the chair-bearers could reach the *yamen*. But her passionate sincerity was rumoured to have

THE MANCHU LADY

greatly affected the whole Court, when it came to their ears, and some of them have, from that hour, taken a certain interest in girls' education.

The Chinese are a logical race. When they see no reason to risk their lives, they decline to do so if they can possibly keep in safety. Once, however, show them a good and sufficient reason, and they will treat Brother Death with as little concern as the fearless of other nations. The only difference lies in the reasons and the purposes.

Now Miss Bowden-Smith loved this lonely unhappy Manchu woman. She, too, was an earnest, if less enthusiastic, student of Confucius, so much so that, in jest, we called her Confucia. Their tastes were similar, for they were both something of ascetics. She was determined that, if she could prevent it, her teacher should not fulfil her desperate intentions. So she informed us one evening that she would no longer be a mere cumberer of the ground, a useless refugee, she had asked the teacher to receive her into her establishment, and the teacher was willing. From her house she could visit such pupils of ours as remained, now all outside, whom she and I shared between us and taught, hoping for better days soon.

She left us, armed with a sheaf of very cogent and patriotic reasons with which to argue with her hostess. It is certainly true that Confucius did not commit suicide, although he lived in times of great misrule. We were relieved to hear, from time to time, that the teacher had agreed to postpone her demise, for we greatly admired the indomitable spirit of the heroic little woman. Finally, and, I believe, entirely by reason of my friend's representations, she promised to put off altogether her supreme sacrifice until there was another outrageous disturbance, like the last, which violated every principle of government as laid down by the Master. Mercifully for Miss Bowden-Smith's peace of mind, no more such outbreaks took place in the North of China during the first few years of the Republic; and the teacher lived some years longer, and saw her schoolgirls go out all the better for the example she daily set them of strict attention to duty and self-discipline.

104
ADOPT AN ELDERLY PRINCESS!
Julia Corner
1853

In certain circumstances, a Chinese might adopt an older relative or family friend who was usually childless. This would assure the elderly that someone would honour them and burn incense at their ancestral tablet at their death. There could also be financial advantages for the younger, adopting party.

In Europe we adopt children, in China the young often adopt old people and call them parents, or fathers and mothers, by adoption. Taou-kwang, on ascending the throne, had adopted as mother a widowed princess of the imperial lineage, and this lady he continued to respect, to love, and almost to idolise. His devoted unvarying affection to her is the best trait in his character, and the pleasantest part of his whole history. The old lady fell sick; he attended on her in person, as he had always done on the like occasions, for the long space of twenty-nine years. On the 19th of January the lady took an airing in the garden, and he rejoiced in the belief that she was convalescent; but only five days after her walk 'she mounted the fairy chariot, and went the long journey.'

The emperor himself drew up the official account of her death and his own great grief. 'We have been happy,' said the paper, 'in attending to her behests, as men are rejoiced by the sun which prolongs their lives; but we shall never see her again, we can never more look upon her affectionate countenance, and we are inconsolable! We received her last orders that mourning should be worn only twenty-seven days; but we cannot be satisfied with this, and therefore, as is right, we ourselves shall put on the filial garb for a hundred days, twenty-seven of which we shall pass in deep mourning. As she required that, since we are nearly seventy years old, we should not give way to deep grief, for the cares of government are heavy, we cannot presume to disobey her, and must endeavour to repress our feelings. Let daily libations be poured out before her in the palace of Contentment. We shall ourselves remain at the palace where her bier is placed, to sacrifice to her manes.' Divine honours were rendered to the old lady throughout the whole empire; and in every city of the empire tablets were erected to commemorate her superhuman virtues. Such is part of the idol-worship of the Chinese; one generation deifies the other.

Taou-kwang passed the twenty-seven days near the coffin, dressed in sackcloth, eating nothing but rice, drinking nothing but water, and sleeping near the remains of the dead on a very hard couch. This seems to have finished the poor old emperor, who died at the end of March or early in April, 1851, after a reign of thirty years.

105
MOURNING RITUALS
Eliza Bridgman
1853

Mourning customs in China differ in many ways from the West. Hired mourners are seen as a form of respect, while wailing is not seen as uninhibited emotion, but as a way to mark the event.

We have had several opportunities of witnessing Chinese funerals. The body of the deceased is dressed in the best suit of clothing, the same as in life, from the cap down to the shoes.

Women have their hair attired and adorned with a profusion of ornaments, and in the wealthy class, the body is clothed in embroidered garments of rich material. . . .

A man never wears mourning for his wife, he would be laughed at by his friends. When a person is known to be dying, the relatives gather around the bed, and call upon the spirit to come back; and the utmost confusion and disorder prevails. When the person expires, these cries cease, and they go laughing and talking about their ordinary employments. Daily, at stated hours, women go into the room where the corpse lies, and wail perhaps half an hour. This continues until after the interment, when at the usual periods, they visit the graves, and weep and offer sacrifices.

One day, passing through a burying-ground near us, where a great proportion of the coffins are above ground, a woman was heard weeping and wailing very loud. Attracted by my appearance, she at once ceased crying, without the least difficulty, and she gratified her curiosity by gazing at the foreign lady, while the tears were still standing on her cheeks. She was asked for whom she was mourning? She said her child. 'How long since the death?' 'Three years.' Passing on, she commenced again, her wailings being heard some distance. She was in a sitting posture, and moved her body backwards and forwards, stopping at pleasure if anything attracted her notice.

PART IX

DRAGON LADIES AND COURT LIFE

'It takes many men to build an empire, but a single woman can tear it down.'

The proverb on the previous page refers to Yang Kuei-fei, China's most famous courtesan who lived during the Tang dynasty. Although women usually achieved power through their men, during the Tang dynasty they were allowed greater freedom and power in their own right. A new teenage concubine, such as Wu Zetian could eventually become Empress through beauty, luck, and ruthlessness. Consequently, not only did Empress Wu dominate, but the two weakling emperors to succeed her yielded to the rule of their wives.

The Empress Dowager Cixi was the last Qing empress and a formidable 'dragon lady'. She also entered the palace as a concubine, but through cunning and determination rose to power as the domineering mother of the young emperor. She was quick to eliminate those who opposed her, but, despite her despotic nature, she was enlightened enough to pass an anti-foot-binding edict in 1902 after pleas from ladies of many nationalities.

For the other ladies of the court, life could be far from glamorous. They had first been inspected by officials on the autumn tour for qualities of perfection. Those ranking highest joined the palace ladies, usually for a period of ten years, commencing when they were between eleven and eighteen. Upon the death of the emperor, his numerous concubines and empresses were expected to enter a convent and pass the rest of their days as nuns.

106
CHINA'S MOST FAMOUS COURTESAN
Shu Qiong
1924

Shu Qiong specialized in writing vivid romantic biographies, such as this one about the eighth-century beauty, Yang Guifei (Yang Kuei-fei). At that time, political disturbances increased and a former official, An Lushan, a lover of Yang Guifei, tried to usurp the throne. Loyal officals declared that only the death of Yang Guifei could save the Emperor and his regime.

Yang Kuei-fei lived in the time of the Tang dynasty (AD 618–907), and for over twenty years was undisputed mistress of the imperial court. Her beauty was said to be unsurpassed, her vivacity unrivalled, and her talents as a musician, singer and dancer were unexcelled. It must be remembered that the accomplishments of a lady in those days were many and complex. Every girl aspiring to shine in society must learn to sing, dance, play music, compose poetry, write a good hand and converse elegantly. Entrance into court meant not only personal power, but also riches for the family.... At the age of sixteen, Kuei-fei had mastered the Five Classics and Chinese history. Her exceptional alertness and activity of mind, combined with her unusual skill and love of music, enabled her to excel all three of her sisters. She took special interest in singing and in playing musical instruments, as well as in the art of dancing. She was adept in the composition of verses. Thus, she was well prepared for any high position which the future might have in store for her.

In AD 735, the Emperor Ming Huang wanted to select a wife for his younger (eighteenth) son, Prince Shou. Kuei-fei's uncle heard the news and used every means, through the influence of a brother official, to spread the fame of her attractions, so that she might be chosen for the exalted position. This was accomplished, much to the delight of the family. Kuei-fei was sixteen when she entered the palace. Her enchanting beauty fascinated the young prince. She proceeded at once to establish herself firmly in the good graces of her husband. By virtue of her charm, she soon became his favourite, and he wrote many poems in praise of her. Notwithstanding all the splendour of court life, Kuei-fei was somehow not perfectly contented with her surroundings, for Prince Shou, though young and handsome, was not in the line of direct succession to the throne. Besides, our ambitious lady desired her name to be recorded in history as one of this world's greatest personages. . . .

She eventually became the favourite of the emperor, Ming Huang.

Soon after their return from Hua-ching Palace, the imperial residence was completely re-decorated. Hundreds of beautiful embroidered garments were made for Kuei-fei by the court ladies. Presents of every description from the imperial clans, as well as from distant and near officials, poured into the court to celebrate her birthday. Sumptuous theatricals and feastings were held in her honour for several days, the best musicians in the capital were engaged, and promotions were conferred upon many dignitaries. Kuei-fei requested the musicians to play a song entitled, 'The Rainbow Skirt and Feather Jacket,' which she had composed herself. She often put on rainbow-coloured garments and danced with the lightness and grace of a fairy during the banquets. In the eyes of the princes, princesses, and other courtiers her many accomplishments were unrivalled. The court had never seen Kuei-fei dance more charmingly. Her speciality on this occasion was the mounting of a round table on which she skilfully performed a classic turn comparable to the Bacchanalian dance of ancient Europe. Her wonderful skill and art so fascinated the emperor that he classed her among the immortal fairies. In his absorbed and besotted mind, no being, human or spiritual, could approach his heart's love in such grace and perfection. So devoted was His Majesty that he ever wished her to appear alongside of him in the imperial chariot. Sometimes she would ride on horseback, with the chief eunuch and maids supporting her, and the emperor riding by her side. Hundreds of court ladies waited eagerly to pay their daily homage to the august sovereign and his favourite. His Majesty enjoyed himself in the society of these ladies, drinking with them, listening to their music,

Yang Guifei prepares for her bath

or strolling with them through the beautiful gardens. He was in favour of continuing the daily feastings and theatricals at all costs. Kuei-fei and her three sisters were thus led into paths of unheard-of extravagances and sensual dissipation. They were daily wafted to ecstasy and transported with joy over the wine-cups of the banquet-hall. Alas, the whole country was burning, but the sovereign not only fiddled, but danced to his own obscene music! While province after province passed through fire and sword to uphold the sway of the falling ruler, he was still thoughtlessly busying himself with new amusements for his countless maidens, or joining his evil genius, the notorious Yang Kuo-chung, in unspeakable orgies and debauchery. The pleasure-loving sovereign remained in blissful ignorance of his country's impending disaster, dwelling contentedly in a court riddled with corruption and fast living.

It was the summer of the year AD 756. The air was unusually dry and sultry. Before the break of dawn, the noise of the frightened masses could be heard in the distance, some in faint, prolonged cries, others in sharp, shrieking notes. The dew was still thick, the dragon robe was soaked, the whole nation's fate rested upon the shoulders of the Son of Heaven. The bodies of the dead littered the roadside and floated on ponds. Men, women, and helpless children huddled together in the streets. Thousands of innocent people, old and young alike, were slain. On reaching a large temple at Ma-wei, the soldiers forming the Emperor's escort mutinied, and killed Yang Kuo-chung, the unpopular minister, as well as Kuei-fei's sisters. On hearing this, the distressed monarch approached the front gate and entreated his soldiers to obey orders and protect his sacred person. The mutineers, however, refused to advance against the enemy and presented a counter-demand, namely, the life of Kuei-fei. 'We are not afraid to die,' they clamoured, 'but we must first kill the hated woman, for she is entirely responsible for this calamity to our nation.'

When he heard these words, the emperor was terrified. His face turned pale and he said in a tremulous voice, 'But Kuei-fei only lived in the Forbidden City and never meddled with state affairs.' The general-in-charge, Chen Hsuan-li, and the head eunuch then prostrated themselves in front of him and in tears cried: 'Your Majesty, this is true, but the situation is helpless. Unless the life of your beloved consort is sacrificed, even the safety of your precious person may not be guaranteed.' The sovereign, realizing now that no power on earth could save Kuei-fei, experienced the most agonizing grief. He lingered for a long while, uncertain what step to take, for he had not the heart to enter the inner court. Seeing his indecision, the chief eunuch again fell upon his knees and beseeched the distracted monarch not to hesitate further. Roused as if from a trance, Ming Huang at last dragged his tired limbs into the inner chamber and for a moment disappeared from the view of the soldiers. Then, leading the trembling Kuei-fei out by the hand, he exclaimed passionately: 'My dearest, I cannot believe that the hour has come when I must perforce leave you for ever and suffer you to perish in this wise. Oh, why has Heaven deserted us so cruelly?'

With dishevelled hair and torn and soiled garments, Kuei-fei knelt down and wept. 'Your humble wife has indeed sinned,' she said. 'To suffer death is no regret. I beseech Your Majesty to take care of yourself. But first allow me to pray to my god Buddha before meeting the fate in store for me.'

To this the emperor replied: 'Oh, I beseech Heaven that my dearly beloved be re-incarnated on the lotus throne.'

He then commanded Kao Li-shih to minister carefully to her needs until the end. Next, he covered his face with the wide sleeves of his yellow imperial robe, and, as he turned back, experienced the utmost despair, feeling as if the whole world had deserted him.

Kuei-fei herself entertained a sense of being cruelly wronged. She was thirsting for some deeper draught of life than had yet befallen her lot. By the tragic irony of fate, she had thus been obliged to face premature death instead. Aloud she cried in lamentation:

'The flowers are withered, the rain is falling,

The bright moon is hidden behind the clouds;

For we who are one in soul are to be separated;

I recall with agonizing memory our vows at the Hall of Immortality.'

107
THE EMPRESS WU
René Grousset
1953

Only a tiny number of women in China have ever had real power, but several of these have been formidable indeed. One, the empress, Wu Zetian (Wu Tse-t'ien), who lived during the Tang dynasty, ruled the country directly, rather than as regent to a child-emperor. Empress Wu combined brutality, murder, and diplomatic ingenuity with Buddhist devotion. Famous for eliminating her enemies and legions of their relatives to dampen revenge, she also decreed that Taoist and Confucian thought, as well as poetry, be required in compulsory examinations.

Wu Tse-t'ien was a former favourite of the emperor T'ai-tsung. She entered the imperial harem in 637, at the age of fourteen, and was outstanding for her wit and beauty. When the future Kao-tsung was still Crown prince, he had seen her among his father's flock of wives, and from that day had nursed a silent love for her. On T'ai-tsung's death his wives and concubines had to cut off their hair and enter a convent. As soon as the official period of mourning came to an end, the new Son of Heaven gave orders for the young woman to be brought out of retirement, and gave her back her position at court. But a secondary role was not enough for this ambitious concubine. According to her enemy the poet Lo Pin-wang, 'her eyebrows, arched like the antennae of a butterfly, would never consent to yield to other women. Hiding her face with her sleeve, she applied herself to slander. Her vixen charms had the power of bewitching her master.' She was prepared to commit any crime, however monstrous, in order to attain her ends. With her own hands she strangled the child she had borne to the emperor and caused the legitimate empress to be accused of the heinous crime.

The account of this drama in the T'ang annals is reminiscent of Tacitus, with an additional *mise en scène* of hypocritical politeness. After the birth of the child, a girl, the empress came to pay a visit to Wu Tse-t'ien. She caressed the infant, took it in her arms and congratulated the young mother. As soon as she had left, Wu Tse-t'ien suffocated the newborn child and replaced it in its cradle. The arrival of the emperor was announced. Wu Tse-t'ien received him, her face glowing with pleasure, and uncovered the cradle to show him his daughter. A horrid sight met his eyes; in the cradle lay the dead body of his child. Bursting into tears, Wu Tse-t'ien was careful not to bring any direct accusation against the woman whose ruin she was determined to bring about. Finally, when questioned, she contented herself with incriminating her attendants. As was to be expected, the latter, so as to divert suspicion from themselves, described the visit which the empress had made a few minutes earlier. The scene had been so cleverly contrived that Kao-tsung was convinced of the empress's guilt. She was degraded and Wu Tse-t'ien promoted to her place (655). Despite the opposition of his father's old comrades, the emperor fell completely under the control of his new consort. Like Agrippina in ancient Rome, she attended the deliberations of the council hidden behind a curtain. Since Kao-tsung continued to pay secret visits to the former empress, Wu Tse-t'ien gave orders for the unhappy woman to have her hands and feet cut off.

From 660 onwards it was Wu Tse-t'ien who directed the affairs of state in the name of the weak Kao-tsung. Through a system of informers which she had established, she was able with impunity to terrorize the court, giving full rein to her jealousy and vindictiveness, and to annihilate her enemies even when they happened to be members of the T'ang imperial family. After bringing about the destruction of the mandarins who opposed her, she forced their widows and daughters to become her slaves. The emperor, weak and helpless, realized the innocence of her victims but did not dare to take any action. It is said that remorse affected his health, but it is possible that his enfeeblement was assisted by the ministrations of his wife. The annalists relate that during the latter days of his life, 'his head swelled up and he became like a blind man. His doctor offered to tap the swollen part, but Wu Tse-t'ien cried out that to lay hands on the imperial face was a crime of *lèse-majesté* which was punishable by death. The doctor held to his opinion and punctured the swelling, whereupon the emperor's eyesight was greatly improved. . . . The empress, pretending that she was delighted, went to fetch a hundred pieces of silk, which she personally gave to the doctor. A month later, however, it was learned that the emperor had suddenly fallen ill and that he had died without witnesses' (December 27, 683). Acting in the name of her son, Wu Tse-t'ien remained absolute mistress of the empire for twenty-two years (683–705).

Despite her unscrupulous behaviour, Wu Tse-t'ien was a woman of superior ability, and more skilled than her unhappy husband in the management of affairs of state. The administrative machinery of the T'ang empire continued to function under her energetic guidance, despite the tragedies that were taking place in the seraglio; and the veteran soldiers almost everywhere held back the barbarians. It was under her government that in the Tarim Basin the Chinese recovered the 'Four Garrisons' of Kucha, Karashar, Kashgar, and Khotan (692). She was less successful in her relations with the Turks of Mongolia, and hardly a year passed without their making sudden raids and pillaging the frontier districts of Kansu, Shensi, Shansi, and Hopei. 'In those times', says the Turkish inscription of Kocho Tsaidam, 'we had so many victorious expeditions that our slaves became slave-owners themselves.'

In internal affairs Wu Tse-t'ien overcame all obstacles. Everyone gave way before the will of this indomitable woman. So great was her audacity that in 684 she went to the length of deposing her own son, the young emperor Chung-tsung, and had herself proclaimed 'emperor' in his place (690). The princes of the blood, ashamed of being ruled over by a former concubine and spurred into action by an appeal from the poet Lo Pin-wang, made an abortive attempt at revolt. Their revolt was put down and their severed heads were brought to the empress. Meanwhile Wu Tse-t'ien realized the necessity of conciliating the Turks of Mongolia so as to put an end to their raids and at the same time gain their support against her enemies. She sent an embassy to their kaghan Bekchor (Mo-chüeh) to ask for the hand of his daughter in marriage to her nephew. The Turk refused this offer with disdain. He did not intend to marry his daughter to the nephew of a usurper, but to the legitimate emperor whom the latter had set aside. Setting himself up as an arbiter between the factions at the imperial court, he declared himself the champion of legitimacy and threatened that, if the T'ang dynasty were not restored, he would come at the head of his hordes and effect the restoration himself. Wu Tse-t'ien was alarmed and formally recognized the rights of Chung-tsung, although in reality she continued as sole ruler herself.

Assured of her power, she satisfied her every whim. Although well on in years, she took a young monk as her favourite and arranged for him to be appointed abbot of one of the principal monasteries of Loyang, 'with leave to enter the palace at any hour of the day or night'. Moreover, quite apart from the personal attractions of her young chaplain, the old dowager was deeply interested in Buddhism. In the character of this extraordinary woman a strong feeling for religion was neighbour to all the impulses of cruelty and lechery and she had phases of manifesting the deepest devotion. Thus between 672 and 675 she ordered and superintended the sculpture of the famous rock Buddha of Lungmen with his entourage of bodhisattvas, monks and guardian kings. Such works, in which the idealism, and mysticism of former times was replaced by a startling realistic violence, doubtless throw some light on the type of Buddhism which was likely to appeal to Wu Tse-t'ien. They also bear witness to the special protection which the sovereign accorded to this faith. A noted recipient of this protection was the pilgrim Yi Ching, a monk from Hopei, who in 671 embarked for India by way of Sumatra. In 695, after twenty-four years in the sanctuaries of India and Outer India, he returned by the sea route, bringing back a large number of Sanskrit texts. On his arrival at Loyang, Wu Tse-t'ien went to meet him with an immense retinue; she accorded him every facility for the work of translation to which he dedicated the rest of his life.

Meanwhile Wu Tse-t'ien's reign was drawing to its close. Hostile public opinion and the threat of Turkish intervention had decided her to effect at least a nominal restoration of the emperor Chung-tsung. In reality she continued to govern alone, aided by her new favourites, the brothers Chang. But a plot was being hatched against her. One night, in the year 705, the conspirators took up arms and invaded the palace. They met the timorous Chung-tsung, the powerless sovereign, acclaimed him emperor and dragged him by force into the apartments of Wu Tse-t'ien. The aged empress, awakened from sleep, alone and defenceless, her favourites slaughtered at her feet, was still capable of resistance. She made one final attempt to intimidate Chung-tsung, and would perhaps have attained her end if the conspirators had given her time, but they held a dagger to her throat and forced her to abdicate (February 22, 705). She died of chagrin some months later, at the age of eighty-two.

108
THE PALACE OF CHASTITY
George Staunton
1799

George Staunton, visiting Beijing as secretary to Lord Macartney's expedition, was fascinated by the eighteenth-century court ladies.

At the death of an emperor, all his women are said to be removed to a particular building within the walls of the palace, where they continue for the rest of their days, secluded from the world. This building is termed the Palace of Chastity.

But to be entrusted with the care of the ladies of the court, or to be allowed to approach to their apartments, it is necessary to be what, without reference to colour, the Turks are said to have termed a black eunuch, which means, that all traces of sex should completely be erased.

109
THE DOWAGER EMPRESS CIXI
Bland & Backhouse
1910

The Dowager Empress Cixi (Tz'u-Hsi, 1835–1908) entered the palace at the age of sixteen as a concubine of low rank. However, she became the mother of the Hsien-feng Emperor's only son. Upon the ruler's death in 1861, the wily, iron-willed mother became co-regent and empress-mother to her emperor-son. She used her position to praise or punish officials and became de facto ruler. However, she evaded the need for modernization, and China lagged behind other nations. After her son's death at the age of nineteen, she appointed her four-year-old nephew as emperor. She continued to increase her power, often through the use of corrupt and willing officials. With their help, she appropriated 'naval funds' to build the extravagant Summer Palace.

The qualities which made up the remarkable personality of the Empress were many and complex, but of those which chiefly contributed to her popularity and power we would place, first, her courage, and next, a certain simplicity and directness—both qualities that stand out in strong relic against the timorous and tortuous tendencies of the average Manchu. Of her courage there could be no doubt; even amidst the chaos of the days of the Boxer terror it never failed her, and Ching Shan is only one of many who bear witness to her unconquerable spirit and *sang froid*. Amidst scenes of desolation and destruction that might well shake the courage of the bravest men, we see her calmly painting bamboos on silk, or giving orders to stop the bombardment of the Legations to allow of her excursion on the Lake. How powerful is the dramatic quality of that scene where she attacks and dominates the truculent Boxer leaders at her very doors; or again when, on the morning of the flight, she alone preserves presence of mind, and gives her orders' as coolly as if starting on a picnic! At such moments all the defects of her training and temperament are forgotten in the irresistible appeal of her nobler qualities.

Of those qualities, and of her divine right to rule, Tzu Hsi herself was fully convinced, and no less determined than His Majesty of Germany, to insist upon proper recognition and respect for herself and her commanding place in the scheme of the universe. Her belief in her own supreme importance, and her superstitious habit of thought were both strikingly displayed on the occasion when her portrait, painted by Miss Carl for the St. Louis Exposition, was taken from the Waiwpu on its departure to the United States. She regarded this presentment of her august person as entitled, in all seriousness of ceremonial, to the same reverence of herself and gave orders for the construction of a miniature railway, to be built through the streets of the capital for its special benefit. By this means the 'sacred countenance' was carried upright, under its canopy of yellow silk, and Her Majesty was spared the thought of being borne in effigy on the shoulders of coolies—a form of progress too suggestively ill-omened to be endured. Before the portrait left the Palace, the Emperor was summoned to prostrate himself before it and at its passing through the city, and along the railway line, the people humbly knelt, as if it had been the Old Buddha of flesh and blood.

STORIES FROM THE PALACE
Daniele Vare
1938

Daniele Vare served as a diplomat in Beijing in the 1930s.

Mme Dàn, who had been lady in waiting to the dowager empress, told me that there was no less confusion and uncertainty in the palace. Tzu-hsi would give an order, and the eunuchs would kneel to receive her commands. After she had spoken, they would depart on their errand. But quite often they would come back and surreptitiously ask the ladies in attendance what it was that the Old Buddha had told them to do.

111
PAINTING THE EMPRESS
KATHARINE CARL
1905

Katharine Carl resided in the imperial palace while she painted the Empress Dowager, observing her and the court in detail unique to foreigners.

We arrived at the Palace in good time the next morning, as Her Majesty and suite were coming out of the Great Audience Hall. She greeted us with a charming smile and made her usual inquiry for my health. We joined her suite and went along to the Throne-room where the portrait had been begun.

On the left of the Throne-room are Her Majesty's sleeping apartments, and behind the openwork partition at the back of the hall is a large ante-chamber where the attendants and Ladies await their turn to make their entrance into the Throne-room. In the rear of the hall is a magnificent five-leaved screen of teakwood, inlaid with lapis lazuli, chalcedony, and many other semi-precious stones. In front of this screen, on a dais, stood an immense, couch-like throne, with a large footstool. These couch-like thrones, where Their Celestial Majesties may recline when holding Audiences, are not at all favored by the Empress Dowager, who always sits extremely erect, without leaning upon a cushion or the back of the throne. Except in the Great Audience Hall, where she uses the traditional throne of state of the Dynasty, she prefers a much lighter and quite modern one, which she has introduced into the Palaces. The thrones favored by Her Majesty are of open carved teakwood, circular in form, with cushions of Imperial yellow. One of these stood in the front part of this hall, on which she sat for the portrait.

The great throne, which I have described above, was hence relegated to the back of the Throne-room and kept for the sake of tradition, but never used by Her Majesty. On either side of it stood two immense, processional fans of peafowl feathers, with ebony handles placed in magnificent cloisonné supports. Superb cloisonné vases stood at either side of these ceremonial fans; and huge bowls of rare old porcelain held pyramids of fruits—apples, sweet-smelling quince, and the highly perfumed 'Buddha's hand.'

And there were flowers everywhere! It was the season of the year when bloomed a sort of orchid, of delicious fragrance, of which Her Majesty is very fond. These were growing in rare porcelain jardinières, placed at intervals around the hall. There were also vases of lotus flowers and bowls of lilies. The combined odors of all

Empress Cixi painted by Katharine Carl in 1903

these fruits and flowers gave a delightful, but not at all overpowering, for the Empress Dowager is so fond of fresh air that there are always windows open in the Palace, even in the coldest weather.

When Her Majesty had her official garments removed (she always changed her dress after the morning Audience), and when the portrait had been placed upon the easel, she came over to look at it. After studying it for some time, she concluded that the nail-protectors on both hands were not artistic, and that she would have the gold ones (set with pearls and rubies) taken off, and show the uncovered nails on the right hand. I was delighted at this decision, for the nail-protectors destroyed the symmetry of the hand and hid the beautiful tips of her fingers.

I came in for my share of presents from the Empress Dowager. At every festival I was remembered, as well as the Princesses and Ladies of the Court, and when presents were sent to the ladies of the Legation, she sent similar ones to me. Many of the presents she made me showed a real consideration for my comfort and displayed much forethought. When the weather became cool, and the Ladies of the Court put on wadded dresses, Her Majesty sent one of her maids to my apartments to get one of my tailor-made dresses. She had the Palace tailors copy this in wadded silk. It was wonderful how well they did it, too, for, as I knew nothing about it, I could give no advice. She ordered a few changes made in the severity of the tailor-costume, thinking it was too hard in its lines. She had a long, soft sash to tie at the side, which, she decided, made it look more graceful. When the Princesses put on furs, Her Majesty, herself, designed for me a long fur-lined garment which she thought would be comfortable to paint in. She had some trouble in arriving at a result which pleased her, which would be warm enough, and which, at the same time, would not interfere with the freedom of movement necessary for me to work with ease. At the time of the Chinese New Year, she sent me two curiously fashioned fur-lined dresses. She had the skirts copied from old pictures. They were not unlike our pleated skirts, with an embroidered panel down the center of the front. The jackets were a sort of compromise between European and Chinese, and the costumes were not only pretty but very comfortable.

112
THE DEATH OF CIXI
Reginald Johnston
1934

Reginald Johnston, friend and tutor to Pu Yi, was later appointed as a Professor of Chinese at the University of London, as well as a British commissioner in China. Pu Yi was Cixi's successor and the last Qing emperor. He succeeded Guang Xu (Kuang-hsu), Cixi's nephew and nominal emperor during her rule.

A member of the imperial family is my authority for a little anecdote relating to the emperor's last interview with his august jailoress. One of his regular duties or punishments was to visit her palace at frequent intervals and to prostrate himself before her throne. It was a pure formality, kept up by the empress-dowager partly because she wished to satisfy herself from time to time that he was still her prisoner, and partly because the sight of his humiliation gave her grim satisfaction. One day, in the autumn of 1908, he went to the Ning-Shou palace to perform the usual ceremonial observance, but his illness was entering its last stage and he knew that he was dying. With drooping head and trembling limbs, supported by eunuchs, he tottered into the throne-hall, obviously on the verge of collapse. As he prepared to go down on his knees, in the usual way, the empress-dowager was struck by his extreme weakness and emaciation. The sight moved her, and the attendant eunuchs observed to their astonishment that there were tears in her eyes and on her cheeks. The ceremony of the emperor's *kotow* before the empress-dowager was usually carried out in complete silence on both sides. On this occasion she suddenly broke the silence with these words: *pu yung hsing li*—'you need not kneel.' But wearily the dying man sank to his knees, and as he did so he murmured in a scarcely audible voice, 'I will kneel. It is for the last time.' And the last time, indeed, it proved to be.

THE DEATH OF CIXI

The death of the empress-dowager, on November 15th, 1908, took place less than a day after that of the emperor. The coincidence inevitably gave rise to the rumour that the 'Venerable Buddha,' knowing her illness to be fatal, and determined that her victim should not survive to triumph over her dead body, took steps to ensure that he should be the first to die. Another story is to the effect that certain palace eunuchs, who had been the agents of her tyranny, had lived in dread of the day when the emperor would be restored to the plenitude of his power, and therefore administered the poison that would end his life and save their own. I do not believe the first story, and although the second one seems much more probable, I am aware of no evidence to support it. I have in my possession a report by a well-informed British medical man, prepared from evidence supplied by the palace physicians, regarding the physical condition and last illness of Kuang-Hsu, and it justifies the belief that he died a natural death—hastened, no doubt, by the barbarous treatment of which he had been the helpless victim for ten long years. After all, perhaps, it would make very little difference to our estimate of the empress-dowager's character whether she brought about his death by methods employed over a period of several years or by a dose of poison taking effect in ten minutes. But if credit is due to her for having refrained from committing murder at a moment when she was herself on her death-bed, we need not begrudge it.

113
VISITING PRINCESSES

Susan Townley
1904

Lady Susan Townley, part of the British legation elite, writes of her privileged glimpse of the Qing court ladies. Several years earlier, the empress's court had been much less friendly towards the capital's Western residents: the siege of the Peking legations in 1900 occurred after the Manchus, who supported the anti-Western Boxers, convinced the Empress Dowager that powerful foreign powers were plotting her forced retirement. Seventy-six foreigners were killed defending the legations over a seven-week period.

One day a big luncheon was given at the British Legation to the Princesses of the Imperial Court. As it is not etiquette for men to see them, it was an exclusively 'ladies' day.' The feast took place in the Legation dining-room, in the very room where not two years before during the siege a roundshot piercing the wall of the room struck the frame of Queen Victoria's portrait, finding its way out through the opposite wall. As I sat beneath that portrait entertaining the adopted daughter of the Empress-Dowager, and the other Princesses of the Court, the thought of that round-shot kept coming back to me, suggesting how quickly events succeed each other, especially in a land like China, when once the West comes into contact with the East!

The hour fixed for their visit was 12.30, and punctually to the hour they began to arrive. I awaited the Princess Imperial according to etiquette at the foot of the steps leading to the front door of the Legation, and shook hands with her as she stepped out of the imperial yellow 'chair' which she alone besides the Emperor and Empresses is entitled to use. In fact so great is the ceremony with which she is treated that any Prince or Mandarin meeting her

Manchu ladies-in-waiting at the court of Empress Cixi

'chair' in the streets would have to dismount or get out of his Cart and kneel in the dust until she had gone by. The next after her to arrive was the Princess Shun Ch'eng, and together we three entered the house. We assembled in the drawing-room, where tea was served, and shortly afterwards luncheon was announced.

It was the prettiest luncheon-party I have ever seen. The broad Manchu head-dresses with the flower and tassel-ornamented paper-cutters of jade set crosswise at the back of the heads made a gay show, whilst the brilliant embroidered silk coats and rouged and powdered cheeks of the little ladies received an additional set-off from the sombre-hued woodwork of the panelled dining-room walls. Even the Chinese servants added to the picture in their crimson sleeveless surcoats worn over long gowns of dark blue silk.

The menu was European, and the guests to their great amusement were given knives, forks and spoons to eat with. Some of them were not very dexterous in their use of them, and no doubt inwardly sighed for the familiar chop-sticks, but they were childishly delighted when they discovered that their images were reflected in the bright silver spoons upside down on the convex side and all right on the other. To my surprise one of them discovered the right solution of the apparent mystery, and explained it to the others.

After luncheon whilst we smoked and drank our coffee Sir Robert Hart's Chinese Band played European music in the courtyard. Great was the interest of the Princesses in these countrymen of theirs, who could play so cleverly on what appeared to them such weird instruments. They listened with wrapt attention, and no doubt on their return to the Palace spoke to the Empress-Dowager of these novel musicians, for shortly afterwards she requested Sir Robert to allow them to play before her, and on a subsequent occasion invited them to spend four days at the Palace, much to the gratification of Signor Incarnaçao, their capable Portuguese Conductor, who must be a musical genius seeing that he has himself and with infinite pains taught each of these Chinese to play a different European instrument. A marvellous feat when one considers that the Chinese music they had previously been accustomed to has only five notes, that it has no sharps, flats or naturals, and that the scale is neither major nor minor but participates of the two.

The Princesses were as playful as kittens. They were all under twenty-five except the Princess Imperial. They ran about the room examining its every detail, the piano offered endless amusement, and they laughed gleefully to see the notes jumping inside when a tune was played! Every detail of our hair and dress came under observation, and afforded interesting matter for comment.

Suddenly they seemed to bethink themselves that the time had arrived for making some changes in their own attire, and, permission having been granted to go to my room, instructions were given to the amahs in attendance, who preceded us upstairs laden with mysterious bundles. A most amusing scene followed, for these little Chinese ladies with much chatter and laughter proceeded to exchange one gay silk coat for another, to make a fresh selection of jewels, and substitute other still lovelier head-dresses for those already in use; powder puffs flew from one hand to another, eyebrows were touched up, and the vivid red patch on lower lips deepened, whilst all the time the amahs bustled about repairing the disorder!

But they capped all their performances when tea-time came by surreptitiously filling their big sleeves with cakes. Observing this manoeuvre we elicited the somewhat remarkable information that they wanted to take them to the Empress to taste! So I hastily sent for more from the kitchen, and had them packed in a biscuit-box, which they took away with them. Whether they ever reached their Imperial destination I cannot say, but suspect they must have been eaten *en route*!

114
LADIES OF THE QING COURT

Katharine Carl
1905

Katharine Carl, an American artist, was invited by the Empress Cixi (Tzu-Hsi) to move into the palace to paint her portrait. The result, in addition to the portrait, was a splendid book describing palace life at the beginning of the twentieth century.

Her Majesty's Ladies-in-waiting are principally Princesses of the Blood or the widows of Imperial Princes. Her first Lady, Sih-Gerga (Fourth Princess), daughter of Prince Ching, the Prime Minister, is a widow of twenty-four. She married, at the age of sixteen, a son of a high Manchu official, Viceroy of Tientsin, and was left a widow a few months later. She is a beautiful young woman, with face a perfect oval, large brown eyes, and a clear, magnolia-leaf complexion of exquisite texture. She would be called beautiful, judged by any standard. She has no children of her own, but, like most ladies of position who are widows or childless, has an adopted son. Adopted children in China are much closer relationships than is a child, by adoption, with us. In many instances their own parents are still living when they are adopted, and even these parents speak of their child as the son of the adopted mother or parents, and bow to her wishes in bringing up the child.

The Northern Chinese and the Manchu ladies use a great deal of paint and powder on their faces; but a widow can never add one artificial iota to the rose of her cheek, to the cherry of her lips, or the lily of her brow. She can nevermore use paint or powder. In most instances the Chinese ladies are but the prettier for this, for they have beautiful skins, and the use of powder and paint is carried to such an excess as to be quite unnatural.

LADIES OF THE QING COURT

Katharine Carl in Chinese dress

There are only eight of Her Majesty's Ladies who live always in the Palace, but this number is increased about four times on festive occasions. The Princess Imperial, the Empress Dowager's adopted daughter, is the first of the Princesses at Court, and, when she comes to the Palace, ranks next to the Empress and the secondary wife of the Emperor.

There are a number of tiring-women and maids in the Palace who are called by outsiders 'slaves'; but they are not slaves, or, if they are so, it is but for a time, a space of ten years. Every spring, the daughters of the lowest of the Manchu families, the Seventh and Eighth Banners, are brought into the Palace to be chosen from, by the Empress and Empress Dowager, for maids and tiring-women. One day, on going to the Palace, I saw a number of ordinary carts near one of the Postern Gates, and I learned they had brought crowds of these girls of the families of the Eighth Banner. They are first passed in review by the Head Eunuch, and he selects from them those he thinks may please Her Majesty. These pass before her, and she tells the Head Eunuch which ones are to remain in the Palace. They are brought to the Palace from the ages of ten to sixteen years. They remain in service for ten years, after which time they are allowed to return to their families; and in case they have been satisfactory and pleased Their Majesties, they are given a comfortable dot and are provided with a handsome marriage outfit, which causes them to make much better marriages than they would otherwise do. During their so-called ten years' slavery in the Palace, they live upon the fat of the land, have beautiful clothes and many advantages. They wear, while in Her Majesty's service, blue gowns, with their hair plainly parted at the side and braided in a single long braid (tied with red silk cords), which hangs down the back. They wear bunches of flowers over each ear. The young Empress and secondary wife, as well as each of the Princesses, have their own maids and tiring-women, who remain in the private quarters of these Ladies.

No Chinese lady of position ever dresses herself or combs her own hair, and she generally has three or four personal maids. These are, in many instances, bought outright from their parents, and might be considered really slaves; but they are treated with great consideration and even friendliness by their mistresses, and have in most instances a happy lot. As these maids are bought when they and their mistresses are children, they grow up together, and though the maid never forgets the respect due her mistress, they are on a much more friendly footing than mistress and maid could ever be in Europe in such cases.

The first of a lady's maids stands behind her at table, no matter how many servitors there may be; goes out with her, sits with her, and sleeps either in her room or at her door, and is almost her constant companion. When the time comes for them to marry, they are given a comfortable outfit by their mistresses, and are cared for to the third and fourth generation; but the children of the so-called slaves are free, unless the mother or parents decide, of their own free will, to sell them, as they have been sold, to some good family.

115
MY MOTHER
Pu Yi
1964

As a three-year-old, Pu Yi, grand-nephew of the Empress Dowager, had been designated her successor. He reigned as emperor from 1909 to 1912 under the regency of his father until the overthrow of the Qing. Here the child-emperor recalls his mother.

My father had two wives, and they bore him four sons and seven daughters of whom all but two are alive today. My father died in 1951 and my own mother in 1921.

My father and my mother were completely different types. It is said that Manchu women are often far more capable than their husbands, and this may well be true. My wife Wan Jung and my mother were far more knowledgeable than myself or my father, particularly when it came to enjoying themselves or buying things. One explanation for the way in which Manchu girls were able to run their households and were treated with respect by their elders in their generation was that they all had the chance of being chosen for service in the palace and becoming imperial consorts; but my own opinion is that as the men were either idling or busy with official business, household management and financial affairs tended to fall on their sisters' shoulders so that the women naturally became rather more able. My mother was a favourite in her mother's home, and Tzu Hsi [Cixi] once said of her: 'That girl isn't even afraid of me.' Her extravagance was a big headache for my father and grandmother, but there was nothing they could do about it. Excluding his land-rents, prince's stipend and 'Money for the Nurture of Incorruptibility' (a form of payment to officials that was supposed to prevent them from accepting bribes), my father had an income of 50,000 taels a year which was always paid in full even during the Republic, but it was never long after he received it before my mother spent it all. Later he tried all sorts of solutions, including giving her a fixed allowance, but none of them worked. He even tried smashing vases and other crockery to show his anger and determination. As he could not bear to lose all this porcelain he replaced it with unbreakable vessels of bronze and lead. My mother soon saw through his tricks and in the end my father would give her more spending money as usual. She spent so much that my grandmother would weep and sigh over the bills sent over by the counting house and my father had no option but to tell his stewards to sell more antiques and land.

116
MY NURSE
Pu Yi
1964

As child-emperor, Pu Yi had an extraordinary childhood with power that only his nurse could control. When Manchukuo was declared an independent state by the Japanese in 1932, Pu Yi was restored to the throne as puppet emperor and brought his nurse to live with him.

Growing up as I did, with people pandering to my every whim and being completely obedient to me, I developed this taste for cruelty. Although my tutors tried to dissuade me from it with their talk about the 'way of compassion and benevolence', at the same time they acknowledged my authority and taught me about that authority. No matter how many stories they told me about illustrious sovereigns and sage rulers of history I still remained the emperor and 'different from ordinary people', so that their advice had little effect.

The only person in the palace who could control my cruelty was my nurse Mrs. Wang. Although she was completely illiterate and incapable of talking about the 'way of compassion and benevolence' or illustrious sovereigns and sage rulers of history, I could not disregard the advice she gave me.

Once I was so pleased with a puppet show given by one of the eunuchs that I decided to reward him with a cake; then an evil inspiration came to me. I opened up a bag filled with iron filings that I used for doing exercises and put some of them into the cake. When my nurse saw what I was doing she said to me, 'Master, who will be able to eat those filings?'

'I want to see what he looks like when he eats the cake.'

'But he'll break his teeth. If he breaks his teeth he won't be able to eat anything, and if he can't eat anything then where will he be?'

I could see that she was right, but I did not want to miss my fun, so I said, 'I just want to see him breaking his teeth this once.' Nurse then suggested that I put dried lentils in instead as it would be great fun when he bit them. Thus she saved that eunuch from disaster.

One time when I was playing with an air-gun, shooting lead pellets at the eunuchs' quarters and making little holes in the paper of their windows, I was really enjoying myself. Then somebody sent for my nurse to come to the eunuchs' rescue.

'Master, there are people in there. You'll hurt someone, if you shoot into the house!'

Only then did it occur to me that there might be people in the room and that they might get injured. My nurse was the only person who ever told me that other people were just as human as myself. I was not the only person to have teeth: other people had them too. Mine were not the only teeth not made for biting iron filings. Just as I had to eat so did others get hungry when they did not eat. Other people had feelings; other people would feel the same pain as I would if they were hit by air-gun pellets. This was all common knowledge which I knew as well as anybody; but in that environment I found it rather hard to remember it as I never would consider others, let alone think of them in the same terms as myself. In my mind others were only my slaves or subjects. In all my years in the palace I was only reminded by my nurse's homely words that other men were the same as myself.

I grew up in my nurse's bosom, being suckled by her until I was eight, and until then I was as inseparable from her as a baby from its mother. When I was eight the High Consorts had her sent away without my knowledge. I would gladly have kept her in exchange for all four of my mothers in the palace, but no matter how I howled they would not bring her back. I see now that I had nobody who really understood humanity around me once my nurse had gone. But what little humanity I learnt from her before the age of eight I gradually lost afterwards.

After my wedding I sent people to find her and sometimes had her to stay with me for a few days. Towards the end of the 'Manchukuo' period I brought her to Changchun and supported her there until I left the Northeast. She never once took advantage of her special position to beg any favours. She had a mild nature and never quarrelled with anybody; on her comely face there was always a slight smile. She did not talk much and was often silent. If someone else did not take the initiative in talking with her she would just smile without saying a word. When I was young I used to find these smiles of hers rather strange. Her eyes seemed to be fixed on something far, far in the distance, and I often wondered if she had seen something interesting in the sky outside of the window or in a picture hanging on the wall. She never spoke about her own life and experiences. After my special pardon I visited her adopted son and found out what suffering and humiliation the 'Great Ching Dynasty' had inflicted on this woman who suckled a 'Great Ching Emperor' with her own milk.

She was born in 1887 to a poor peasant family named Chiao in a village of Jenchiu County in Chihli (now Hopei Province). There were three other people in her family: her parents and a brother six years older than herself. The fifty-year-old father rented a few *mou* of low-lying land which was parched when it did not rain and flooded when it did. What with rents and taxes they did not get enough to eat even in good years. In 1890 there were disastrous floods in northern Chihli and her family had to leave their village as refugees. Her father thought of abandoning her several times during their wanderings, but he always put her back into one of the baskets slung from his carrying pole. The other basket contained the tattered clothes and bedding that was all the property they had in the world. They did not have a single grain of food. When she later told her adopted son about how she had been in such danger of being abandoned, she had not a word of complaint against her father; she only repeated that he had been hungry for so long that he could no longer carry her. He had not been able to beg a scrap of food on their journey as everyone they met had been reduced to more or less the same state.

Finally the two parents with their son of nine and daughter of three managed to drag themselves to Peking. They had originally planned to take refuge in the house of a eunuch who was a relative of theirs, but when he refused to see them, they had to drift round the streets as beggars. Peking was full of tens of thousands of refugees who slept in the streets moaning with hunger and cold. At this very time the court was carrying out large-scale building at the Summer Palace and my family was spending money like dirt on my grandfather Prince Chun's funeral. Meanwhile the victims of the floods, whose sweat and blood had provided that money, were on the brink of death and selling their own children. The Chiao family wanted to sell their daughter but could find no buyer. The prefect of Shuntienfu opened a congee kitchen as a measure to prevent disturbances and so they were able to stay for a while. A barber took on the nine-year-old boy as an apprentice, and this enabled them to last out the winter, albeit with difficulty.

With the coming of spring the refugees thought of their land and faced the prospect that the congee kitchen would soon close, so they drifted off home again. Back in the village the Chiaos spent several more cold and hungry years, and in 1900 the allied armies of the foreign powers devastated the district. The daughter of the family was now a girl of thirteen, and she fled again to Peking where she stayed with her brother the barber. But he was unable to support her, so when she was sixteen she was half sold and half married to a yamen-runner named Wang. Her husband developed tuberculosis, but lived a rather loose life. After three years as a down trodden slave she gave birth to a daughter, shortly after which her husband died, leaving his wife, daughter and parents destitute.

This was just about the time that I was born, and the household of Prince Chun was looking for a wet-nurse for me. She was chosen from among twenty applicants for her healthy and pleasant appearance and the richness of her milk. For the sake of the wages with which she could support her parents-in-law and her daughter she accepted the most degrading conditions: she was not allowed to return home or to see her own child, she had to eat a bowl of unsalted fat meat every day, and so on. For two ounces of silver a month a human being was turned into a dairy cow.

In the third year in which she was my nurse her own daughter died of malnutrition, but my family kept this news from her lest it should affect the quality of her milk.

In the ninth year a woman servant quarrelled with a eunuch and the High Consorts decided to expel them and my nurse as well. This docile and long-suffering woman, who had borne everything in those nine years with a slight smile and a set stare, only then discovered that her own child had long been dead.

PART X

GODDESSES, GHOSTS, AND BELIEFS

'Young, she is a Guanyin: old, she's a monkey.'

CHINESE WOMEN

The Chinese have inherited an extended tradition of intertwined religions, myths, and superstitions. Guanyin, the Goddess of Mercy, has long been China's most beloved deity, offering compassion, fertility, and easy childbirth. Originally a god arriving in China with traders and missionaries as part of Buddhism from India, Guanyin was a male incarnation of Amitabha. He decided to become a female to teach women the way to the Western Paradise.

In Taoism, female immortals influenced the lives of those on earth, but humans themselves are viewed as a small part of the universe. The *Analects*, based on the teachings of Confucius (*c.* 551–479 BC), focus on the state and the family, underscoring the importance of admirable conduct of women toward their sons, husbands, and ancestors.

Buddhism and Taoism offered women the retreat of nunneries—something that appealed to wealthy widows. Although in Buddhism women were considered temporarily lower than men, they could seek future salvation for themselves and their families.

Most convents in China served as refuges for women, and places of prayer and spiritual exploration. Nuns often came from impoverished families unable or unwilling to care for girls, while others were actual foundlings.

Bound feet suggest one of these Qing dynasty women became a nun as a widow

117
THE BELL GODDESS

Jin Shoushen

Jin Shoushen (1906–68) collected and retold Beijing folktales. In this story, a new goddess is added to China's pantheon.

Before 1924, the people of Beijing and its northern suburbs every evening at seven o'clock would hear the continuous ding-dong of a bell—xie! xie! xie!—a most pleasing sound. Then, especially in the cold winter, mothers would tell their children, 'Time for bed. They're striking the bell in the Bell Tower [built in Beijing in 1272] and the Bell Goddess wants her slipper ['xie']. Go to sleep now. Don't disturb the Bell Goddess.' If children asked why the Bell Goddess wanted her slipper, their mothers would tell them this story.

Long ago, before the invention of clocks and watches, all provincial and county towns had drum towers. At seven in the evening, drums were sounded to let the citizens know the time. As Beijing was the capital, of course its drum tower had to be much higher and bigger than those in provincial and county towns, and a big bell tower had to be built as well to keep it company. So the Emperor issued an imperial edict and ordered the Minister of Works to build a great bell tower and cast a bell weighing ten tons.

The Minister of Works lost no time in summoning all the best foundrymen from the provinces to Beijing, to discuss how to cast this great bell. When these skilled craftsmen were assembled, they talked the matter over and the Minister of Works put the best-known of them, Master Deng, in charge of all the rest. First they set up a large foundry west of the Bell Tower, and the workmen moved in to live there.

Master Deng was a family man with a wife and a lovely daughter, an intelligent girl who could read and write, and they were very comfortably off. They lived in an alley not far from the foundry, and when he went home in the evening they would laugh and chat together without a care in the world.

Each time Master Deng came home, his daughter would ask, 'Dad, has the bell been cast yet?'

'It soon will be,' he told her, smiling. 'Very soon.'

Time slipped by, and when twenty days had passed the bell was finished—a big cast-iron bell. Master Deng reported this to the Minister of Works, who immediately informed the Emperor, requesting him to inspect it. He was sure that after hearing the big bell the Emperor would reward him. The bell was set up and the Emperor arrived, but at the sight of it his face darkened.

'Why not cast a bronze bell?' he demanded. 'Instead of this ugly black thing!'

When the bell was struck, the Emperor flew into a rage. 'What sound is that?' he roared 'Those cracked notes won't even carry to my palace, let alone all over the city!' He penalized the Minister and warned him, 'I give you three months, no more, to cast a ten-ton bronze bell. In fine weather its sound must carry to all four suburbs, and on windy days to forty *li* away. If you fail to make it, or botch it, I'll cut off your head!' Then, with a swish of his sleeves, he stormed back to the palace.

The Minister of Works was frightened out of his wits. After the Emperor had left he bellowed at Master Deng, 'Why lose face for me like this! I give you two months, no more, to cast the bell the Emperor wants. If you fail, or botch it, you'll be the first to lose your head. I won't spare one of the other workmen either!' This said, he got into his sedan-chair and left.

Master Deng and his mates were livid.

'He never told us he wanted a bronze bell!' one pointed out.

'He gave us iron not bronze!' another said.

They angrily took down the iron bell and left it lying on the ground, then discussed how to cast a bronze one. Master Deng went home fuming. At the sight of him his daughter asked, 'Haven't you finished the bell, dad? Why are you angry?'

'Finished it?' Her father told her what had happened, making the girl angry too.

She could only say consolingly, 'Well, you can think out a way to cast a bronze one.'

Master Deng went on going to the foundry every morning and coming home in the evening. For the first six weeks or so all seemed

THE BELL GODDESS

to be well, but then a change came over him and he kept frowning and sighing. Questioned by his wife, he said nothing. Questioned by his daughter, he simply said, 'It's all right.' It dawned on the clever girl that her father was anxious because they had not succeeded in casting the bronze bell. Either molten bronze would not set, or it set in the wrong shape. For some time Master Deng had been off his food. His worried mates pulled long faces.

'We're really stumped,' they said. 'When the two months are up we'll be executed!'

When Deng's daughter knew this she was frantic too. Every single day she worried over her father, trying to comfort him when he came home and weeping with her mother when he was out. Soon the time would run out. The intelligent, lovely girl was at her wit's end.

Finally the deadline for casting the bell was reached. The day before, Master Deng had not gone home, making his wife and daughter fearfully anxious. So when she got up that morning, the girl told her mother she meant to go to the foundry.

'How can a girl like you go into the foundry?' her mother objected. When her daughter insisted she agreed, 'All right then. But come straight home to set my mind at rest.'

The girl changed into clean clothes and new embroidered slippers, then went to the foundry. The sun had just come out as she went in and found her dad and his mates milling round the great smelting cauldron, covered with sweat. In the sunshine their faces streaked with grime made them seem a horde of demons.

'It's me, dad!' she called.

Master Deng turned, and at sight of her his heart ached. He asked anxiously, 'What are you doing here?'

'Because you didn't come home, mum told me to come and ask how you're getting on with the bell.'

Before Deng could answer, one of the workmen put in, 'The bell, eh! This bronze won't come right and today is the last day left. At sunset we'll all be dead men. Better hurry home, lass.'

Hearing this, and looking at her dad and his mates, her heart bled for them. She thought: If dad and all these good uncles are to lose their lives because of a bell, I don't want to go on living. I'd rather die first! She gritted her teeth and braced herself to dash over to the great cauldron. Splash! She vaulted into it, spattering molten bronze in all directions.

When she darted forward the workmen had yelled, 'Look out! Stop her!'

At first Deng had been stupefied. At this cry he charged after her, but was too late to stop her. All he managed to catch hold of was one embroidered slipper. He held it, choking with sobs, for by now his daughter had become a wisp of blue smoke in the cauldron. Her father broke down, and the workmen all shed tears too, till suddenly one youngster shouted:

'Stop crying—look! The molten bronze has changed!'

The others crowded round to look and, sure enough, the molten bronze was giving off an extraordinary radiance. Sure now that they could cast it into a bell, they dried their eyes and set to work, and just as the sun was sinking in the west the new bronze bell, eight inches thick, was cast. So at last Master Deng and his mates had finished the task given them by the Emperor.

This new bronze bell was hung in the Bell Tower. Every evening at seven o'clock it is given eighteen swift strokes, then eighteen slow ones, then eighteen neither swift nor slow, and this sequence is repeated, making a hundred and eight strokes in all, each tailing off: xie! xie! xie!

Mothers hearing that sound say sadly, 'The Bell Goddess is asking for her slipper again.'

The foundry was dismantled, but that place is still called The Foundry, and there someone built a Temple of the Bell Goddess. Some say it was the Emperor who built it, others that it was Master Deng's mates, his daughter's uncles. But no matter who built that temple, the story of the Bell Goddess has been handed down. And what about the big iron bell? That was left lying in The Foundry for hundreds of years, but in 1925 it was moved to the back of the Bell Tower and set up straight. All who see it remember the story of the Bell Goddess.

118
CHINESE TEMPLES
Lord Macartney
1798

Lord Macartney was not the first to observe the similarities between Buddhism (Fojiao) and Catholicism.

It was observed by one that there is so great an apparent likeness between the worship of some of the priests of Fo and the Romish form, that a Chinese, on entering the church of the latter, might fancy himself in one of his own temples. On a Chinese altar, behind a screen, may be seen a representation in the person of Shin moo, or the sacred Mother, sitting with a child in her arms, and a glory round her head, with lights constantly burning before it. It would be difficult to separate the idea of this from that of the Virgin Mother.

A Guanyin Goodess of Mercy, drawn by Thomas Allom in 1843

119
TAOIST DEITIES
Adele Fielde
1894

Adele Fielde viewed her years in China as an opportunity to describe Chinese beliefs and mythology to Westerners.

The genii are divinities of the Taoist sect, immortals intermediate between gods and men, and they have the power of making themselves invisible, or of taking at will the shape of any animate or inanimate object. The Eight, who are the oldest and greatest of their kind, are supposed to have an habitation in the highest heavens, and to be under the immediate tutelage of the Supreme Ruler.

The eight genii, seven male and one female, have each a recorded personal origin. It is said that the first genie was an old woman who lived among the mountains, and there found and ate a fruit which made her immortal. Having herself partaken of a fig from the tree of life, she acquired, after a thousand years, the power to discern in others a fitness for continued existence. She perceived that Tek Kuai Li, who had killed himself by hard study, ought to live forever, and she sent a messenger to his distant grave to resuscitate him. When Tek Kuai Li emerged from the tomb, his legs were mortified, and so the messenger slew a dog, and used two of its legs for making new ones for Tek Kuai Li. He afterwards made new legs of clay for the dog, and sent it off alive and well; but Tek Kuai Li's legs were of unequal length, so that he ever afterward limped. When he returned from the grave to his parents, they did not recognize him, and declined to receive him as their son. He therefore went and pursued his studies with the old dame who revived him, and who is called the Mother of the Genii. He carries a crutch, and is the special patron of conjurers.

The eighth genie, O Sien Ko, was a pious woman who kept an inn. She was so cleanly that Lu Tong Pin, who frequented her house, thought she deserved immortality, and led her to become a genie. She is said to have invented boats. Her first craft was a mere raft, without means of propulsion. But one day when she was washing clothes in the river, she took a hint from a fish that was rowing with its fins and steering with its tail, and she then put oars and a rudder upon her boat. She carries a lotus-flower, and helps in housewifery.

120
THE TERRORS OF BELIEF
George Morrison
1895

'Peking Morrison,' as George Morrison was nicknamed, became an astute observer of Chinese rituals and beliefs. Here, he empathizes with the intensity of true beliefs as he describes a town in Shanxi Province.

There are several temples in Tongchuan, and two beyond the walls which are of more than ordinary interest. There is a Temple to the Goddess of Mercy, where deep reverence is shown to the images of the Trinity of Sisters. They are seated close into the wall, the nimbus of glory which plays round their impassive features being represented by a golden aureola painted on the wall. The Goddess of Mercy is called by the Chinese *Sheng-mu*, or Holy Mother, and it is this name which has been adopted by the Roman Catholic Church as the Chinese name of the Virgin Mary.

In the Buddhist Temple are to be seen, in the long side pavilions, the chambers of horrors with their realistic representations of the torments of a soul in its passage through the eight Buddhist hells. I looked on these scenes with the calmness of an unbeliever; not so a poor woman to whom the horrors were very vivid truths. She was on her knees before the grating, sobbing piteously at a ghastly scene where a man, while still alive, was being cast by monsters from a hill-top on to red-hot spikes, there to be torn in pieces by serpents. This was the torture her dead husband was now enduring; it was this stage he had reached in his onward passage through hell; the priest had told her so, and only money paid to the priests could lighten his torment.

121
THE BENEVOLENT GUANYIN
Robert Douglas
1882

Here is a brief observation on childbirth by Robert Douglas of the British Museum and Professor of Chinese at the University of London. Guanyin (Kwan-yin) is also Goddess of Children.

Water, in which scented herbs and leaves have been fused, is used in the ablutions, and when the process is over all present join in offering sacrifices to the Goddess of children for the mercy she has vouchsafed. For a hundred days the Chinese mother remains in the house, and at the end of that time goes with her infant to the temple of Kwan-yin—the Goddess of matrons—to return thanks for the possession of a child.

122
A CONTEST OF THE GODS
Howard Levy
1974

This folktale, retold by Howard Levy, centres on a contest between the Goddess of Mercy, Guanyin, and the God of Wealth, Cai Shen.

There is a temple located on the very top of a rarely visited mountain, and in the temple the two statues of The God of Wealth and The Goddess of Mercy sit face to face. One night the two gods had a conversation, and here is what they said:

'A man's wealth all depends on me,' said The God of Wealth. 'If I want someone to be rich he is rich, and if I want someone to be poor he is poor.'

'You're wrong,' replied The Goddess of Mercy, 'because a man's wealth depends entirely on the fate I bestow. If I don't give him a good fate you can't make him wealthy, no matter how hard you try.'

The God of Wealth started to argue with her, and finally he proposed a contest to see which god was more powerful. The God of Wealth, carrying a large gold ingot, strolled out of the temple with The Goddess of Mercy close behind. They were nearing a bridge, when from the distance two men approached, Chang the Third and Li the Fourth. 'See those two men?' said The God of Wealth. 'You try to give them a luckless fate, and I'll show you what I can do about it.'

The Goddess accepted the challenge, whereupon The God of Wealth placed the large gold ingot right in the middle of the bridge, where they couldn't miss it. And do you know what happened? Chang and Li were returning home from a visit to a wine shop and they were a little tipsy, wobbling on their feet and singing loudly. Said Chang to Li, 'Hey you know, Li old buddy, I've been over this bridge so many times I can walk it with my eyes closed.'

'Really? Well if you can so can I!'

And the two men closed their eyes and walked over the bridge, failing to see the gold. 'You see!' said The Goddess of Mercy to The God of Wealth. 'If I don't give them a good fate they can't find money even though it's right before their eyes!'

'I'm still somewhat dubious, Goddess, so let's have another test. I'm going to hide the gold ingot in that pile of hay over there. Now let's see if you can bestow good fortune.'

'That will be easy,' replied The Goddess. 'I'll give the good luck to Chang the Third.

The God of Wealth hid the gold ingot under the pile of hay. Chang and Li walked on past the bridge, but suddenly Chang turned to Li and said,

'I'm sorry Li but I can't go back to my wife in this condition. I think I'll take a nap first to sober up.'

'Do what you want,' Li replied, and he walked away.

Chang looked around for something soft to sleep on and when he saw the pile of hay he headed for it and tipsily threw himself down on it. But feeling something hard underneath he took hold of it and uncovered the gold ingot. Delighted with his good luck, he sobered up in a hurry and rushed home to tell his wife the good news, and The Goddess won her bet.

Happy the man who is blessed with good fortune!

123
THE BUSINESS OF CONFESSION
Matteo Ripa
1720

Father Ripa, a Jesuit priest living in Beijing in the early eighteenth century, opened services and special chapels for Chinese women. Confession, however, raises some problems.

On my return to Peking I established a chapel in the house of one of my penitents who lived near the Palace, so that the Christian women of the neighborhood might perform their religious duties. This scheme having succeeded beyond my expectations, I erected another chapel in Peking, and one at Chan-choon-yuen, both for the exclusive service of women, who, owing to the excessive jealousy with which they are kept, could not enter the place of worship destined for men. The Jesuits had a church for women at Peking, but it was only opened once in six months. In other places where two churches could not be procured, the two sexes went to the same, but at different times; and on the day appointed for the women, it was necessary to place two guards at the door to prevent the intrusion of men.

To show how jealously the women of China are watched, and how cautious the missionaries ought to be, I will relate what happened to me at Chan-choon-yuen. One day when I was in the above-mentioned chapel, confessing in turn several women who were stationed behind a curtain, I observed a man passing to and fro before the door and watching my actions. When my duty was over, I asked the beadle who the man was, and what he wanted; and he replied, with a smile, that he was a heathen but lately married to a Christian, who had stipulated that she should be allowed the free exercise of her religion. On the preceding day she had told him that in the morning she would come to Atso-koong-foo, which means 'to do the business,' this being the manner in which the

Chinese express confession. Not understanding what business his young bride could have to perform with another man, he had given her permission to come, but had followed her by stealth, in order to watch her proceedings. The beadle, having been informed of this, took no notice of him, in order that his mind might be relieved from any jealous suspicions. After he had watched for some time, finding that I remained seated and immoveable, he approached the beadle, and said he thought we were mad, as we sat doing nothing while we pretended to have business to transact. The beadle explained the mystery to him, by informing him that the women on the other side of the curtain came one after the other to confess their transgressions, and that, after suitable correction and instructions, if repentant I absolved them, upon which explanation he went away apparently satisfied.

124
LETTERS FROM ANHUI
Marguerite Owen
1934–37

Marguerite Goodner Owen sailed to China in 1933 as a missionary with the China Inland Mission. While teaching at a school in Northern Anhui Province, she wrote letters relating her work and friendships, and her romance and marriage to Harry Owen, one of the few unmarried male missionaries in China. These letters were transcribed and presented to the author on her ninetieth birthday.

Last Thursday . . . in the evening I was invited to a feast. Just the women of our household were invited—to the home of the wife of the head official of the city. He is a very fine moral and honest official, and she is a Christian. She is a graduate of a school in Peking and speaks a little English. She is a graduate nurse, and a very charming young woman.

July 13, 1934
Last night, Marjorie S. received 3 magazines—McCalls, L. Home Journal & S.E.P., and did we pounce on them. The lovely pictures, advertisements, riotous colors etc were all so typically American. . . . not that they're classics, but just a spice of something different!

I wish you [could] sit here in the glow of my little lamp, and listen to the girls studying across the hall—all at the tops of their voices—typical Chinese fashion! It's a most amusing sound—to say the least.

June 27, 1934
My Dearest Agweet—
I do hope for your sake it's not as hot in Texas as it is in North Anhwei. You drip from morning till night, and wherever you go your fan goes too! . . .

The whole place is a ferment of excitement now, for graduation is Saturday. I wish you could peek in my room! There are 12 lovely pairs of embroidered shoes that the bigger girls have made to wear graduation day. They really are exquisite—all shades and designs! . . .

We're planning all sorts of drills and songs, and tho' it takes time it's well-worth the effort. We're planning a may-pole drill for the wee ones— and tho' they'll probably do it all wrong in the end— they do look so cute trying to skip to music and weave in and out! I'm playing for the entire program—so it will be a busy day for me. All the Chiao-sï [missionaries] are wearing white silk Chinese gown[s] & I'm having a lovely new one made. Last Thursday evening I bought the material—soft, cream-colored silk—only 70¢ a yard—and 5 yards makes a gown. Marjorie had a remnant of pale green pongee that will make lovely buttons and edging. I'll wear white shoes and stockings—foreign in this point, and do my best to add to the pleasure of the day.

July 18, 1934
If it was hot Wednesday—Thursday was hotter—Friday still hotter & Friday night I couldn't sleep. The *mouth* thermometer went over 106 lying on the mantle in Marjorie's room! Saturday was almost as bad. Really July 12–14 was as hot a 48 hours as I ever spent! Then just as we were about exhausted—a lovely cool breeze sprang up temporarily. . . . Several (between 10 & 20) died in & around Fowyang those days. . . .

We had a lovely communion service [Sunday] morning—the most blessed Chinese one I've attended. The church was comparatively cool—and there was a quiet reverence rarely found in Chinese audiences (they just don't understand church decorum until they've been taught years).

Wednesday—Aug. 1—1934
[Thursday evening] Miss P'eng took Grace & me shopping. . . . It was raining slightly and the streets were slippery and so queer-looking in the dim light of various lanterns. I did wish for a movie camera that takes night pictures. Much of the filth and dirt of the day is hidden at night and the streets of even this ordinary city become almost picturesque!

CHINESE WOMEN

Nov. 4, 1936
Let me introduce you to a few of the women with whom I have the joy of fellowship. Mrs. Ning is a little white-haired woman of fifty odd years, who has been a Christian about two years. Her husband has taken a second wife who makes life in the home practically unbearable for Mrs. Ning. Since her own children are grown, she is more or less free to come to the city to study or to go out preaching, She has many relatives—or so-called relatives in the surrounding villages and towns, and has witnessed faithfully to most of them. She has learned to read the phonetic script haltingly, but still needs help to read with understanding.

Peter's Mother has a surname, but is known, as most country women in this district are known, only as the mother of her oldest child. (Women don't have given names unless they go to school and even then they are only used with their maiden surnames. Therefore it is difficult to know how to address them— 'Sister-in-law', 'old Mother' and 'Grandmother' attached to their surnames are the common titles of address.) Peter's Mother is a comparatively young woman, alone except for her small boy Peter. Five of her children died and when conditions became too difficult, her husband went off to earn money as a soldier. He wrote once and sent some money, but for over a year there has been no word of him, which leaves Peter and his mother quite destitute. She is a young Christian just learning to read and with no real knowledge of the Scriptures, but with earnest devotion and love of the Lord. In spite of her adverse circumstances, she is happy and rejoicing and witnesses gladly to neighbors and distant relatives. Life is not easy for her, but it's a joy to give her new hope and comfort in the Scriptures and teach her more of His word.

Big Sister Wang, as she is known, is a young widow utterly alone in the world, a far more pitiable circumstance in China than in America where a single woman is not the anomaly she is here. Since she is young and attractive and has no-one to protect her, her half sister-in-law is making every attempt to sell her. While she is working for the Ho family and for us and is on our compound, the attempts are of no avail. She was married when she was quite young and lost her only child a few years later; then her husband died a year ago, after a long and painful illness. She was saved during his illness (he was a Christian) and has grown much in grace through these last months. She is eager to know more of the Bible and is learning to read in the spare time when she is not busy with her needlework, at which she is very clever.

These are but three out of many but they are typical of most in that they are young in the faith, illiterate and unable to nourish themselves in the Word of God, and tested by difficult circumstances. Of course, some of the Christians have comfortable easy lives, but in the month I've been here, I've listened to dozens of pathetic stories: unhappy family relationships, persecuting relatives, grinding poverty, and the desolation of being alone in the world. However, it's a glorious privilege that is ours to teach these new believers to comfort the broken-hearted, and to lead them into a deeper fellowship with the all-sufficient Saviour.

Besides the activities in the station itself, I have been riding to an outstation every other week to lead a women's meeting there. Mrs. Yang, a voluntary worker from Fowyang district, has come to help us temporarily, and we are taking the opportunity of going with her to visit in the surrounding villages. This past week we had some special classes for the 'grandmothers' among the believers. Over twenty came to the four days of classes, the youngest of which was fifty-three, the oldest, seventy-eight! At present, a group of voluntary workers are preaching daily in one of the market-towns twelve miles away, using the Kuoyang Gospel tent. We are hoping to join them soon, and I have already made one flying trip on my bicycle. It was encouraging to see the crowds, who came and to note their attentiveness.

Marguerite Owen with Chinese women

125
LETTERS FROM SICHUAN
Astrid Peterson
1931–50

Astrid Peterson, an educational missionary in Sichuan Province, represented the American Baptist Foreign Mission Society from 1930 to 1951. She was born of Swedish parents in 1901 and left over 300 pages of her letters which were collected shortly before her death in 2000. They record the interactions of a devout Christian, eager to convert, educate, and befriend Chinese women.

Suifu, Szechwan, West China, December 27, 1931
Monday I unpacked the tea set that I bought in Japan and it was in perfect condition. I also sorted out the Christmas presents for the Suifu people. We played tennis for a while in the afternoon. In the evening I heard Miss Stalling at the church. She was one of the Shanghai delegates. She spoke in English and had an interpreter.

Tuesday Miss Mao and Miss Song visited me for a while. They are two of the teachers in the school. Miss Mao has just returned from America. She has studied three years in America, graduating from a university. Her home was down river but she is gradually improving in the Szechwanese dialect. She is a very fine girl. Of course she speaks English very well. That day I wrapped the Christmas presents. In the evening I escorted the school girls over to the church.

January 3, 1932
Yesterday noon Miss Mao invited me to a Chinese meal. Mrs. Wood and the three children were there too. You should see the children use chops sticks.

Miss Mao became a good friend, and on May 1, 1932, she wrote to Astrid's mother:

Dear Mrs. Peterson:

You will be surprised to get this unexpected letter. If you knew what a grand time Astrid and I are having together, once in a while you wouldn't be surprised that you would hear from me.

I wonder if you would adopt a Chinese girl for Astrid's sister. She already considers me as her sister. I am three years older than she is but you would not think so if you knew how I act sometimes. Anyway, I hope that I am not too old for her.

We all like Astrid very much. She is such a dear. I am looking forward for her mutual help. I already am getting her help even though we don't see each other very much. I mean real heart to heart talk.

I am sure that you are thinking of her and worrying about her all the time and you can't help it but hereafter I will look after her as my own sister and will help her as much as I possibly can. I don't have any sisters or brothers neither parents so she can get her only sister's care abundantly.

I hope that you will write to me too sometimes if you have time. You can write in Swedish so Astrid can read it to me.

When I have a good picture of myself, I will send you one. Don't be disappointed when you see it, as I am not a good looking girl.
Sincerely,
Edna Mao

Fighting between Guomindang and Communist troops soon added daily problems.

Suifu, Szechwan, West China, November 20, 1932
I still have no letter to answer for we have received no foreign mail since three weeks ago tomorrow. There is still fighting down the river about 50 miles away so of course that accounts for the delay in mail. I don't think that it will be lost but just delayed. Just now the city is flooded with soldiers who are retreating at other places. They are a most pitiful looking bunch of men. We don't think there will be any fighting here at Suifu, but there could be a turn over of officials and thus a change of soldiers. The common people are rather afraid for they are expecting an airplane.

This last sentence I wrote just before we ate dinner and now it is Sunday evening. We had just finished our soup when we heard the sound of an airplane. We went out to see it but stayed under the porch. It flew right over our house. It flew about and around Suifu for twenty minutes. It dropped bombs. There were three steamers down the river and the bombs were aimed at them.

Suifu, Szechwan, West China, December 17, 1933
Tuesday after school the two principals and Lettie and I met to discuss plans for next fall as to teachers and the students we expect to go on to college. Some that go on to college have to have student aid.

Wednesday afternoon the three evangelists from Shanghai called the 'Bethel Band' arrived. There are two women and a man. They led the prayer meeting that night. The two women, Mrs. Chen and Miss Fu, are living here with us. They are using my bedroom and I am sleeping in the guestroom, which has a smaller bed. These people are real old time evangelists, I mean in believing in rebirth, that we must be born again. My, but it does my heart good to hear some Chinese preach the gospel with power. . . .

It was this afternoon when some of the girls were at the meeting held at the Y.M.C.A. that the ice broke. We came back to school and the two women led a real revival meeting. Some of the girls were church members and others were not. They confessed that they had sin and wanted to be born again. We were all down on our knees and many of the girls shed tears because of their sins and accepted Christ as savior and were really saved. This is the first real revival that I have seen since I came to China. My how good it did my heart to see people really born again. I guess there were about thirty girls involved. After they ate their supper about fifty of them went over to the C.I.M. where the evangelists spoke tonight. We walked over and the girls again showed much concern over their souls. Tomorrow we have two meetings with the girls and we do hope that we shall see great results.

Saturday afternoon and evening, except when I was at the students meeting in the afternoon from about 3:00–5:00, Lettie and I sorted out the White Cross Christmas gifts the girls are to receive on Saturday.

I am housekeeper this month. Even with having the guests and these extra meetings I have been feeling well. I do thank God for the strength for each day, for there are so many little things that come up, such as buying things, calling the carpenter, having an organ fixed or a blackboard mended, etc.

Suifti, Szechwan, West China, October 20, 1935
Friday was the day set for our middle school trip. It rained in the morning but we waited until 9:00 o'clock and then later it turned out to be a clear day. We went to a place called Swei Liean Chi Kwan. There was a waterfall in a little stream running into the Min River. We stopped at a temple not far from the falls. Each girl brought her own eats, or rather several girls went together and ate in groups, but the students are responsible for their own eats. We teachers ate together. Miss Crawford was along too. We walked back too. I should imagine it was about nearly a ten-mile walk for the day. It was especially nice walking back. We had to cross the river outside the city going and coming. The girls always sing when they go in a boat. Everything turned out fine and everyone seemed happy. The only thing was that Miss Li could not find her sweater when we were going home. We thought someone must have taken it. Well to my surprise yesterday morning the nun from the temple came here with the sweater. It had fallen under a place and thus we were unable to find it. To have this old woman come all this distance with the sweater was an act of honesty that reminded me of the stories of Abraham Lincoln.

Suifi, Szechwan, West China, November 23, 1935
We had a rather tragic week of deaths. Within 24 hours two girls from the junior III class died. They were day pupils so died in their homes. It was probably typhoid fever and other complications. There were 21 girls in the class. The girls have of course been rather upset but have done pretty well in their work even if they have been to two funerals. They made many paper flowers to put on frames that they put up at the gate of the dead girls' homes. One girl was buried Friday morning and one Thursday morning.

Suifu, Szechwan, West China, December 11, 1938
Mama, thank you ever so much for your Christmas gift. It is entirely too much for you to give. Your gift I will use to furnish my cottage that I have bought in the mountains if conditions are such that I get to live in it.

The gift from the church I will use for married women and girls too old to go to ordinary schools. This special school, attended by about 50 women, has been run by tuitions and funds that Miss

Nelson received from friends in America. She has now gone to Yachow, and thus will give up support of the school.

Suifu, Szechuan, West China, October 20, 1940
Thursday evening the women evangelistic workers, Mrs. Hsu, Mrs. Han, Mrs. Yen, and Miss Teng, and I together with Dr. Fu and Miss Teng of the Woman's Hospital were invited to the Medical House to meet with Mrs. Liu. After that Mrs. Liu spoke to the Woman's Hospital staff. There was an air raid alarm that beautiful moonlight night, but fortunately it was only the first alarm so Mrs. Liu could give her talk.

After returning from her furlough back hame to California, Astrid Peterson wrote:

Ipin, Szechuan, West China, June 4, 1946
I really feel terribly sorry that I have not written more than once since I arrived but the reason is that on the third day I started to work and really have not had time. Today is a holiday, Dwan Yang, one of the three important holidays. . . .

I have charge of the Women's evangelistic work. The three workers are Mrs. Yen, Mrs. Han, and Miss Wen. They are all very good. Mrs. Han spends most of her time teaching Bible in the Primary School and in the High School. She surely is excellent in that work. Miss Wen is half time women's work and the other half the evangelistic work at the hospital. Mrs. Yen now lives at the hospital and has some responsibility there in the mornings and evenings for the student nurses. Some very good work has been done by these people. We still go visiting in the homes and then on Wednesday and Friday afternoons we have the women's Bible classes at church. We also continue our monthly Home Problem Discussion Group. We are to meet next week.

I'm not much of an organist but when there is no one who can do it better one must help out. Thus I play for church, prayer meeting, practice with the choir, and with all who give special numbers. All this seems to take a good deal of time.

June 25, 1946
In the early days the men far outnumbered the women in church membership, but during these last few years it seems easier to win

the girls and women. One sad part about the girls is that so many marry non-Christians and thus there is not a complete Christian home. That seems to be why some of our girls who were so earnest in Christian service while in school grow weak when in a home of their own. The Chinese church needs more Christian families.

126

A SUPERNATURAL WIFE

Herbert Giles

1923

Female ghosts abound in Chinese folklore, and they are often both benevolent and useful.

A certain Mr Chao, of Ch'ang-shan, lodged in a family of the name of T'ai. He was very badly off, and, falling sick, was brought almost to death's door. One day they moved him into the verandah, that it might be cooler for him; and, when he awoke from a nap, lo! a beautiful girl was standing by his side. 'I am come to be your wife,' said the girl, in answer to his question as to who she was; to which he replied that a poor fellow like himself did not look for such luck as that; adding that, being then on his deathbed, he would not have much occasion for the services of a wife.

The girl said she could cure him; but he told her he very much doubted that; 'And even,' continued he, 'should you have any good prescription, I have not the means of getting it made up.'

'I don't want medicine to cure you with,' rejoined the girl, proceeding at once to rub his back and sides with her hand, which seemed to him like a ball of fire.

He soon began to feel much better, and asked the young lady what her name was, in order, as he said, that he might remember her in his prayers. 'I am a spirit,' replied she; 'and you, when alive under the Han dynasty as Ch'u Sui-liang, were a benefactor of my family. Your kindness being engraven on my heart, I have at length succeeded in my search for you, and am able in some measure to requite you.'

Chao was dreadfully ashamed of his poverty-stricken state, and afraid that his dirty room would spoil the young lady's dress; but she made him show her in, and accordingly he took her into his apartment, where there were neither chairs to sit upon, nor signs of anything to eat, saying, 'You might, indeed, be able to put up with all this; but you see my larder is empty, and I have absolutely no means of supporting a wife.'

'Don't be alarmed about that,' cried she; and in another moment he saw a couch covered with costly robes, the walls papered with a silver-flecked paper, and chairs and tables appear, the latter laden with all kinds of wine and exquisite viands.

They then began to enjoy themselves, and lived together as husband and wife, many people coming to witness these strange things, and being all cordially received by the young lady, who in her turn always accompanied Mr Chao when he went out to dinner anywhere.

One day there was an unprincipled young graduate among the company, which she seemed immediately to become aware of; and, after calling him several bad names, she struck him on the side of the head, causing his head to fly out of the window while his body remained inside; and there he was, stuck fast, unable to move either way, until the others interceded for him and he was released.

After some time visitors became too numerous, and if she refused to see them they turned their anger against her husband. At length, as they were sitting together drinking with some friends at the Tuan-yang festival, a white rabbit ran in, whereupon the girl jumped up and said, 'The doctor has come for me;' then, turning to the rabbit, she added, 'You go on: I'll follow you.' So the rabbit went away, and then she ordered them to get a ladder and place it against a high tree in the back yard, the top of the ladder overtopping the tree. The young lady went up first and Chao close behind her; after which she called out to anybody who wished to join them to make haste up. None ventured to do so with the exception of a serving-boy belonging to the house, who followed after Chao; and thus they went up, up, up, up, until they disappeared in the clouds and were seen no more. However, when the bystanders came to look at the ladder, they found it was only an old door-frame with the panels knocked out; and when they went into Mr Chao's room, it was the same old, dirty, unfurnished room as before. So they determined to find out all about it from the serving-boy when he came back; but this he never did.

BIBLIOGRAPHY

Abeel, David, *Journal of a Residence in China*, New York: J. Abeel Williamson, 1836.
Abel, Clarke, *Narrative of a Journey in the Interior of China*, London: Longman, Hurst, Rees, Orme and Brown, 1819.
Alley, Rewi, *Travels in China: 1966–71*, Peking: New World Press, 1973.
Andersson, Johan Gunnar, *The Dragon and the Foreign Devils*, Boston: Little, Brown and Co., 1928.
Andors, Phyllis, *The Unfinished Liberation of Chinese Women, 1949–1980*, Bloomington: Indiana University Press, 1983.
Anon., A Complete *View of the Chinese Empire*, London: G. Cawthorn, British Library, 1798.
Anon., *An Authentic Account of An Embassy from the King of Great Britain to the Emperor of China*, Philadelphia: Robert Campbell, 1799.
Baker, Hugh, *Chinese Family and Kinship*, New York: Colombia University Press, 1979.
Barrow, John, *Travels in China*, Philadelphia: W. H. McLaughlin, 1805.
Beguin, Giles and Morel, Dominque, *The Forbidden City: Center of Imperial China*, New York: Discoveries, Harry N. Abrams, 1997.
Bing Xin, *The Photograph*, trans. Jeff Book, Beijing: Panda Books, 1992.
Birch, Cyril, ed., *Anthology of Chinese Literature*, Vol. 2, New York: Grove Press, 1972.
Birch, Cyril, *Chinese Myths and Fantasies*, Oxford: Oxford University Press, 1992.
Bird, Isabella, *The Yangtze Valley and Beyond*, London: John Murray, 1899.
Birrell, Anne, trans., *New Songs from a Jade Terrace*, London: George Allen and Unwin. 1982.
Bland, J. O. P., and Backhouse, E., *China Under the Empress Dowager: Being the History of the Life and Times of Tzu Hsi*, London: William Heinemann, 1910.

Boothroyd, Ninette and Detrie, Muriel, ed., *Le Voyage en Chine: Anthologie Des Voyageurs Occidentaux du Moyen Age à la Chute de L'Empire Chinois*, Paris: Editions Robert Laffont, 1992.
Brassey, Annie, *Around the World in the Yacht 'Sunbeam'*, New York: Henry Holt and Company, 1879.
Bridgman, Eliza Gilbert, *Daughters of China*, New York: Robert Carter and Brothers, 1853.
Brown, Brian, *The Wisdom of the Chinese: Their Philosophy in Sayings and Proverbs*, London: Brentano's, 1922.
Bruce, Clarence Dalrymple, *In The Footsteps of Marco Polo*, Edinburgh and London: William Blackwood and Sons, 1908.
Bryan, William Jennings, *The Old World and Its Ways*, St. Louis: The Thompson Publishing Co., 1907.
Buck, Pearl S., *Pavilion of Women*, New York: The John Day Company, 1946.
Buck, Pearl S., *The Good Earth*, New York: John Day Co., 1931.
Cao Xueqin, *The Story of the Stone*, 5 vols., London: 1986.
Carl, Katharine A., *With the Empress Dowager*, New York: The New Century Co., 1905.
Cass, Victoria, *Dangerous Women: Warriors, Grannies and Geisha of the Ming*, Lanham: Rowman & Littlefield, Inc., 1999.
Chang, Chi-Yu, *The Essence of Chinese Culture*, Taipei: China News Press, 1957.
Chang, Jun-mei, *Ting Ling: Her Life and Work*, Taipei, Taiwan: Institute of International Relations, 1978.
Chang, Pang-Mei Natasha, *Bound Feet and Western Dress*, New York: Doubleday Dell Publishing Group, Inc., 1996.
Chao, Pan, *Instruction for Chinese Women and Girls*, trans. Mrs. S. L. Baldwin, New York: Eaton and Mains, 1988.
Chen Jianing, ed., *The Core of Chinese Classical Fiction*, Beijing: New World Press, 1996. (orig. 1990)
Cheng Naishan, *The Blue House*, Beijing: Panda Books, Chinese Literature Press, 1989.
Childhood in China, William Kessen, ed. New Haven: Yale Univesity Press, 1975.
China Body and Soul, E.R. Hughes, ed., London: Secker and Warburg, 1938.
China: Social and Economic Conditions, Philadelphia: American Academy of Political and Social Science, 1912.

Chinese Fairy Tales and Fantasies, Roberts, Moss, ed. and trans., New York: Pantheon Books, 1979.
Chinese Poetry: Through the Words of the People, Bonnie McCandless, ed., New York: Ballantine Books, 1991.
Chinese Women Writers: A Collection of Short Stories by Chinese Women Writers of the 1920s and 30s, Jennifer Anderson and Theresa Munford, trans., Hong Kong: Joint Publishing Company, 1985.
Chun, Jinsie, *I Am Heaven*, Philadelphia: Macrae Smith, 1973.
Chung, Priscilla Ching, *Palace Women in the Northern Sung*, 960–1126, Leiden: E. J. Brill, 1981.
Contemporary Chinese Women Painters, Beijing: Foreign Languages Press, 1995.
Contemporary Chinese Women Writers II, Beijing: Panda Books, Chinese Literature Press, 1991.
Contemporary Chinese Women Writers, III, Beijing: Panda Books, Chinese Literature Press, 1995.
Contemporary Chinese Women Writers IV, Beijing: Panda Books, Chinese Literature Press, 1995.
Contemporary Chinese Women Writers V: Three Novellas by Fang Fang, Beijing: Panda Books, 1996.
Corner, Julia, *China: Pictoral, Descriptive and Historical*, London: Henry G. Bohn, 1853.
Couling, Samuel, *The Encyclopaedia Sinica*, Oxford University, 1917.
Croll, Elizabeth, *Chinese Women Since Mao*, London: Zed Books, Ltd. and Armonk, New York: M. E. Sharpe, 1983.
Cutter, Robert Joe, and William Gordon Crowell, *Empresses and Consorts*, Honolulu: University of Hawai'i Press, 1999.
Davin, Delia, *Women-Work: Women and the Party in Revolutionary China*, Oxford: Oxford University Press, 1979.
Davis, Sir John Francis, *China: A General Description of That Empire and Its Inhabitants*, London: John Murray, 1857, 2 vols.
Dawson, Raymond, *The Chinese Chameleon: An Analysis of European Conceptions of Chinese Civilization*, London: Oxford University Press, 1967.
Dennys, N. B., *Folk-lore of China*, London: Trubner and Co., 1876.
Departed But Not Forgotten, Beijing: Women of China, 1984.
Der Ling, *Old Buddha*, New York: Dodd, Mead and Co., 1934.
Ding Ling, *A Yanan Collection*, Peking: People's Literature Publishing House, 1954.

Doolittle, Revd Justus, *Social Life of the Chinese: with some account of their Religious, Governmental, Educational and Business Customs and Opinions*, 2 vols., New York: Harper and Brothers, 1865.

Douglas, Robert K., *China*, London: Society for Promoting Christian Knowledge, 1882.

Douglas, Robert K., *The Story of Nations: China*, New York: G. P. Putnam's Sons, 1904.

Dragon Tales: A Collection of Chinese Stories, Beijing: Chinese Literature Press, Panda Books, 1994 (1988).

Duke, Michael S., *Blooming and Contending: Chinese Literature in the Post-Mao Era*, Bloomington: Indiana University Press, 1985.

Dundes, Lawrence (The Earl of Ronaldshay), *A Wandering Student in the Far East*, Edinburgh and London: William Blackwood and Sons, 1908.

Dyer Ball, J., *The Chinese at Home*, New York: Fleming H. Revell Co., 1912.

Ebrey, Patricia Buckley, *The Inner Quarters: Marriage and the Lives of Chinese Women in the Sung Period*, Berkeley: University of California Press, 1993.

Ebrey, Patricia Buckley and Watson, James L., eds., *Kinship Organization in Late Imperial China: 1000–1940*, Berkeley: University of California, 1996.

Evans, Harriet, *Women and Sexuality in China*, Oxford: Polity Press, 1997.

Fairbank, John King, *China: A New History*, Cambridge, Massachusetts: The Belknap Press of Harvard University Press, 1992.

Fan Hong, *Footbinding, Feminism and Freedom*, London and Portland, Oregon: Frant Cass, 1497, 1997.

Fielde, Adele, *A Corner of Cathay*, New York: Macmillan and Co., 1894.

Fitzgerald, C. P., *The Empress Wu*, Vancouver: University of British Columbia, 1968.

Forster, Lancelot, *The New Culture in China*, London: George Allen and Unwin Ltd., 1936.

Forsyth, Robert Coventry, *The China Martyrs of 1900*, New York: Fleming H. Revell, 1904.

Fortune, Robert, 'A Foreigner in China Eighty Years Ago', Shanghai: *The China Digest*, September 24, 1932.

Freeman-Mitford, A.B., *The Attaché at Peking*, London: Macmillan and Co., 1900.
Garnier, Francis, *De Paris au Tibet*, Paris: Librairie Hachette, 1887.
Giles, Herbert, *Gems of Chinese Literature: Prose*, Shanghai: Kelly and Walsh, 1923.
Giles, Herbert, *Quips from a Chinese Jest Book*, Shanghai: Kelly and Walsh, Ltd., 1925.
Giles, Herbert, *The Civilization of China*, London: Thornton, Butterworth, Ltd., 1911.
Graves, Revd R. H., *Forty Years in China or China in Transition*, Wilmington, Delaware: Scholarly Resources, Inc., 1972.
Grousset, René, *The Rise and Splendor of the Chinese Empire*, Berkeley: University of California Press, 1953.
Gutzlaff, Charles, *China Opened*, London: Smith, Elder and Co., 1838.
Gutzlaff, Charles, *Journal of Three Voyages Along the Coast of China*, London: Frederick Westley and A. H. Davis, 1834.
Hart, Henry H., 'Seven Hundred Chinese Proverbs', *Harvard Journal of Asiatic Studies*, vol. 2, no. 2, 1937.
Hegel, Robert and Hessney, Richard, eds., *Expressions of Self in Chinese Literature*, New York: Columbia University Press, 1985.
Hershatter, Gail, *Dangerous Pleasures: Prostitution and Modernity Twentieth-Century Shanghai*, Berkeley: University of California Press, 1997.
Hillard, Katharine, *My Mother's Journal*, Boston: George H. Ellis, 1900.
Hodous, Lewis, *Folkways in China*, London: A. Probsthain, 1929.
Holcomb, Chester, *The Real Chinaman*, New York: Dodd, Mead, & Co., 1895.
Honig, Emily, and Gail Hershatter, *Personal Voices: Chinese Women in the 1980's*, Stanford: Stanford University Press, 1988.
Hosie, Lady Dorothea Soothill, *Portrait of a Chinese Lady and Certain of her Contemporaries*, New York: William Morrow and Co., 1930.
Hosie, Lady Dorothea Soothill, *Two Gentlemen of China*, London: Seeley Service and Co. Ltd., 1929.
Hou, Helena, *Return to Peking*, Taipei, Taiwan: The China Publishing Co, 1977.
Hsiao-hsiao-sheng, *Chin Ping Mei: The Adventurous History of Hsi Men and His Six Wives*, New York: G. P. Putnam's Sons, 1940.

BIBLIOGRAPHY

Hsia, H. J., *The Fair Sex in China: They Lift Up Half of the Sky*, Albuquerque, N.M.: American Associates Publishing, 1992.

Huang, Martin W., *Literati and Self-Representation: Autobiographical Sensibility in the Eighteenth Century Chinese Novel*, Stanford: Stanford University Press, 1995.

Huc, M., *Recollections of a Journey Through Tartary, Thibet and China During the Years 1844, 1845 and 1846*, trans. Mrs. Percy Simnett, London: Longman, Brown, Green and Longmans, 1852.

Hunter, William C., *Bits of Old China*, Shanghai: Kelly and Walsh, Ltd., 1911.

Huo Da, *The Jade King: History of a Chinese Muslim Family*, Beijing: Panda Books, Chinese Literature Press, 1992.

Hussey, Harry, *Venerable Ancestor: The Life and Times of Tz'u Hsi*, New York: Doubleday and Co., 1949.

I Wish I Were a Wolf: The New Voice in Chinese Women's Literature, Beijing: New World Press, 1994.

Jackson, Beverly, *Splendid Slippers: A Thousand Years of an Erotic Tradition*, Berkeley, California: Ten Speed Press, 1997.

Jaschok, Maria and Miers, Suzanne, eds., *Women and Chinese Patriarchy*, Hong Kong: Hong Kong University Press, 1994.

Jenner, Delia, *Letters from Peking*, London: Oxford University Press, 1967.

Johnson, Kay Ann, *Women, the Family and Peasant Revolution in China*, Chicago: University of Chicago Press, 1983.

Johnston, Reginald, *Twilight in the Forbidden City*, London: Victor Gollancz, 1934.

Kao Ming, *The Lute (P'i-p'a chi)*, Jean Mulligan, trans., New York: Columbia University Press, 1980.

Kates, George N., *The Years That Were Fat*, Cambridge, Mass.: The M.I.T. Press, 1952.

Kazoko, Ono, *Chinese Women in a Century of Revolution, 1850-1950*, Stanford: Stanford University Press, 1989.

Kliene, Charles, 'The Marriage Maker', *Journal of the North-China Branch of the Royal Asiatic Society*, Shanghai: Kelly and Walsh, Ltd., 1921, pp. 139-155.

Ko, Dorothy, *Teachers of the Inner Chamber: Women and Culture in Seventeenth-Century China*, Stanford: Stanford University Press, 1994.

Kristeva, Julia, *About Chinese Women*, New York: Marion Boyars, 1993.

Lady in the Picture: Chinese Folklore, Peking: Chinese Literature Press, Panda Books, 1995. (orig. 1993.)

Lai, T. C., and Gamarekian, S. E., translators and adaptors, *The Romance of the Western Chamber*, Hong Kong: Heinemann Asia, Swindon Book Company, Ltd., 1979.

Larson, Wendy, *Women and Writing in Modern China*, Stanford: Stanford University Press, 1998.

Lee Lily Xiao Hong, ed., *Biographical Dictionary of Chinese Women: The Qing Period, 1644–1911*, Armonk, New York: M. E. Sharpe, 1998.

Lecomte, Louis, *Un Jesuite a Pekin: Nouveaux Memoires sur L'Etat Present de la Chine: 1687–1692*, Paris: Phebus, 1990. (orig. 1697.)

Legge, James, *The Works of Mencius in The Chinese Classics, vol. 11*, Oxford: Clarendon Press, 1895.

Leong Liew Geok, ed., *More Than Half the Sky: Creative Writings by Thirty Singaporean Women*, Singapore: Times Books International, 1998.

Levy, Howard, trans., *A Feast of Mist and Flowers: The Gay Quarters of Nanking at the End of the Ming*, Yokohama, Japan, 1966 (privately printed).

Levy, Howard, *Harem Favorites of an Illustrious Celestial*, Taipei: Chung-T'ai Printing Co., 1974.

Levy, Howard, trans., *One Hundred Chinese Stories*, Taipei: The Orient Cultural Service, 1974.

Li He, *Goddesses, Ghosts, and Demons: The Collected Poems of Li He (Li Chang-ji 790–816)*, San Francisco: North Point Press, 1983.

Li Po—A New Translation, Sun Yu, trans., Hong Kong: The Commercial Press, Ltd., 1982.

Li Yu-ning, ed., *Chinese Women Through Chinese Eyes*, Armonk, New York: M. E. Sharpe, 1992.

Li Zhen, *Real Love, Zhenzheng de Aiqing*, Peking: Youth Publishing House, 1956.

Lin Yutang, *Imperial Peking: Seven Centuries of China*, New York: Crown Publishers, 1961.

Lin, Yutang, *Lady Wu: A True Story*, Melbourne: William Heinemann Ltd., 1957.

Lin, Yutang, *Widow, Nun and Courtesan*, Westport, Connecticut: Greenwood Press, Publishers, 1951.

Little, Archibald, *Gleanings from Fifty Years in China*, Philadelphia: J. B. Lippincott Co., c. 1909.

BIBLIOGRAPHY

Little, Mrs Archibald (Alicia), *The Land of the Blue Gown*, London: A. and C. Black, 1908.

Mackerras, Colin, *The Rise of the Peking Opera: 1770–1870*, Oxford: Clarendon Press, 1972.

Mann, Susan, *Precious Records: Women in China's Long Eighteenth Century*, Stanford: Stanford University Press, 1997.

McLaren, Anne E., trans, *The Chinese Femme Fatale: Stories from the Ming Period*, Sydney: Wild Peony, University of Sydney East Asian Series No. 8, 1994.

Medhurst, W. H., *The Foreigner in Far Cathay*, London: Edward Stanford, 1872.

More or Less, Half the Sky: Chinese Women Parade, Beijing: China Features, 1995.

Morrison, George, *An Australian in China*, London: Horace Cox, 1895, reprinted, Taipei: Ch'eng Wen Publishing Company, 1971.

Mowry, Hua-yuan Li, *Chinese Love Stories from 'Ch'ing-shih'*, Hamden, Conn: Archon Books, 1983.

Naquin, Susan and Rawski, Evelyn S., *Chinese Society in the Eighteenth Century*, New Haven: Yale University Press, 1987.

Nevius, John L., *China and the Chinese: A General Description of the Country and Its Inhabitants*, London: Sampson Low, Son, and Marston, 1869; reprinted, Asian Educational Services, 1991.

Ng, Janet and Wickeri, Janice, eds., *May Fourth Women Writers: Memoirs*, Hong Kong: Renditions Paperback, Research Centre for Translation, Chinese University of Hong Kong, 1996.

O'Hara, Allen R., *The Position of Women in Early China*, Baltimore-Washington: Archbishop M. Curley, 1946.

Parker, E. H., *China: Her History, Diplomacy and Commerce, from the Earliest Times to the Present Day*, New York: E. P. Dutton and Co., 1917.

Payne, Robert, *Chungking Diary*, London: William Heinemann Ltd., 1945.

Pfeiffer, Ida, *A Lady's Second Journey Round the World*, New York: Harper and Brothers, 1856.

Polo, Marco, *Book of Ser Marco Polo*, Henry Yule and Henri Cordier, ed., Greenwood Press, Armonica Book Co., 1964 (St. Helier: 1871 first edition; London: John Murray, 2 vols. 1975).

Polo, Marco, *The Travels of Marco Polo*, Thomas Wright, ed., London: Henry G. Bohn, 1854.

Prime, Edward D., *Around the World: Sketches of Travel*, New York: Harper and Brothers, 1872.
Pu Yi, Aisin-Gioro, *From Emperor to Citizen*, Peking: Foreign Language Press, 1964, 2 vols.
Pun Ngai, 'Becoming Dagongmei (Working Girls): The Politics of Identity and Difference in Reform China', *The China Journal*, No. 42, July, 1999.
Ripa, Father Matteo, *Memoirs During Thirteen Years' Residence at the Court of Peking in the Service of the Emperor of China*, New York: Wiley and Putnam, 1846.
Robertson-Scott, J. W., *The People of China*, London: Methuen & Co., 1900.
Roper, Myra, *China—The Surprising Country*, London: Heinemann Ltd., 1966.
Roses and Thorns: The Second Blooming of the Hundred Flowers in Chinese Ficton, 1979–80, Perry Link, ed., Berkeley: University of California Press,1984.
Salisbury, Charlotte, *China Diary*, New York: Walker and Company, 1973.
Schafer, Edward H., *The Divine Woman: Dragon Ladies and Rain Maidens in T'ang Literature*, Berkeley: University of California Press, 1973.
Seagrave, Sterling, *The Soong Dynasty*, London: Sidgwick and Jackson, 1985.
Seton, Grace Thompson, *Chinese Lanterns*, New York: Dodd, Mead and Co., 1924.
Sewell, William G., *The People of Wheelbarrow Lane*, London: George Allen and Unwin Ltd., 1970.
Shang, Xizhi, compiler, *Tales of Empresses and Imperial Consorts in China*, Hong Kong: Hai Feng Publishing Co., 1994.
Shastri, Brajkishore, *From My China Diary*, Delhi: Siddharta Publications Ltd., 1954.
Shen, Mark T., 'Shanghai As A Country-Woman Sees It', in *The China Critic*, Shanghai, 1936.
Shen, Rong, *At Middle Age*, Beijing: Panda Books, China Literature Press, 1987.
Shimer, Dorothy Blair, ed., *Rice Bowl Women: Writings by and about the Women of China and Japan*, New York: New American Library, a Mentor Book, 1982.

Shi Nai'an and Luo Guanzhong, *Outlaws of the Marsh*, Sidney Shapiro, trans., Beijing: The Commercial Press, 1986.
Shu Chiung, *The Most Famous Beauty of China: Yang Kuei-Fei*, London: Brentano's Ltd., 1924.
Sitwell, Osbert, *Escape with Me!*, New York: Harrison-Hilton Books, Inc., 1940.
Siu, Bobby, *Women of China: Imperialism and Women's Resistence, 1900–1949*, London: Zed Press, 1982.
Smedley, Agnes, *China Fights Back: An American Woman with the Eighth Route Army*, New York: Vanguard Press, 1939.
Smith, Albert R., *To China and Back*, Hong Kong: Hong Kong University Press, 1974 (1859).
Smith, Arthur H., *Chinese Characteristics*, New York: Fleming H. Revell Company, 1894.
Smith, Arthur H., *Proverbs and Common Sayings from the Chinese*, Shanghai: American Presbyterian Missionary Press, 1914.
Smith, Arthur H., *Village Life in China*, New York: Fleming H. Revell Co., 1899.
Smyth, George B., et al., *The Crisis in China*, New York: Harper and Brothers, 1900.
Snow, Edgar, ed., *Living China: Modern Chinese Short Stories*, Westport, Conn.: Hyperion Press, 1989. (First reprint, 1973 from 1937 by John Day in association with Reynal and Hitchcock, New York. Edgar Snow 1905–1972.)
Soothill, W. E., *China and England*, London: Oxford University Press, 1928.
Soothill, W. E., *The Analects of Confucius*, published by the author, 1910.
Spence, Jonathan, *The Death of Woman Wang*, New York: The Viking Press, 1978.
Spence, Jonathan, *The Gate of Heavenly Peace: The Chinese and Their Revolution*, New York: The Viking Press, 1981.
Stacy, Judith, *Patriarchy and Socialist Revolution in* China, Berkeley, California: University of California Press, 1983.
Staunton, George, *An Authentic Account of an Embassy from The King of Great Britain to the Emperor of China*, Philadelphia: Robert Campbell, 1799.
Stockard, Janice E., *Daughters of the Canton Delta*, Stanford: Stanford University Press, 1989.

Taylor, Charles, *Five Years in China*, New York: Derby and Jackson, 1860.
Terrill, Ross, *Madame Mao: The White-Boned Demon*, Stanford: Stanford University Press, 1999.
The Courtesan's Jewel Box: Chinese Stories of the X–XVII Centuries, Peking: Foreign Languages Press, 1957.
Thomson, John Stuart, *China Revolutionized*, Indianapolis: The Bobbs-Merrill Co., 1913.
Thomson, John Stuart, *The Chinese*, Indianapolis: The Bobbs-Merrill Co., 1909.
Ting, Jan C., *An American in China*, New York: Paperback Library, Coronet Communications, Inc., 1972.
Townley, Lady Susan, *My Chinese Note Book*, London: Methuen & Co, 1904.
Tracy, Jane A., *See China With Me*, Boston: The Stratford Co, 1930.
Vare, Daniele, *Laughing Diplomat*, New York: Doubleday and Co., 1938.
Wang, Anyi, *Lapse of Time*, Beijing: Panda Books, 1997 (1988).
Warner, Marina, *The Dragon Empress: Life and Times of Tz'u-hsi, 1835–1908, Empress of China*, London: A Hamish Hamilton Paperback, 1984.
Wattress, T., 'Chinese Fox-Myths', *Journal of the North-China Branch of the Royal Asiatic Society*, Shanghai: 1874, pp.58–65.
White, Martin K., and Parish, William, *Urban Life in Contemporary China*, Chicago: University of Chicago Press, 1984.
Widmer, Ellen and Kang-I Sun Chang, eds., *Writing Women in Late Imperial China*, Stanford: Stanford University Press, 1997.
Wilhelm, Richard, *Chinesische Volksmarchen*, Jena: Eugen Diedrichs, 1927.
Wilhelm, Richard, *The Soul of China*, New York: Harcourt, Brace and Co., 1928.
Wilkinson, Hiram Parkes, *The Family in Classical China*, Shanghai: Kelly and Walsh, 1926.
Williamson, Isabelle, *Old Highways in China*, New York: American Tract Society, c. 1875.
Wise, Michael, ed., *Travellers' Tales of Old Hong Kong and the South China Coast*, Brighton, U.K.: In Print Publishing, Ltd., 1996.
Wolf, Margery, *Revolution Postponed*, Stanford: Stanford University Press, 1985.

Wolf, Margery, *Women and the Family in Rural Taiwan*, Stanford: Stanford University Press, 1972.

Wolf, Margery and Witke, Roxane, eds., *Women in Chinese Society*, Stanford: Stanford University Press, 1975.

Wright, G. N. and Allom, Thomas, *China in a Series of Views*, London: Fisher, Son and Co., 1853, 2 vols.

Wu, Yenna, *The Chinese Virago: A Literary Theme*, Cambridge: Council on East Asian Studies, Harvard University, 1995.

Yao, Esther S. Lee., *Chinese Women: Past and Present*, Mesquiete, Texas: Ide House, 1983.

Ying Bian, ed., *The Time is Not Yet Ripe*, Beijing: Foreign Languages Press, 1991.

Yue Nan and Yang Shi, *The Dead Suffered Too: The Excavation of a Ming Tomb*, Zhang Tingquan, trans., Beijing: Chinese Literature Press, Panda Books, 1996.

Zhang Jie, *Love Must Not Be Forgotten*, Beijing: Panda Books, The Chinese Literature Press, 1986.

Zhang, Kangkang, *The Invisible Companion*, trans. Daniel Bryant, Beijing: New World Press, 1996.

Zhang Souchen et al., *Traditional Comic Tales*, Beijing: Panda Books, The Chinese Literature Press, 1983.

Zhu Hong, trans., *The Serenity of Whiteness: Stories By and About Women in Contemporary China*, New York: Ballantine Books, 1991.

Zurndorfer, Harriet, ed., *Chinese Women in the Imperial Past*, Leiden: Brill, 1999.